LANG/BAUMANN
MODELS

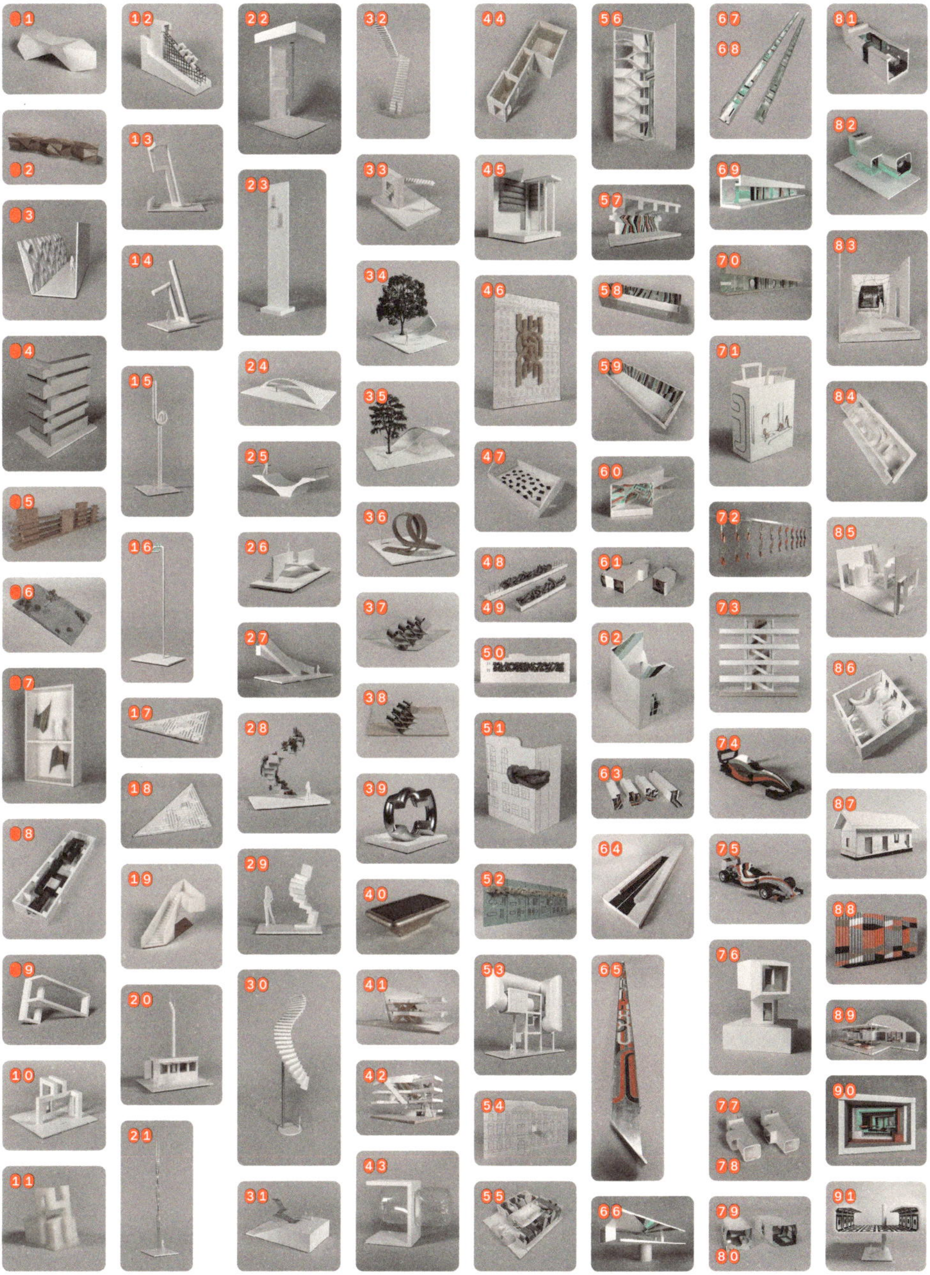

L/B MODELS

N°

PAGE

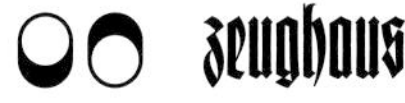

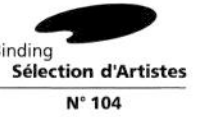

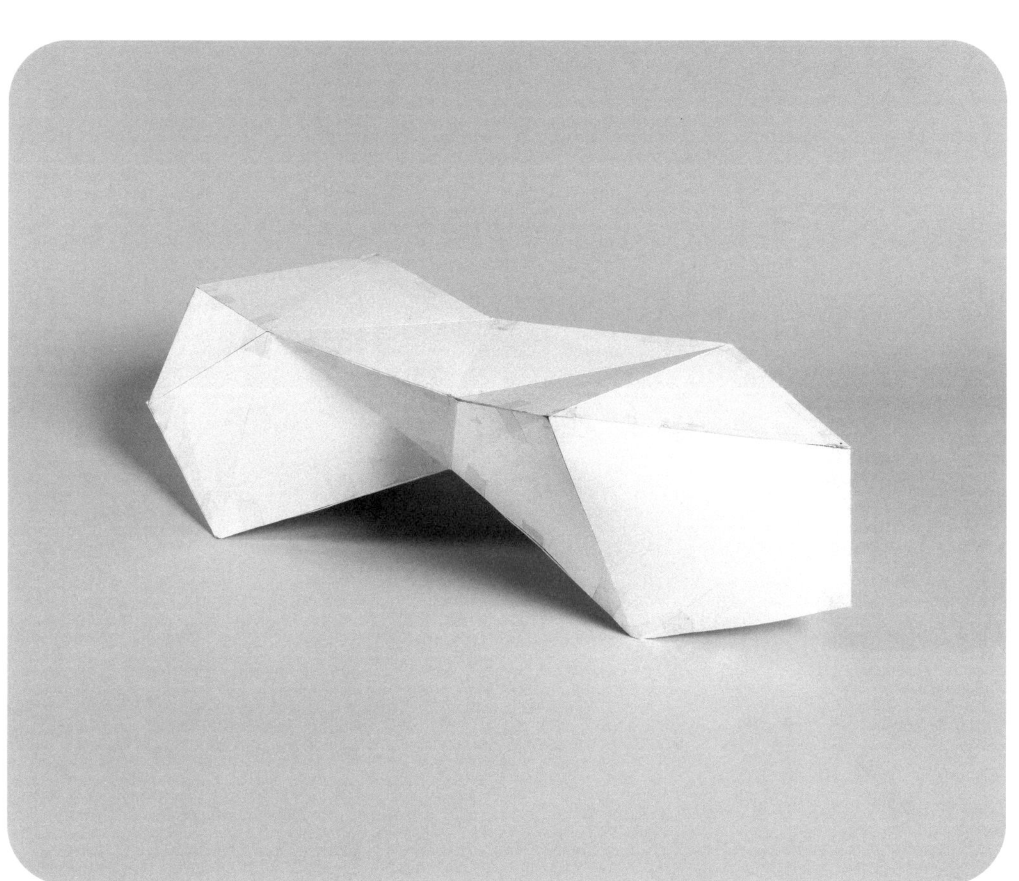

01 GOLDEN TABLE #2
1:5 | 2011

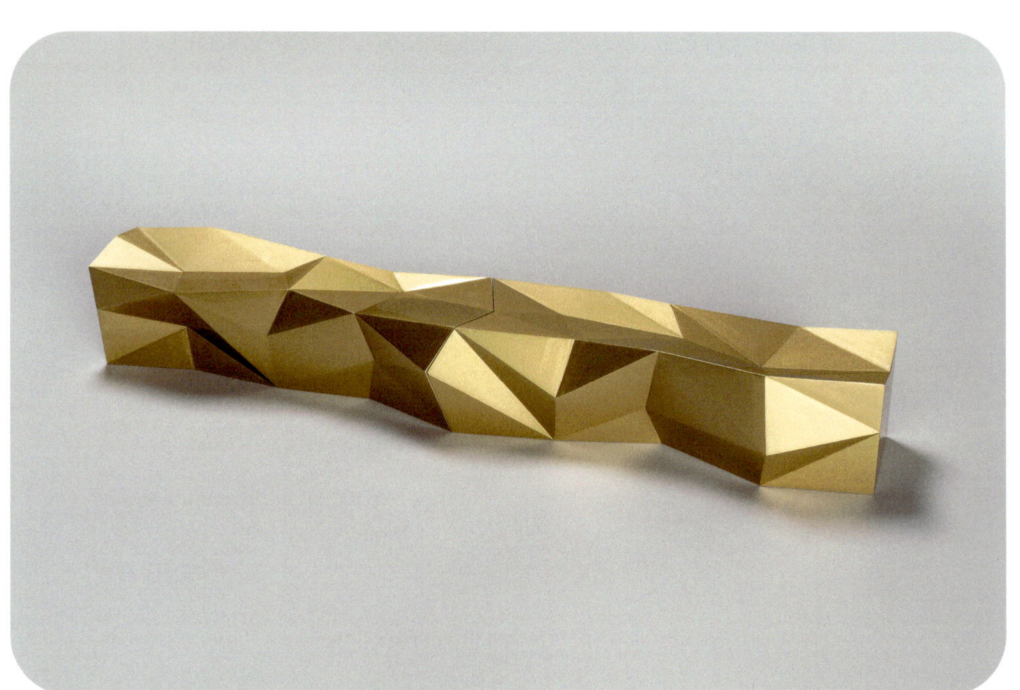

02 GOLDEN TABLE #2
1:10 | 2011

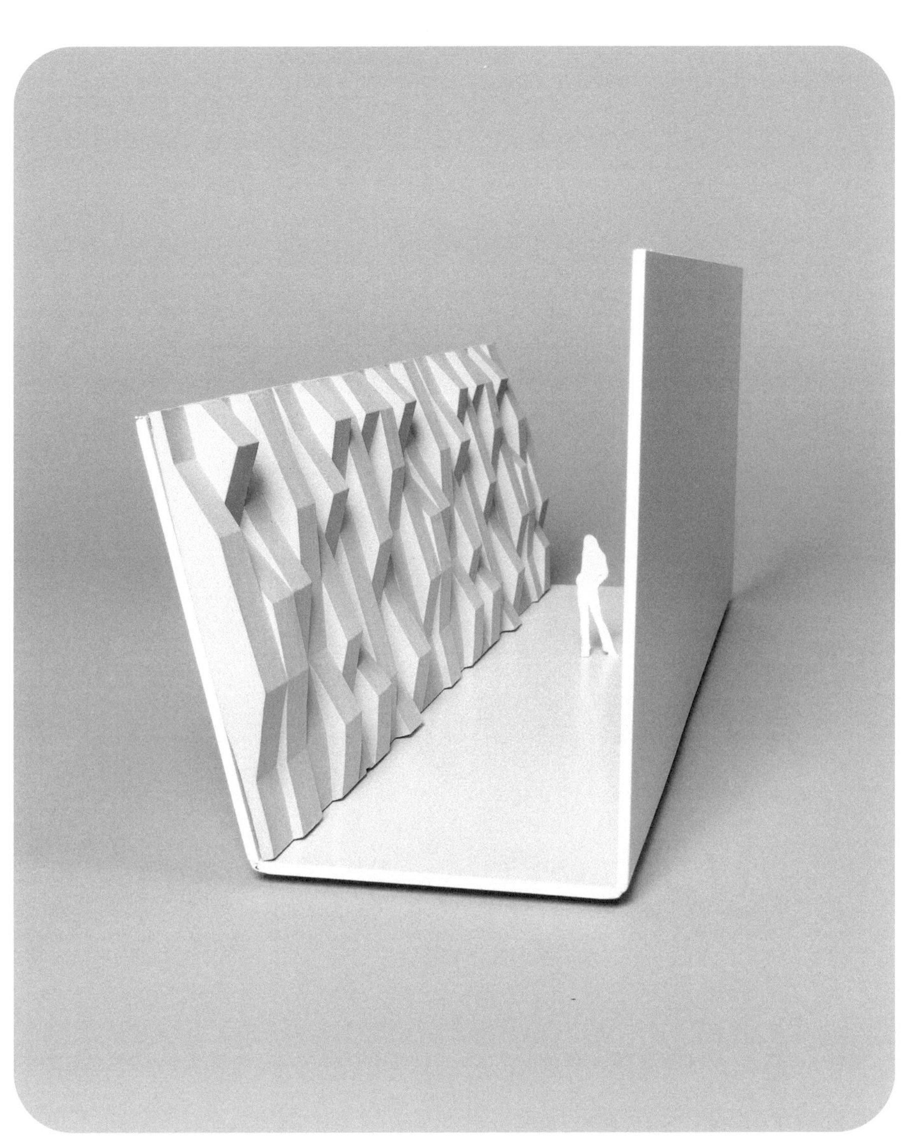

03 BEAUTIFUL ENTRANCE #7
1:50 | 2018

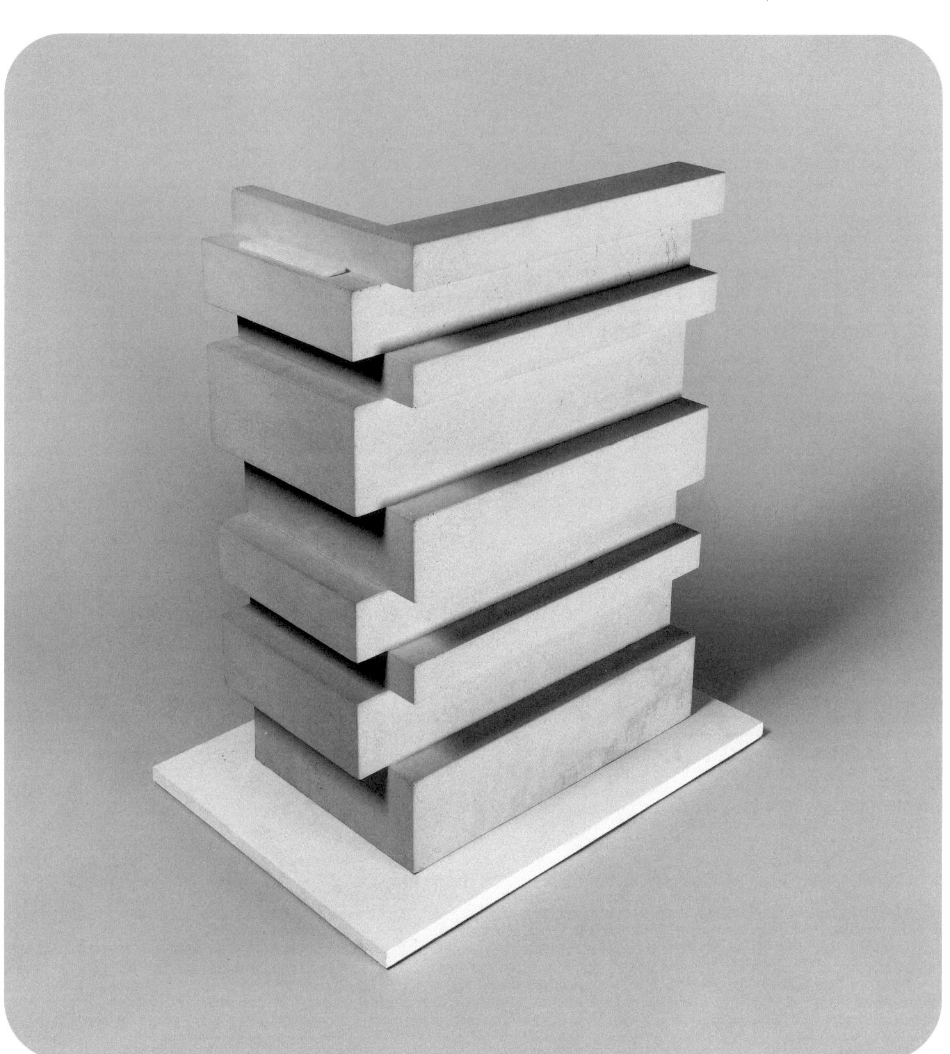

04

E9
1:50 | 2011

05

VORNAMEN
1:100 | 1997

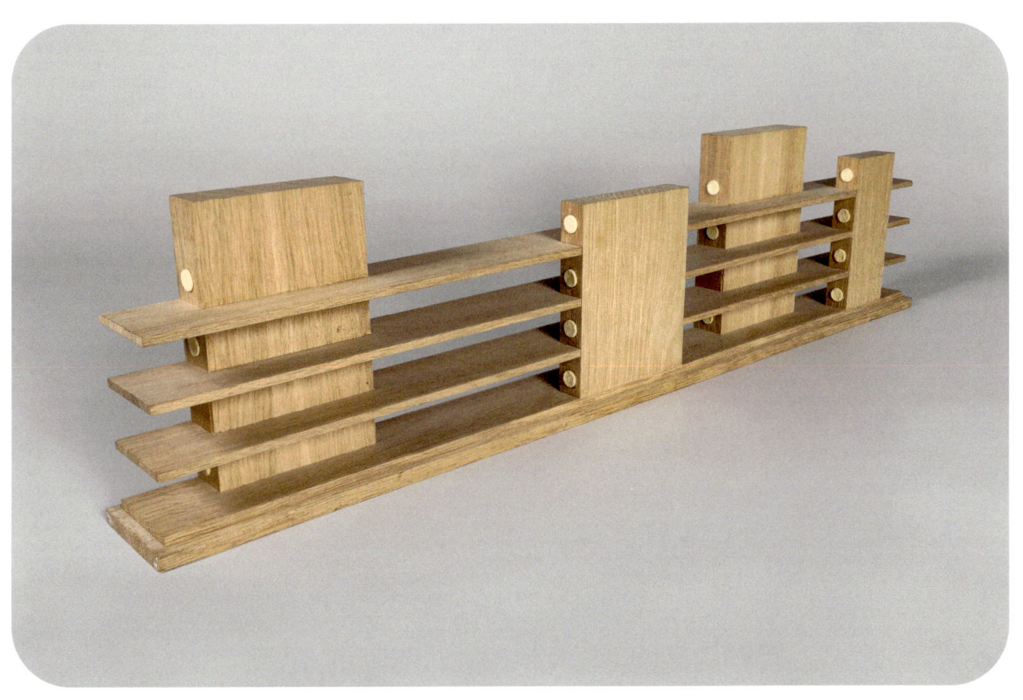

06

E15
1:100 | 1996

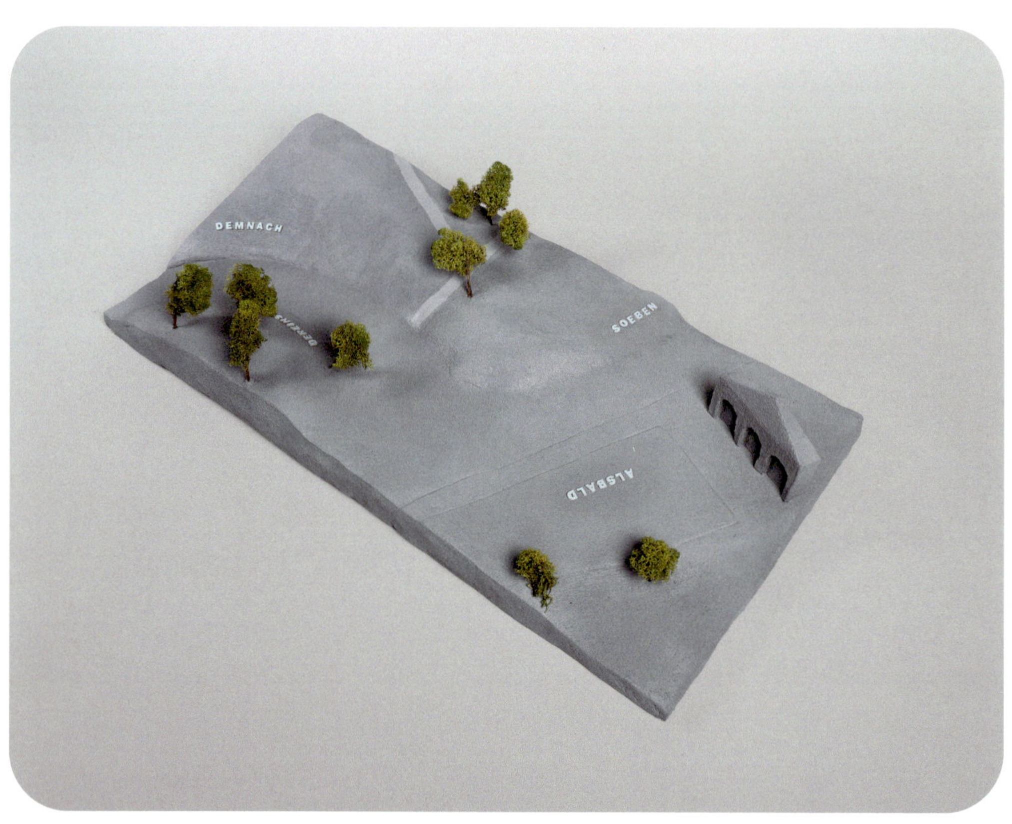

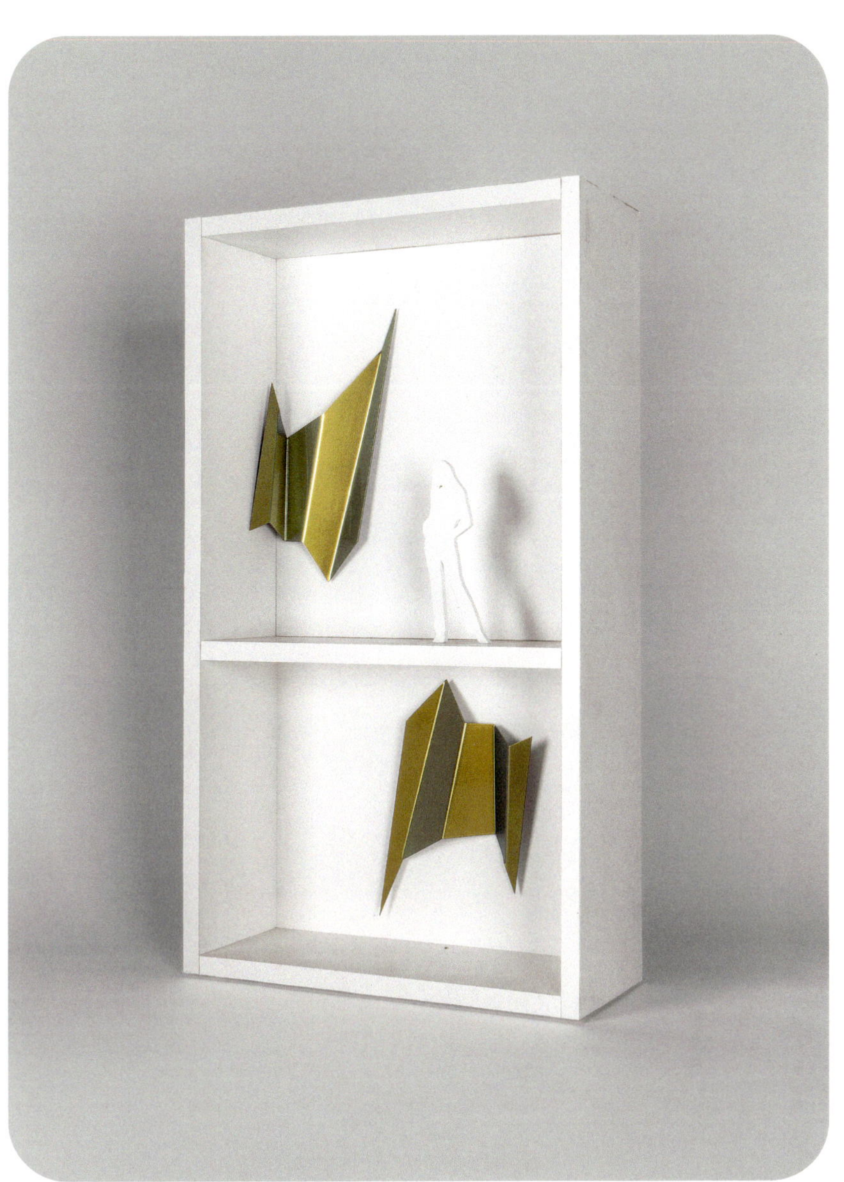

07 WAVES
1:12 | 2016

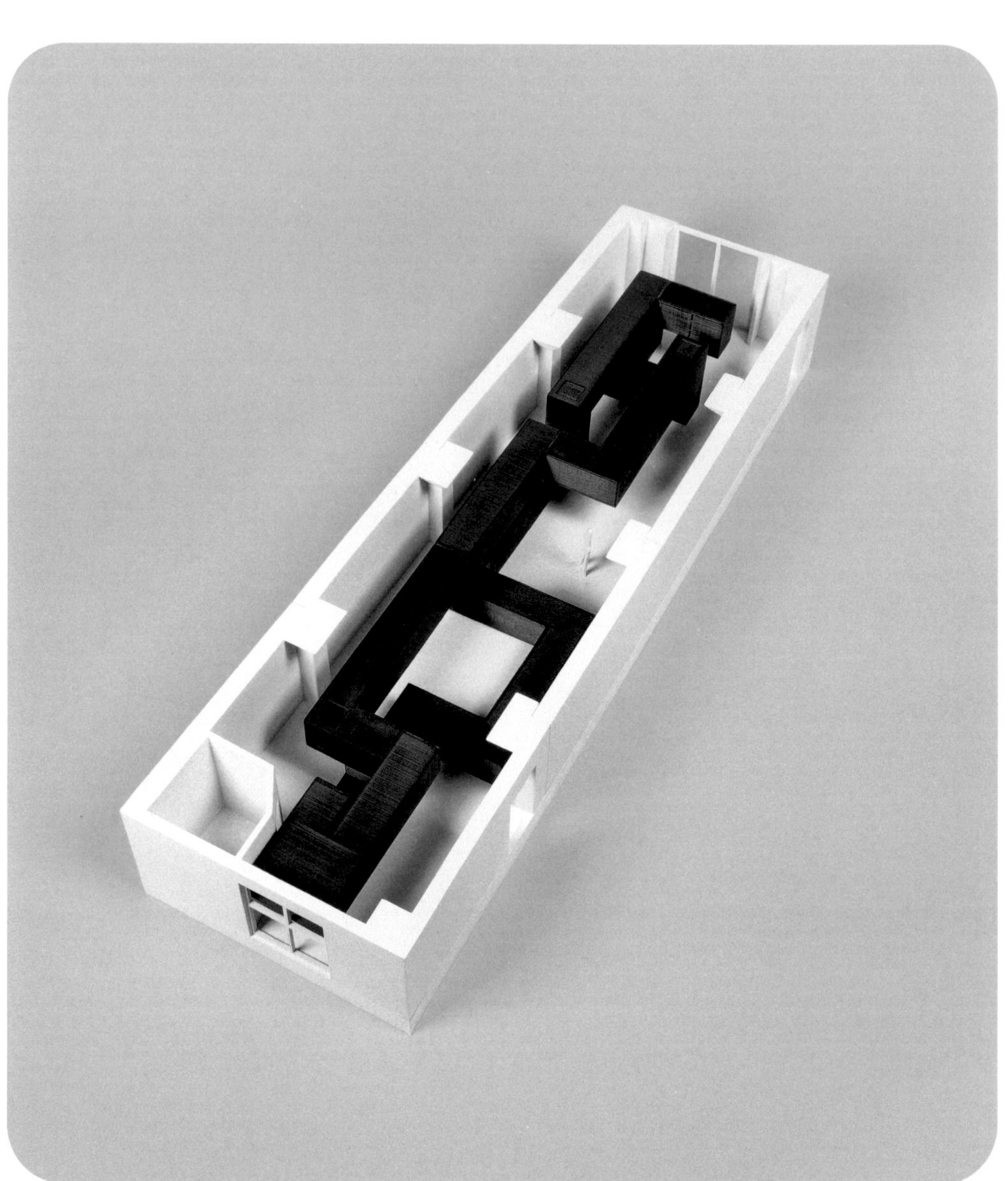

08 BEAUTIFUL TUBE
1:40 | 2023

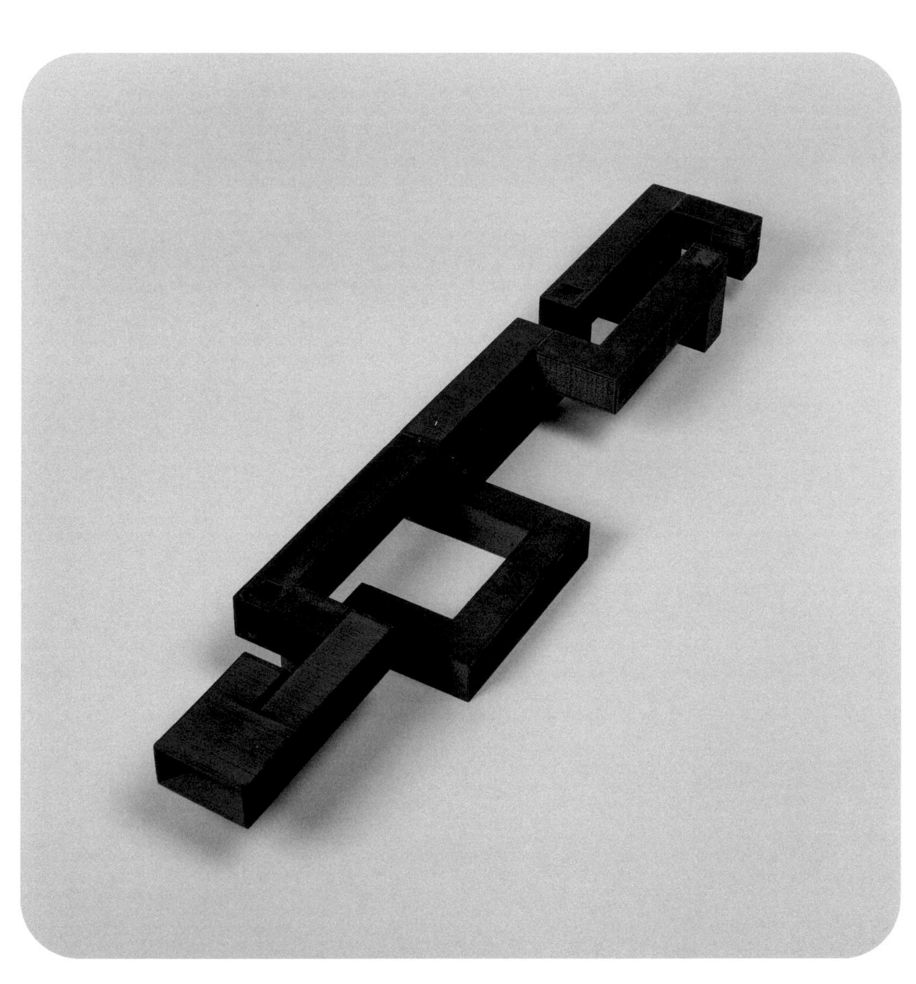

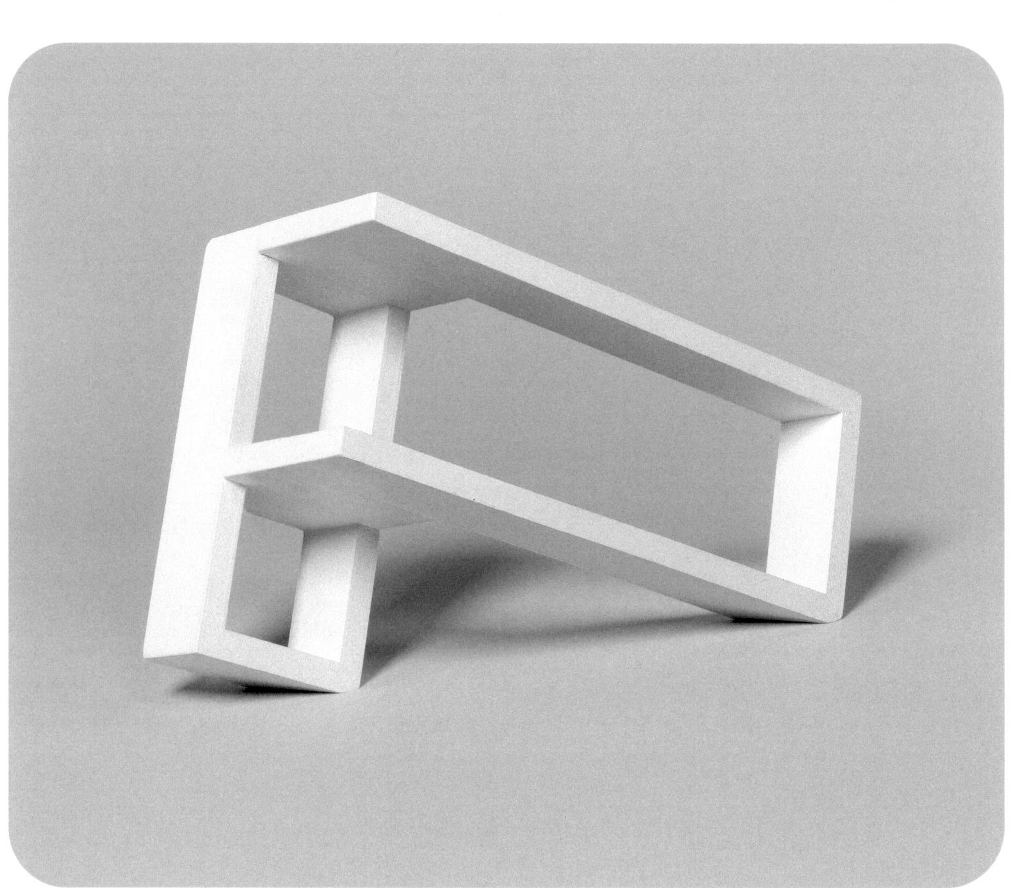

09 UP #5
1:33 | 2022

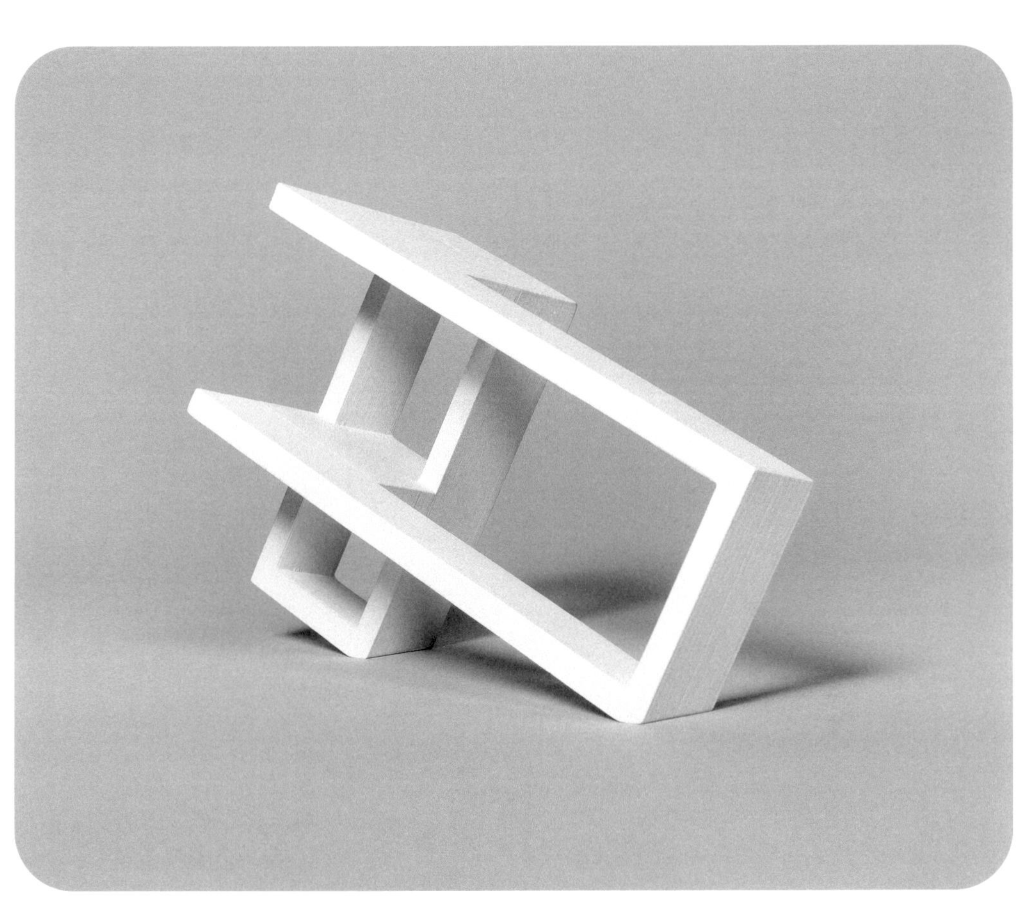

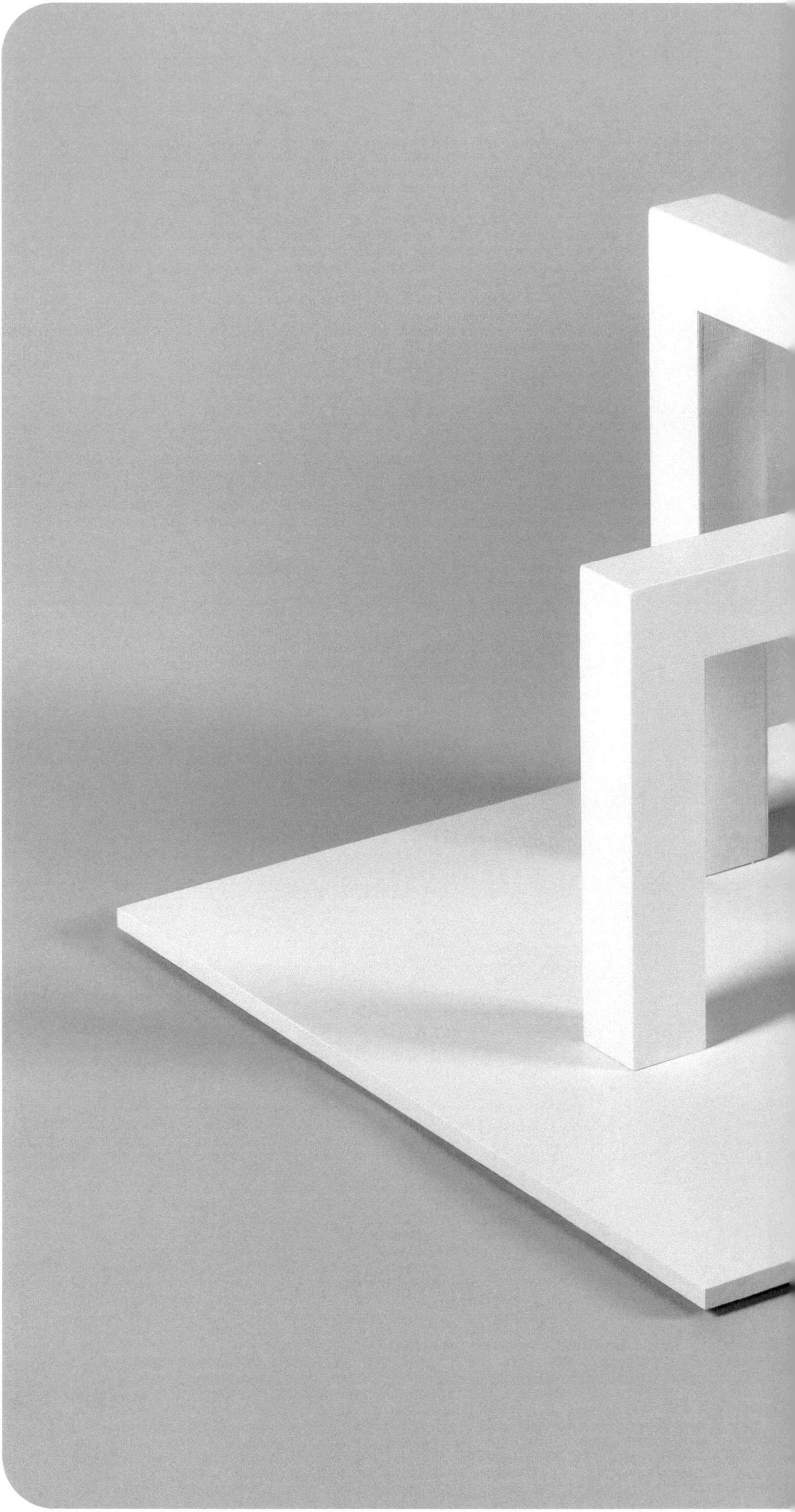

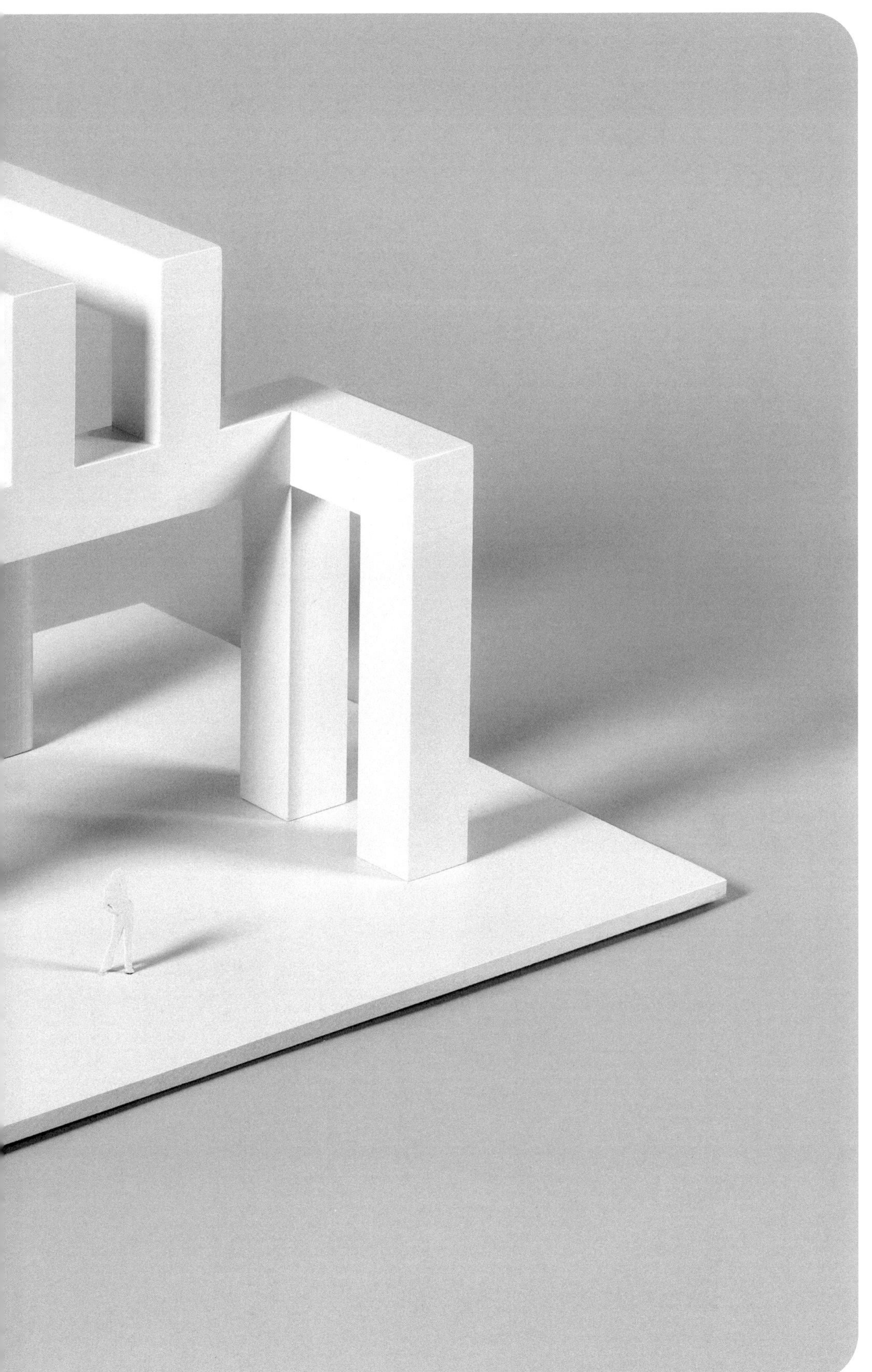

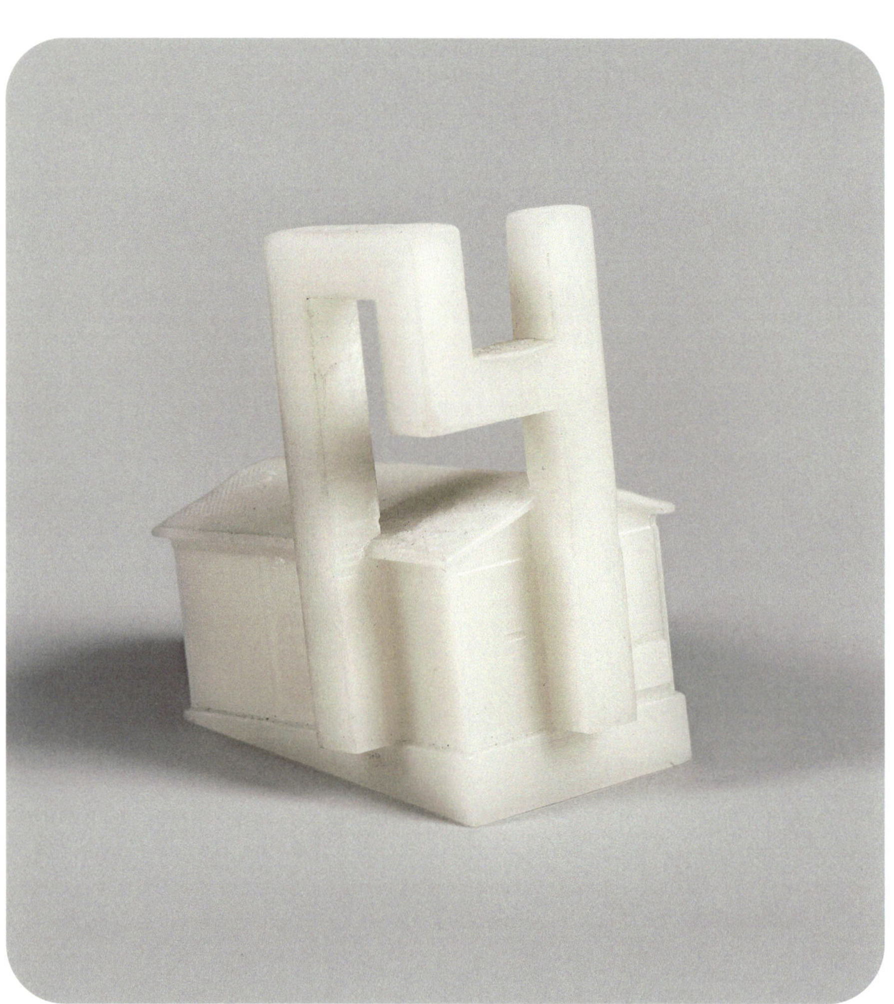

11

UP #1
1:200 | 2014

12 SPIRALS #3
1:100 | 2013

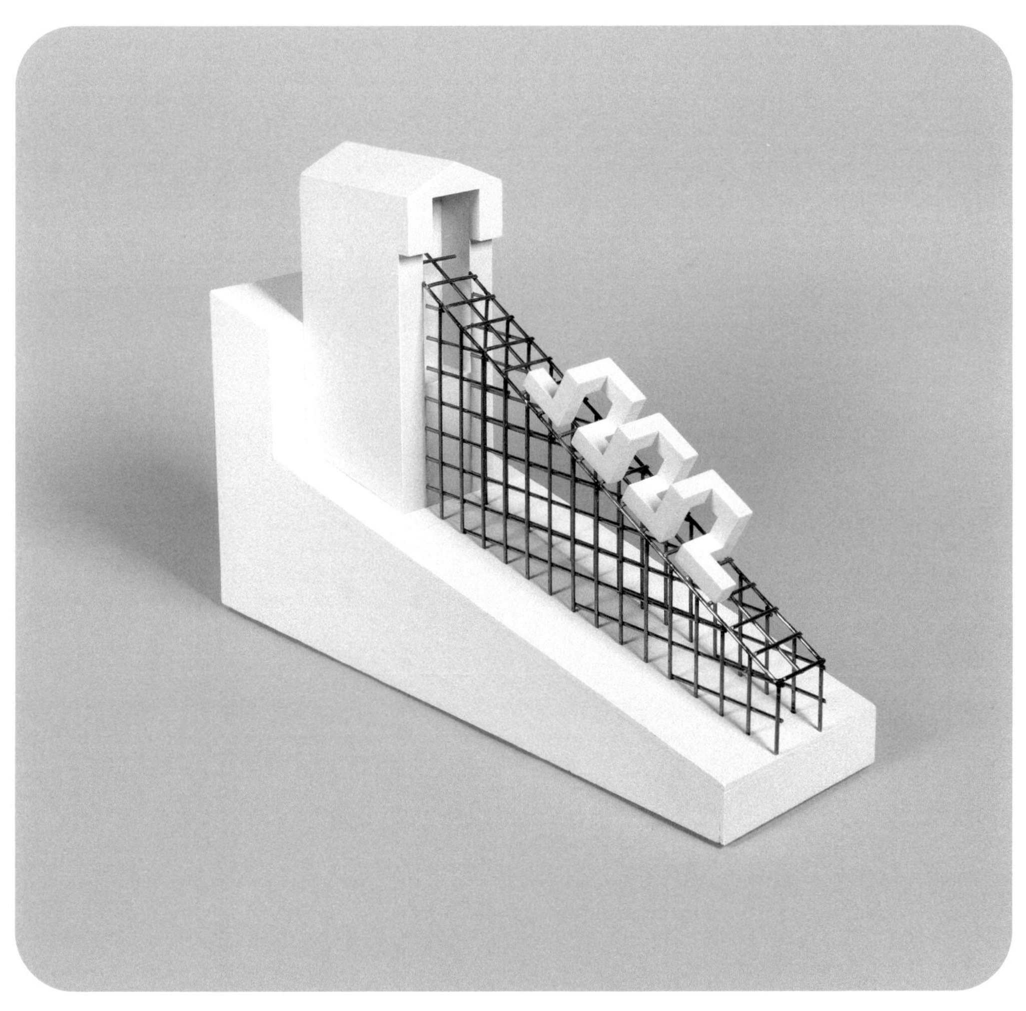

13 UP
1:30 | 2020

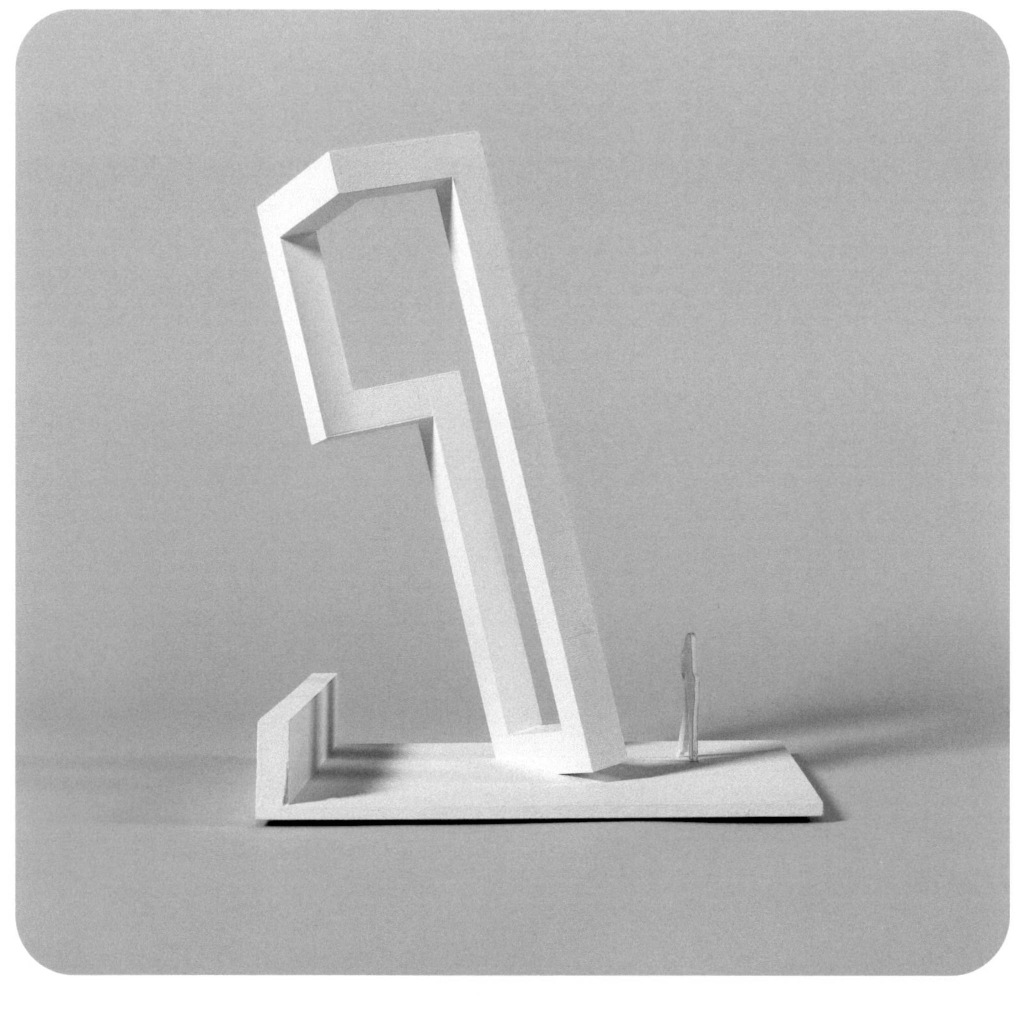

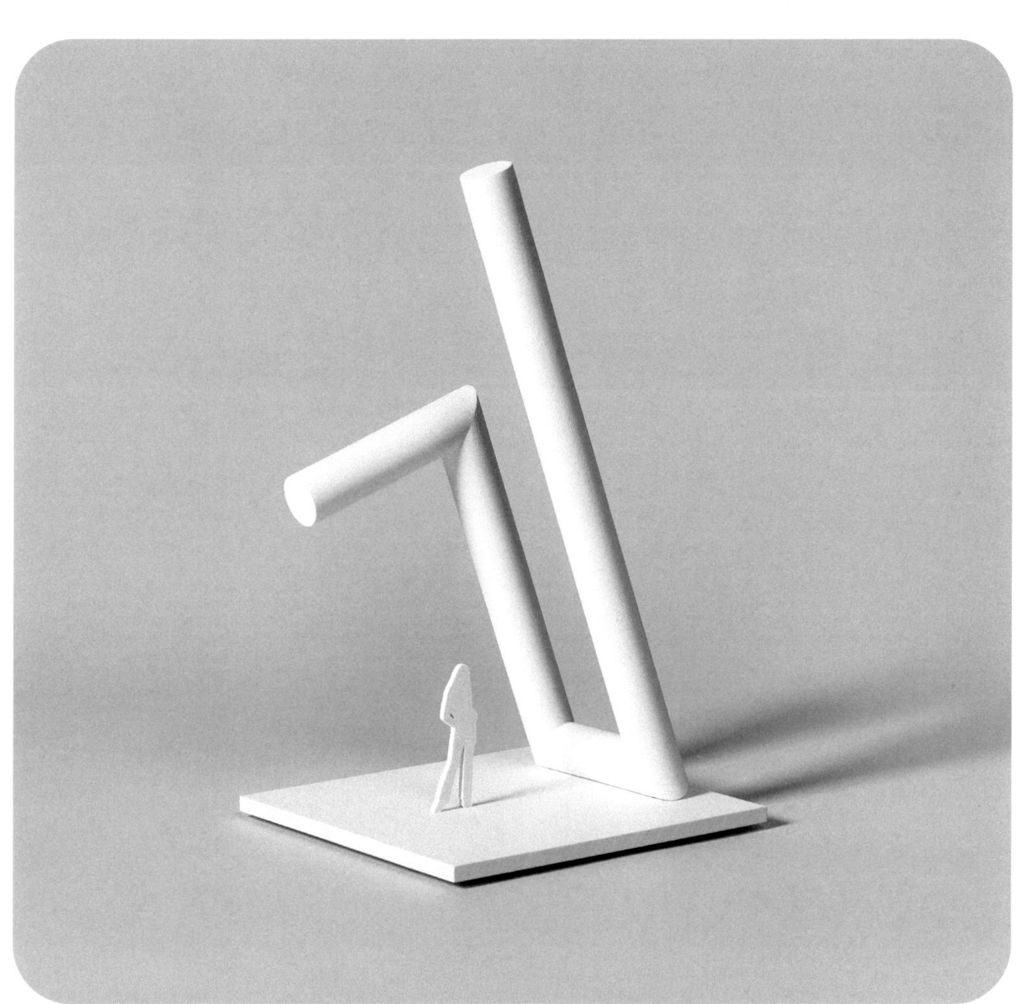

UP #4
1:35 | 2020

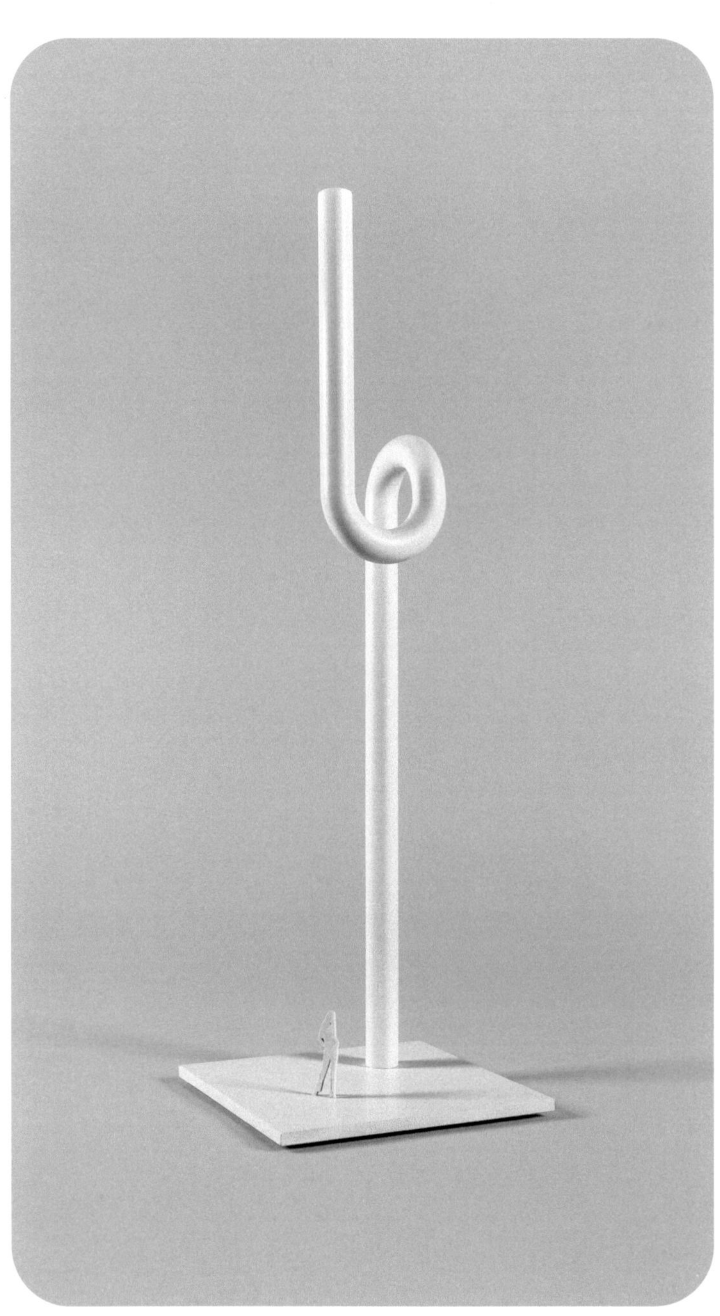

15

UP #7
1:40 | 2023

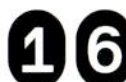

BEAUTIFUL VIEW #1
1:50 | 2019

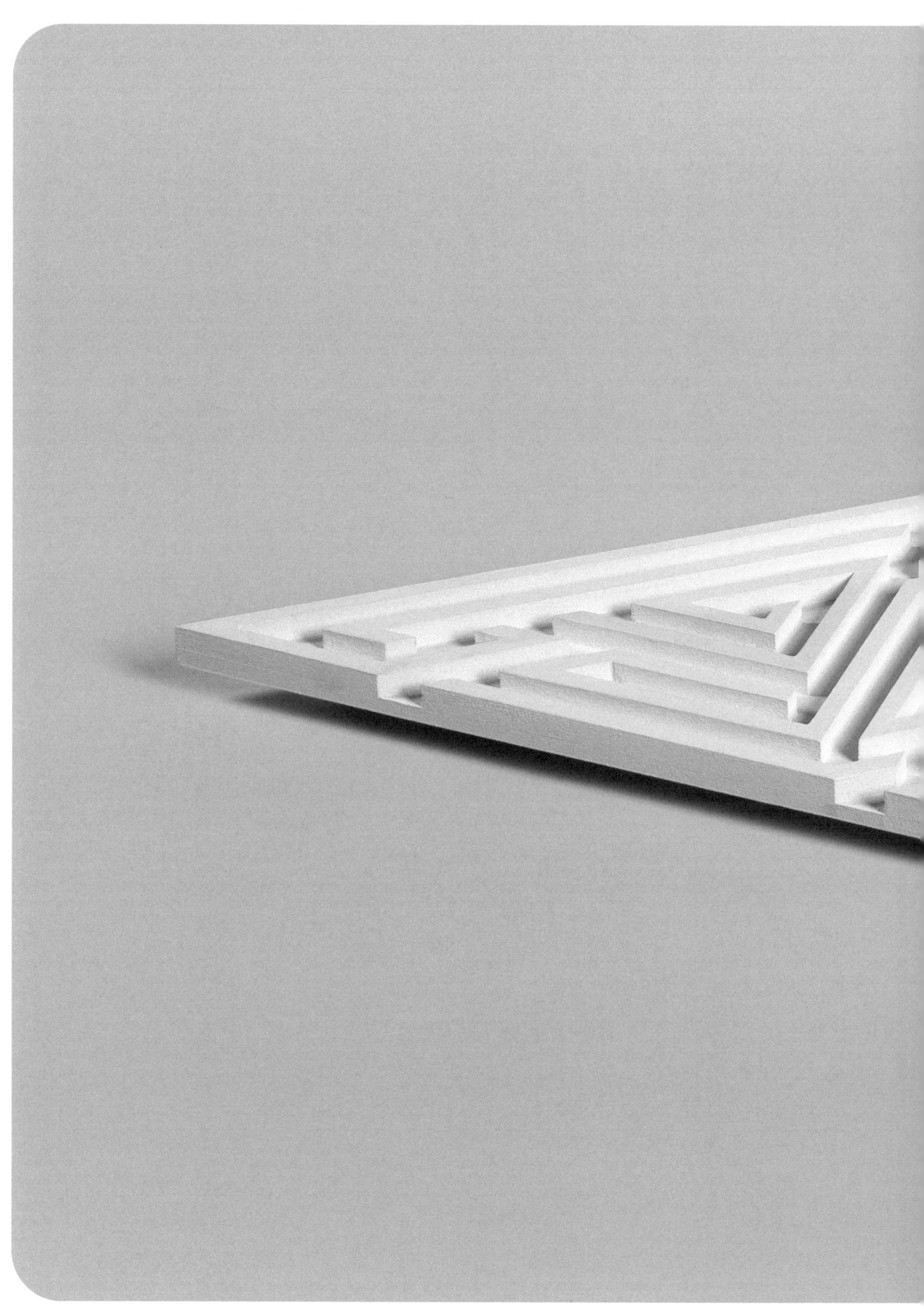

17 DIVING PLATFORM
1:150 | 2014

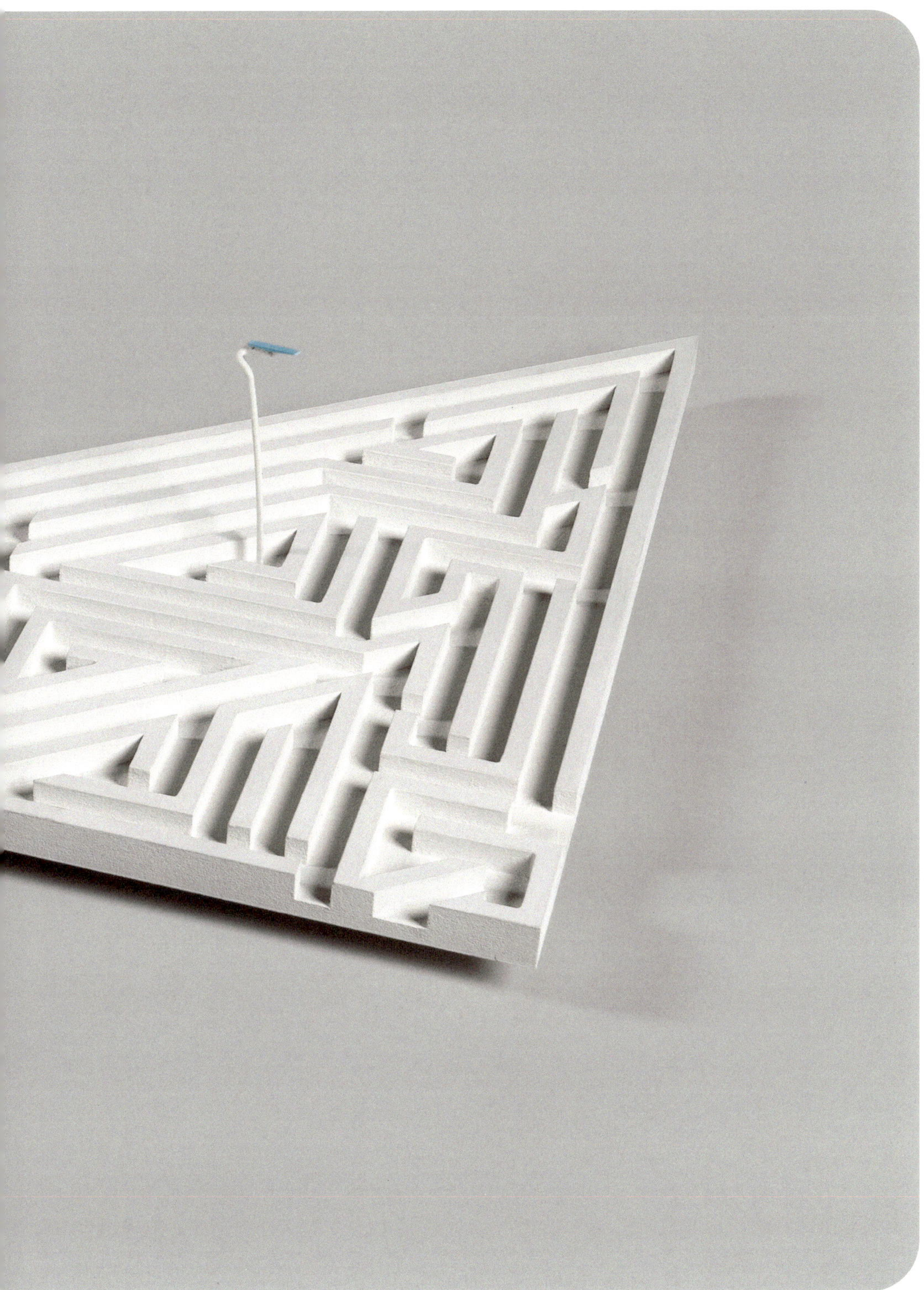

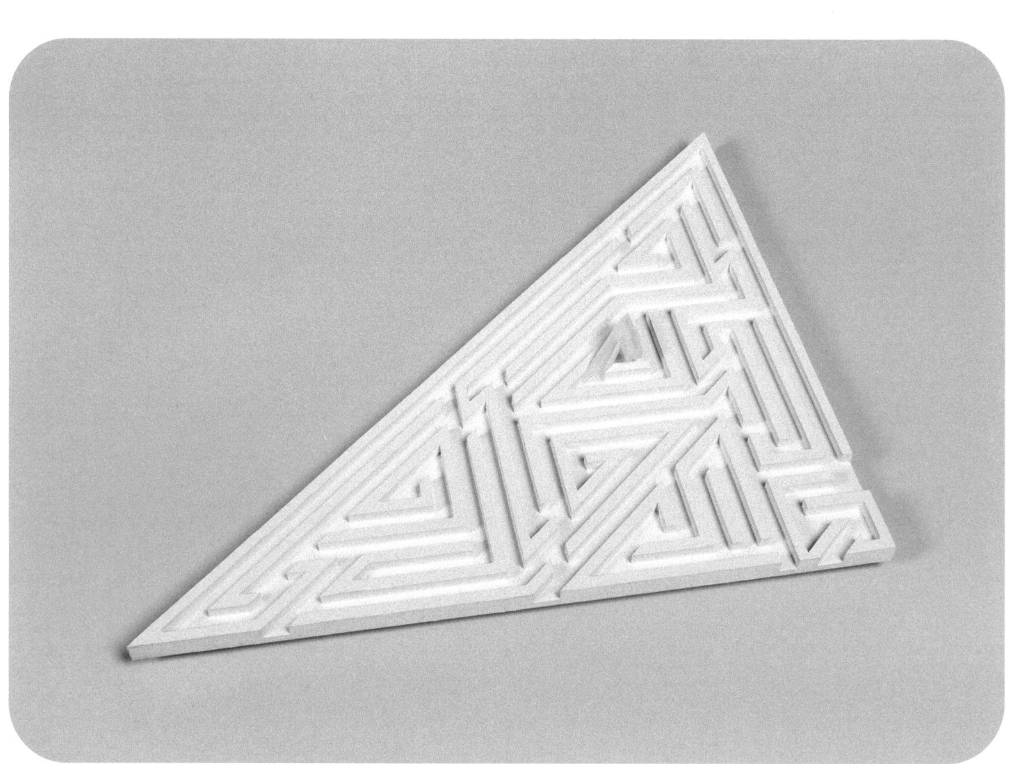

18

BEAUTIFUL STEPS
1:150 | 2014

19 BEAUTIFUL VIEW #1
1:50 | 2019

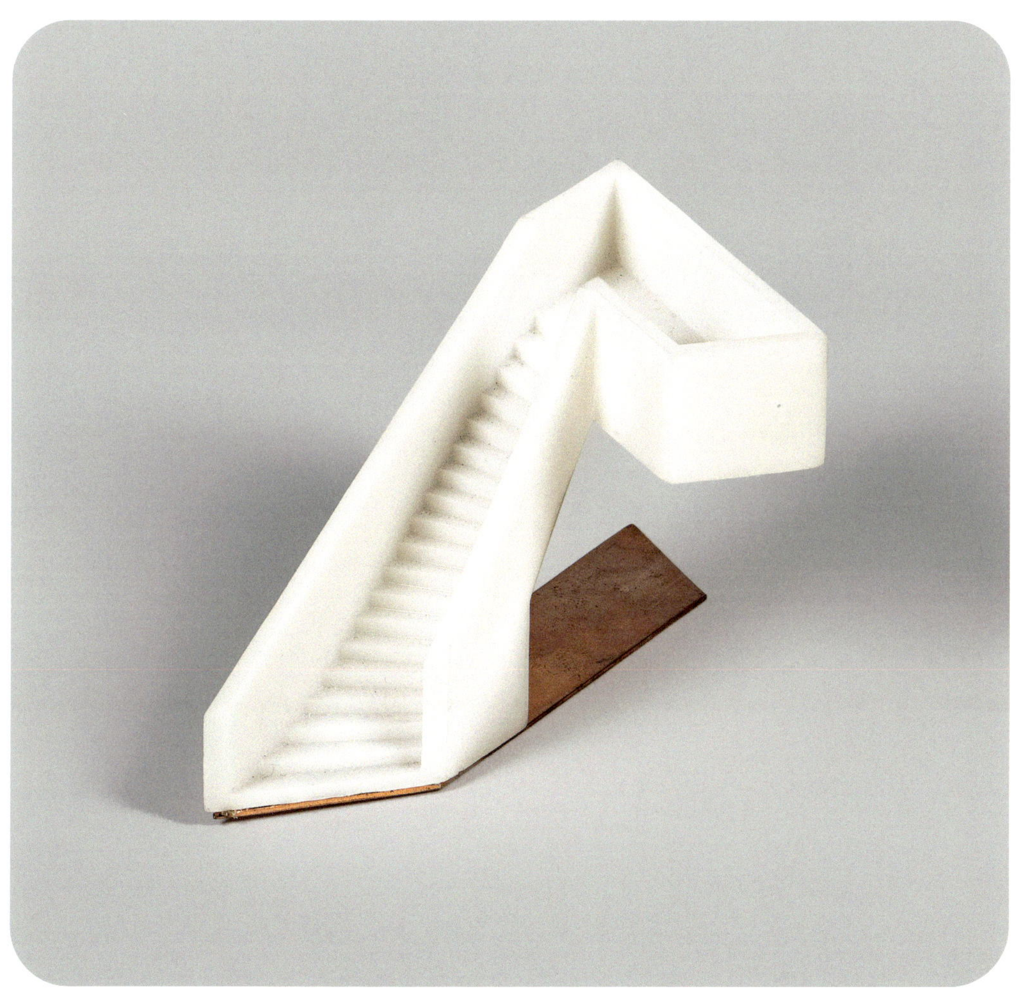

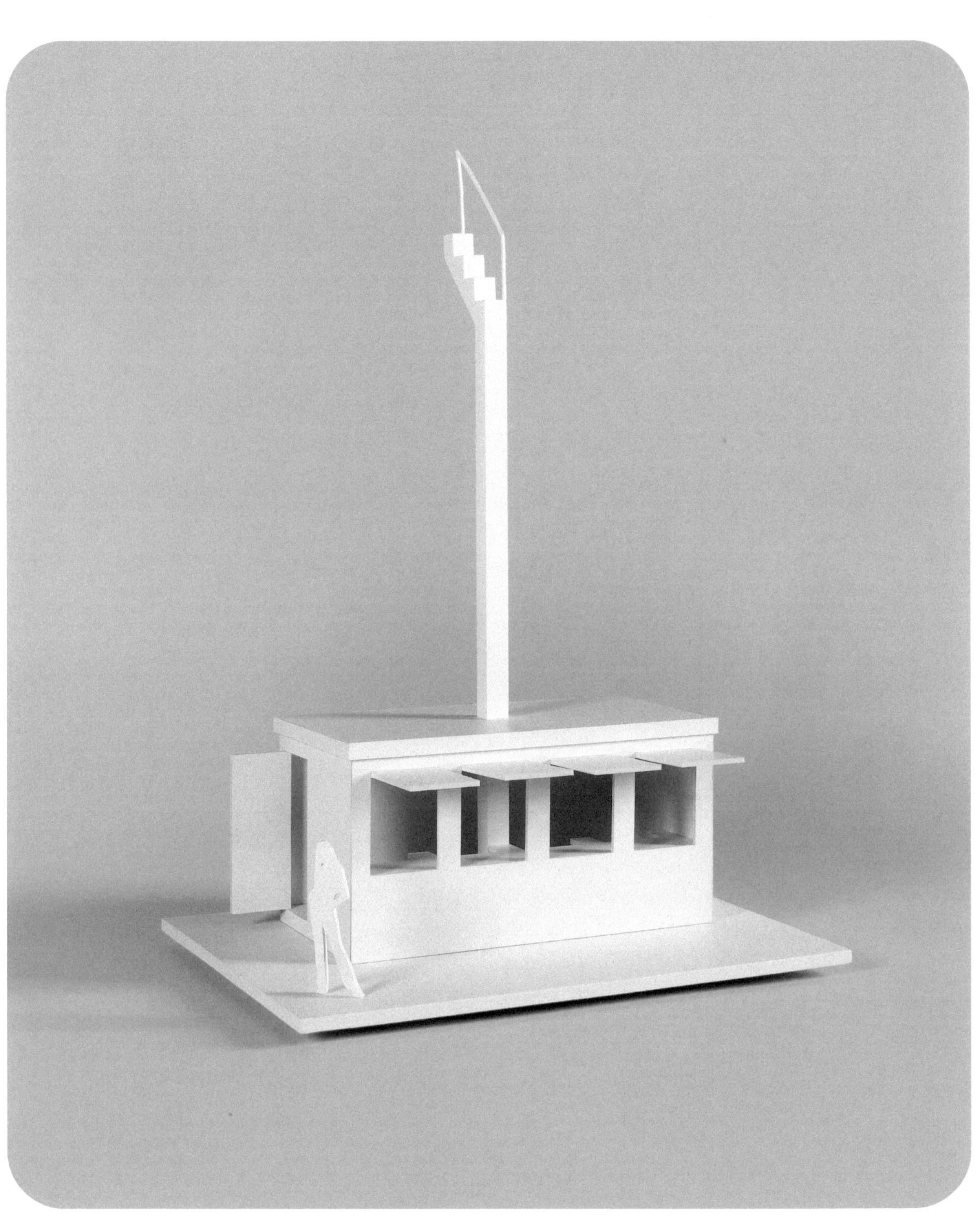

20 PLACES DÉPLACÉES
1:20 | 2019

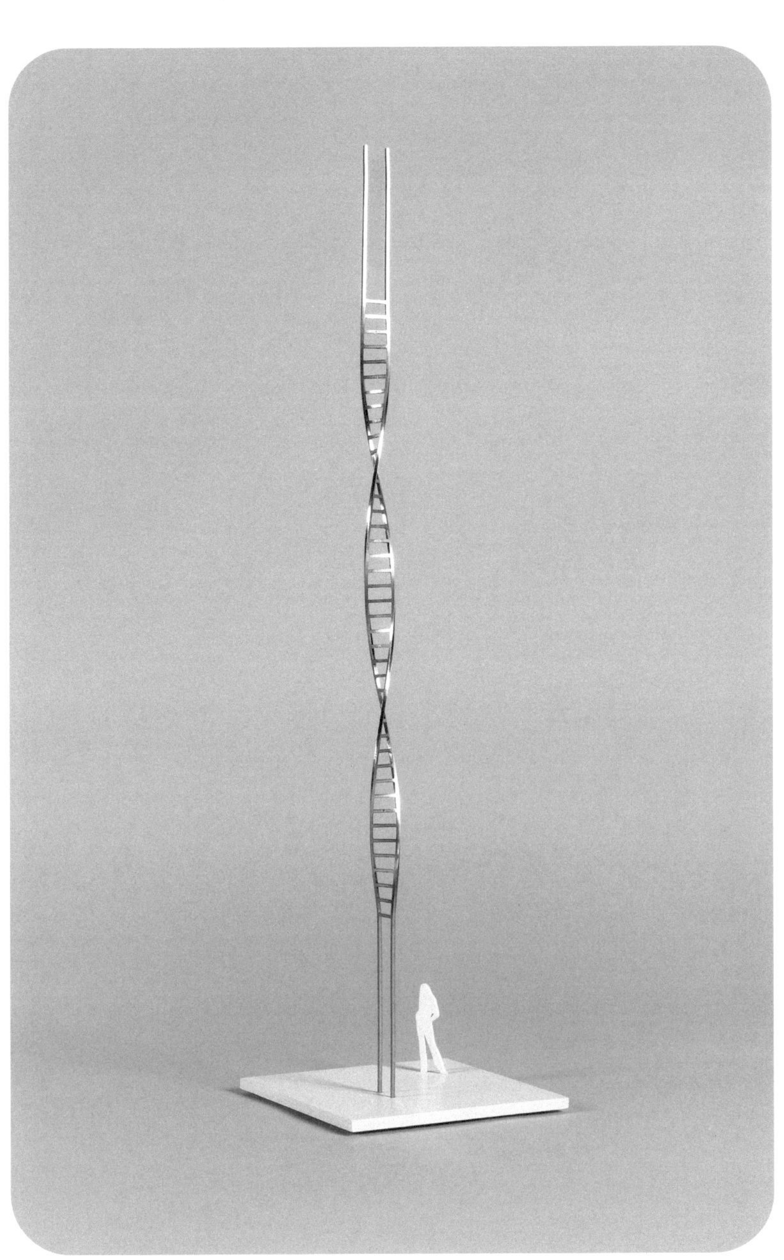

21

S42
1:33 | 2013

22

BEAUTIFUL STEPS #16
1:25 | 2018

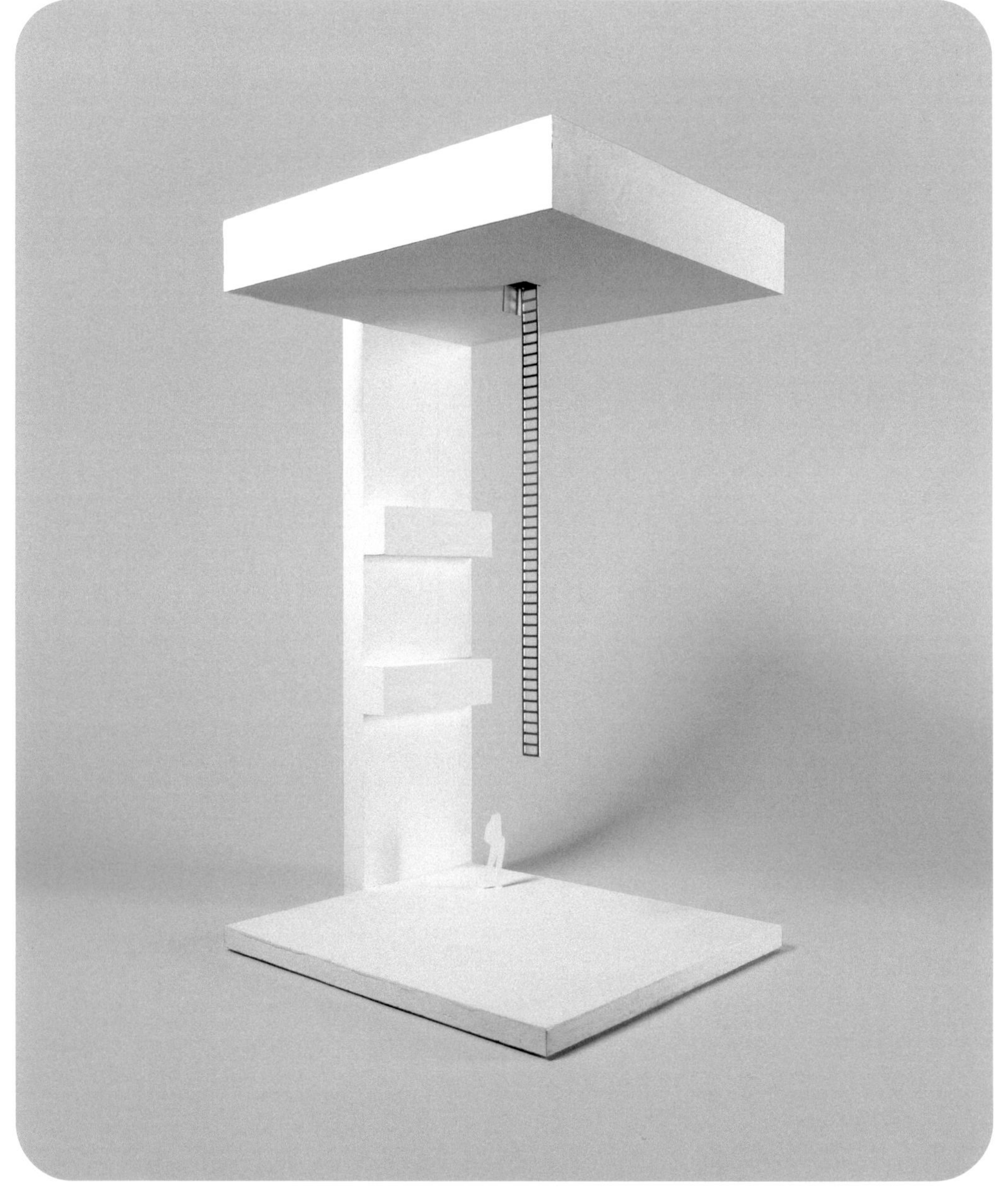

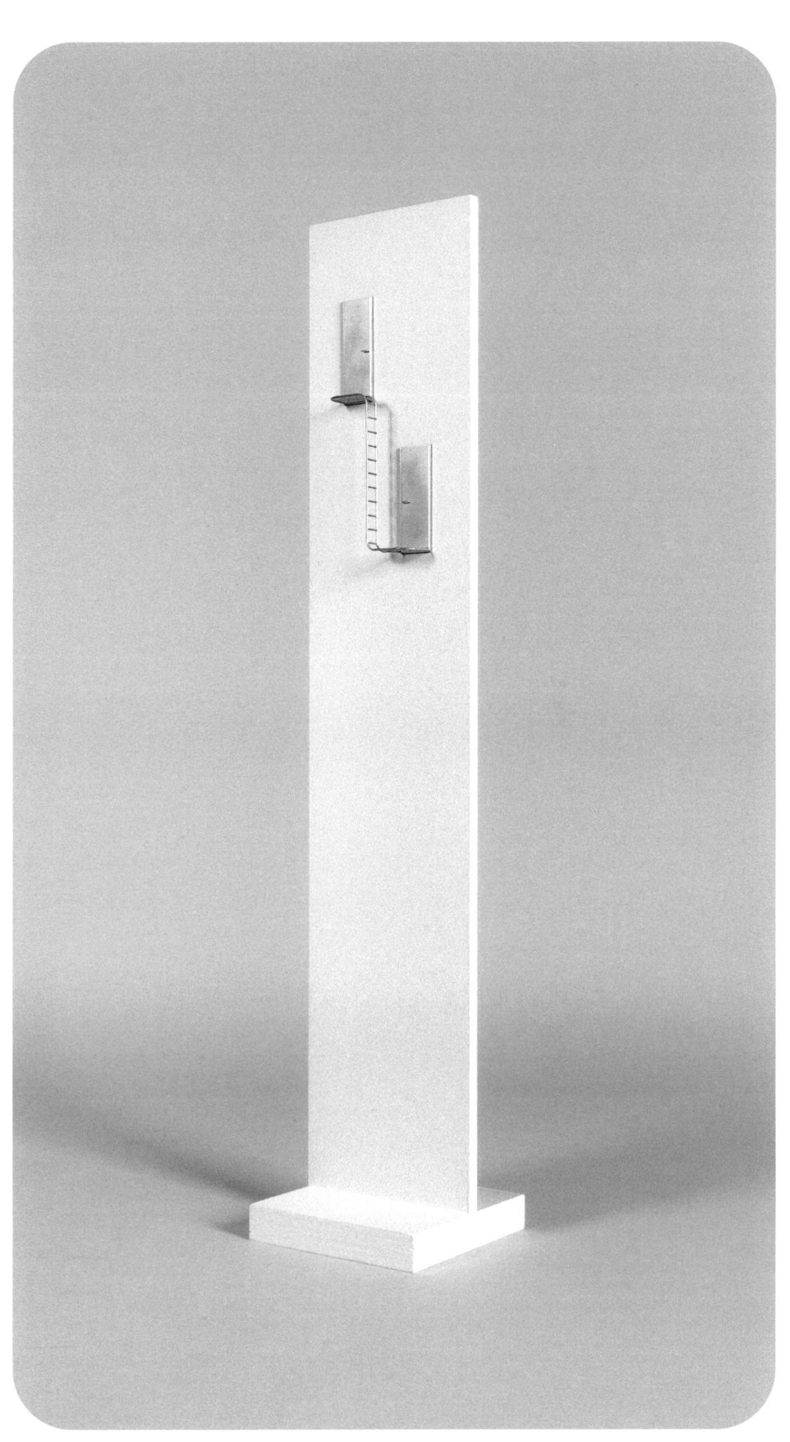

23 BEAUTIFUL STEPS #15
1:25 | 2013

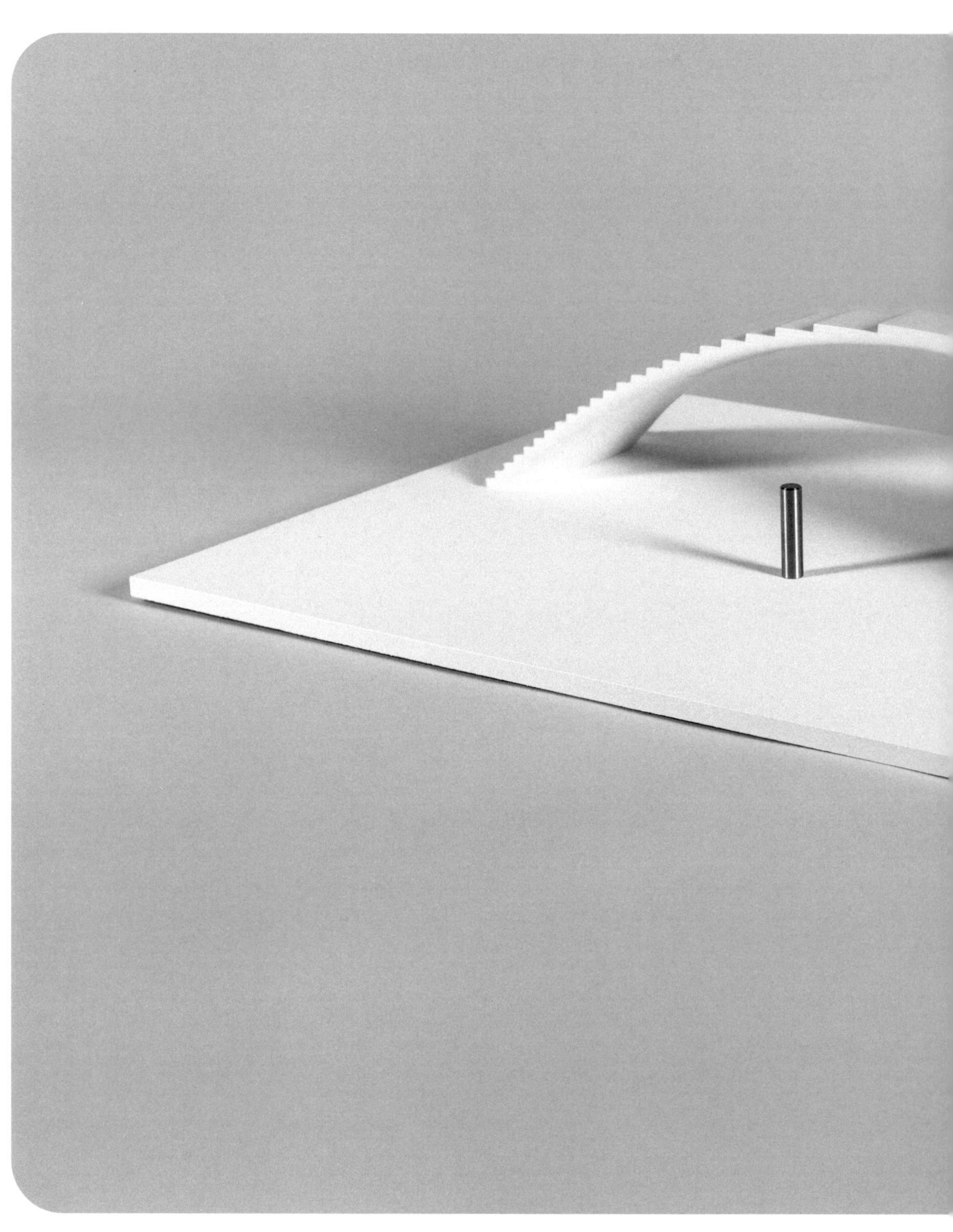

BEAUTIFUL BRIDGE #3
1:40 | 2023

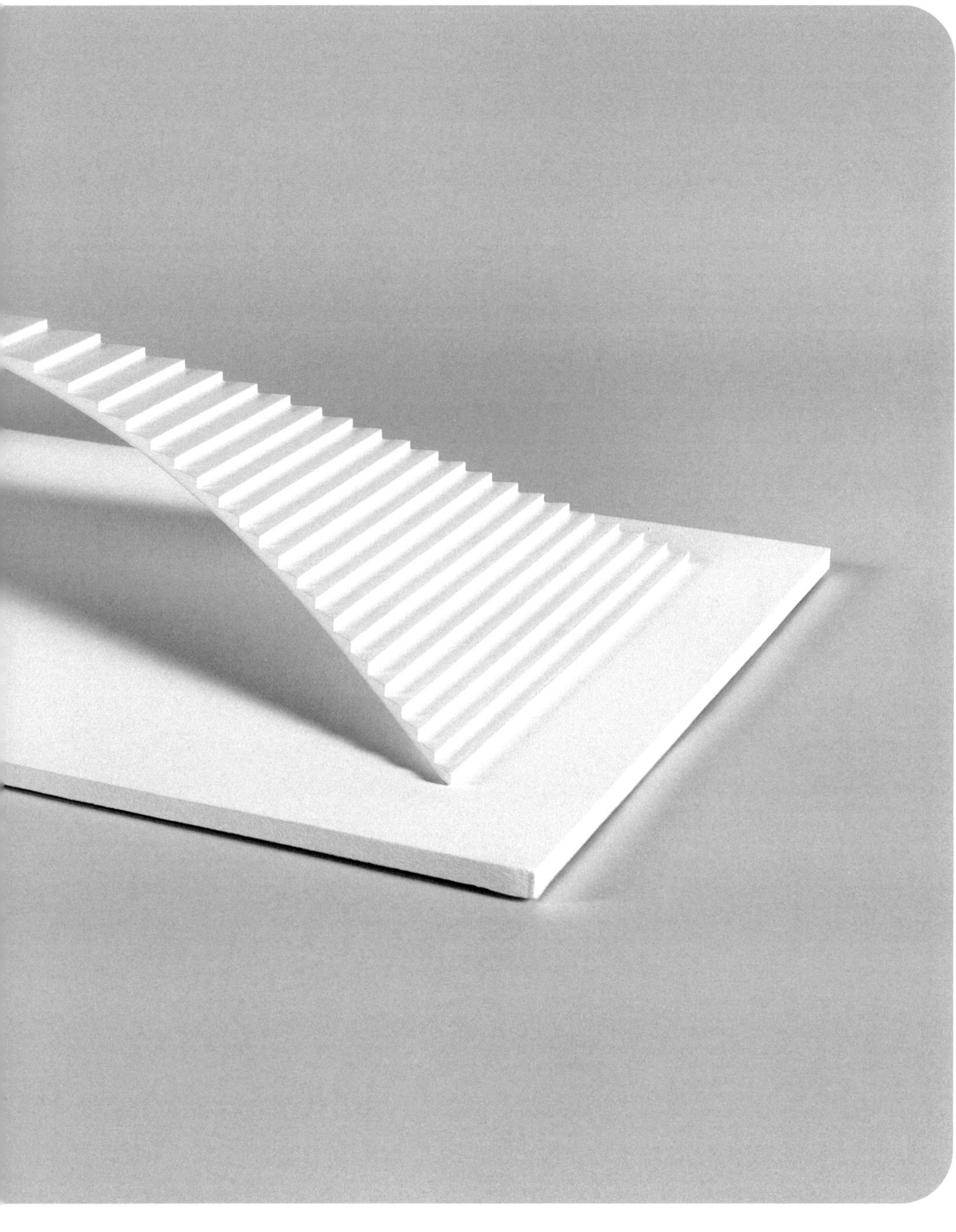

25 E3
1:30 | 2016

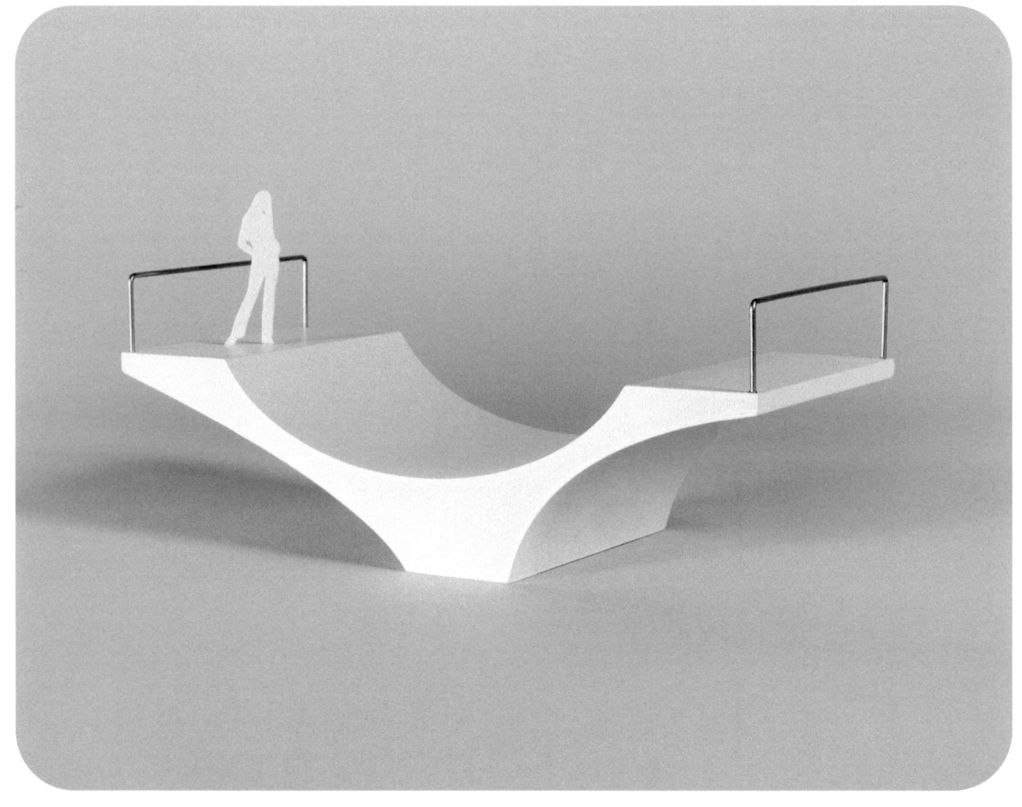

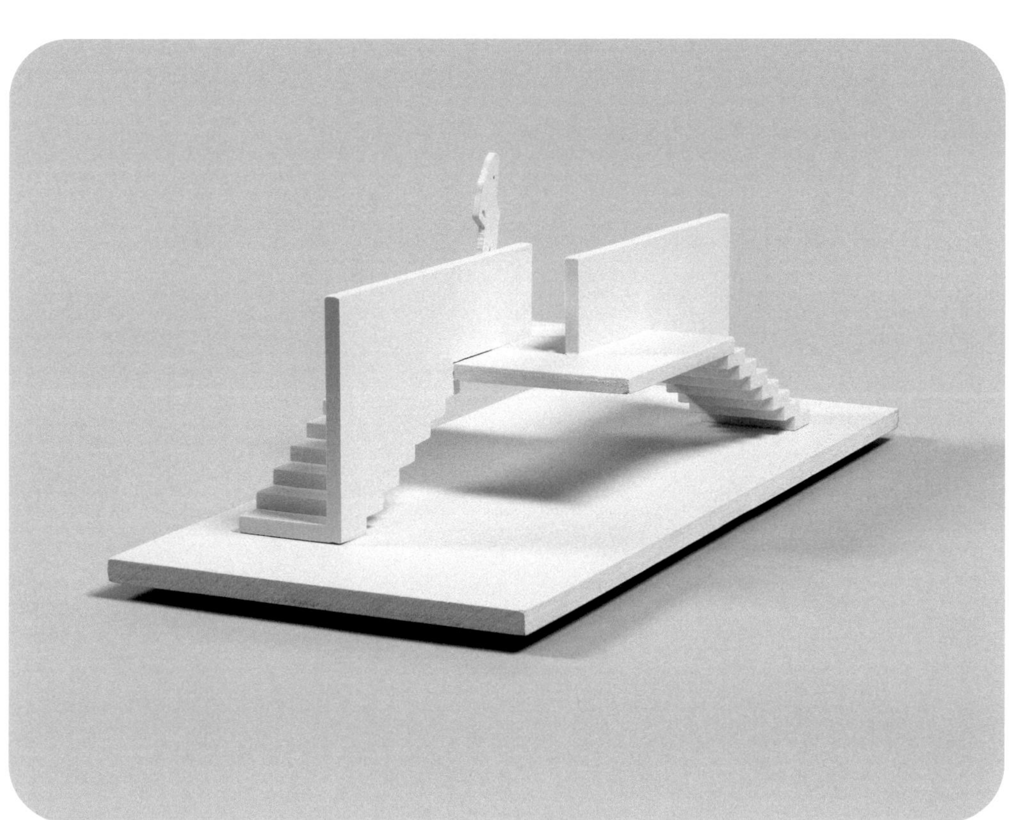

26

T15
1:25 | 2019

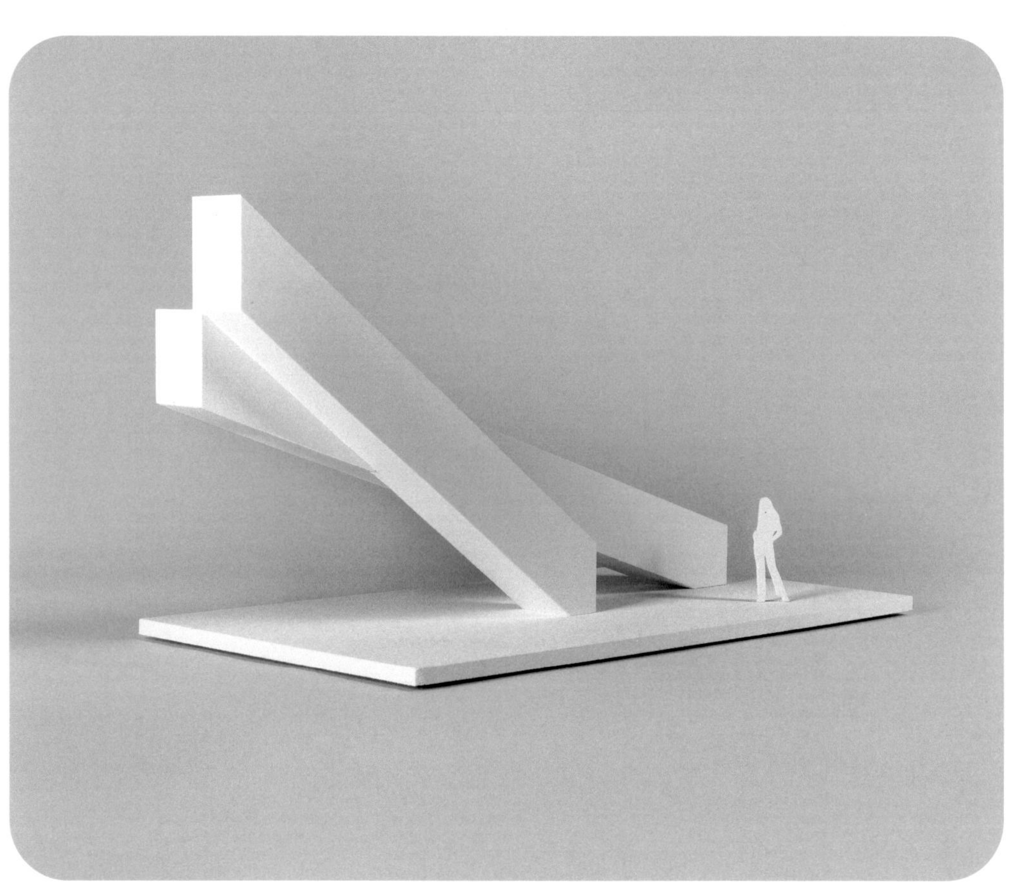

27 BEAUTIFUL STEPS #11
1:25 | 2016

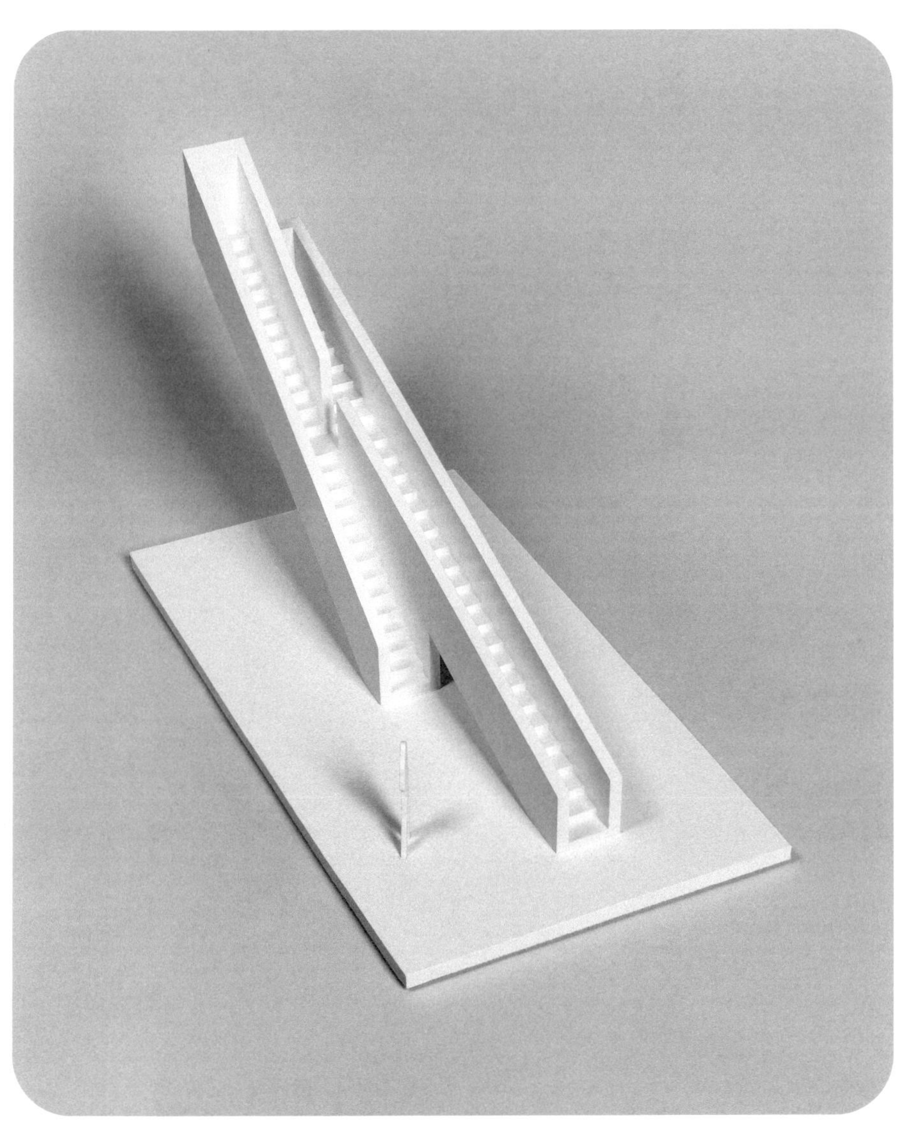

T12
1:25 | 2016

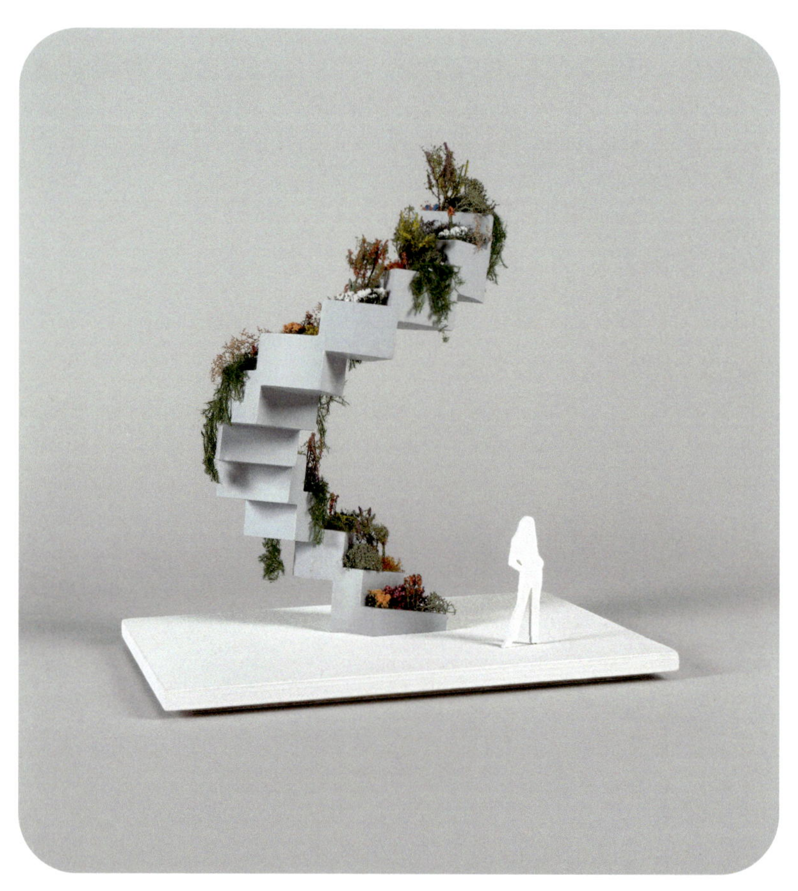

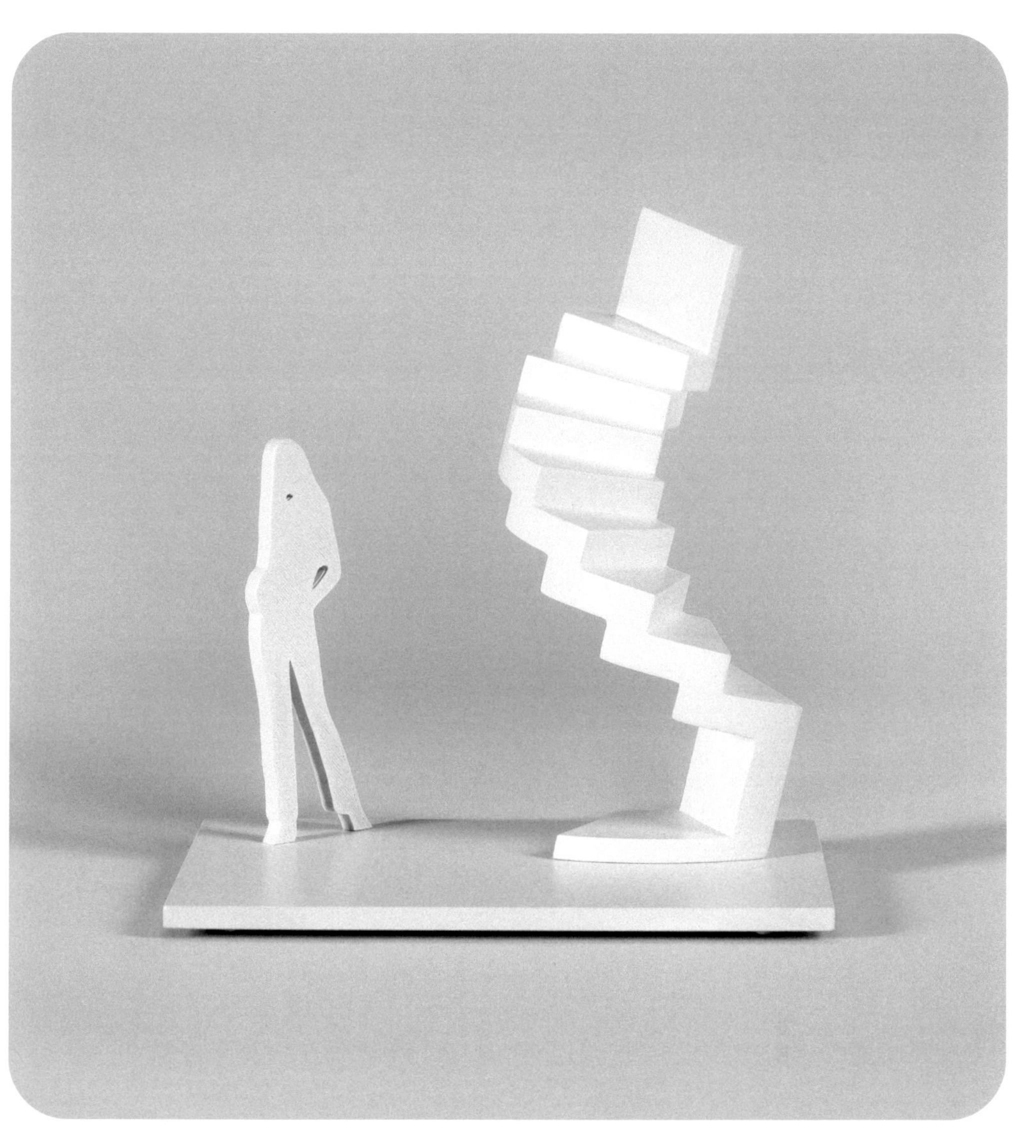

29 BEAUTIFUL STEPS #13
1:20 | 2015

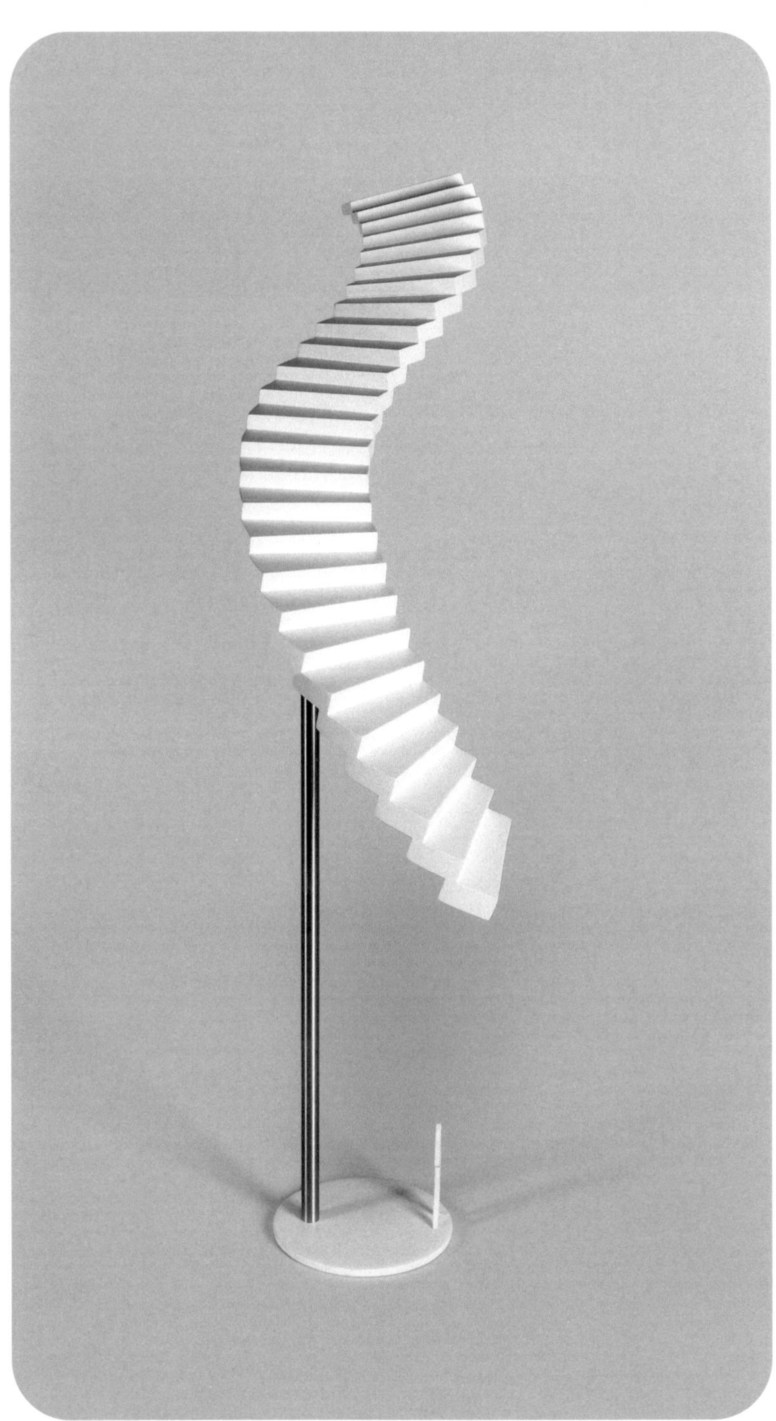

30 BEAUTIFUL STEPS
1:30 | 2022

31

BEAUTIFUL STEPS #7
1:33 | 2013

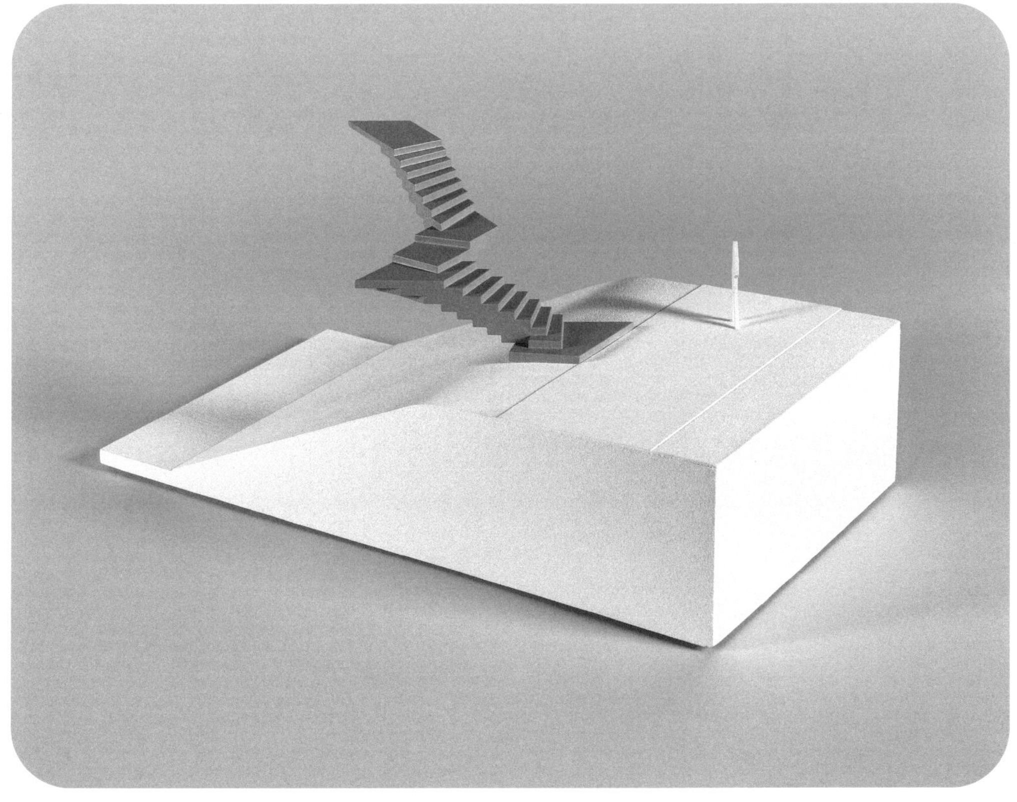

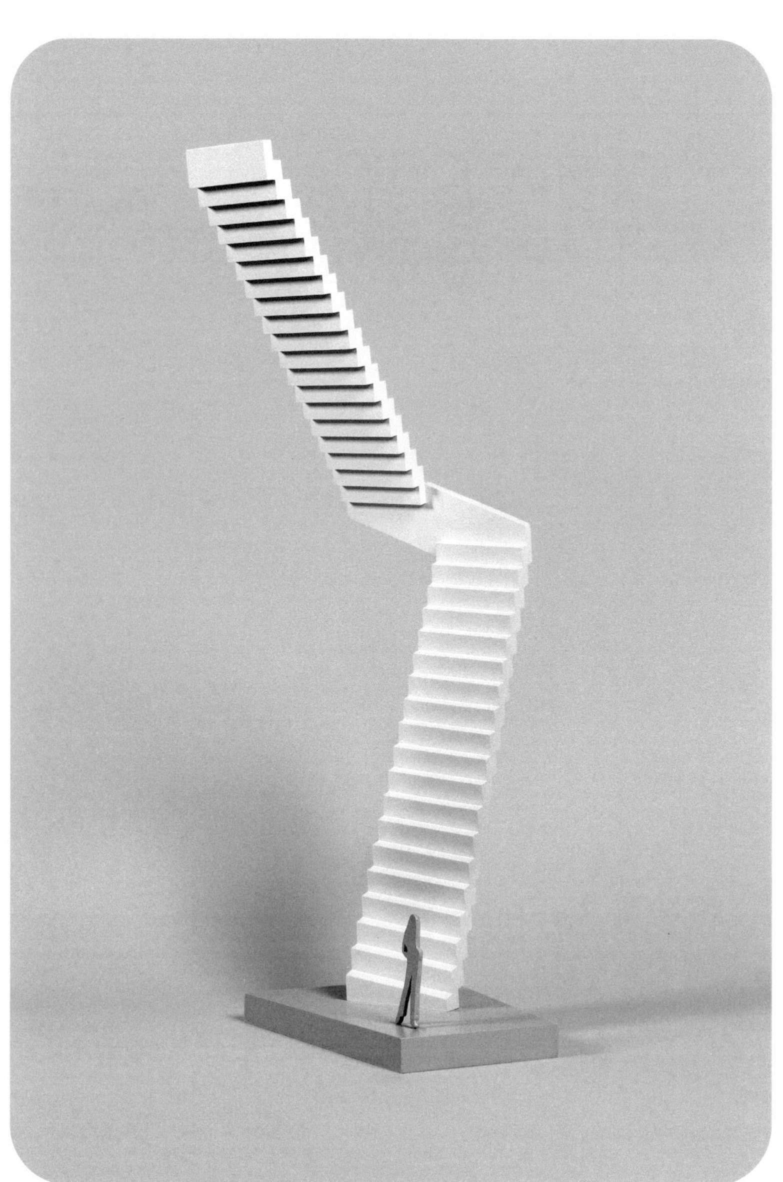

32 BEAUTIFUL STEPS
1:20 | 2010

S20
1:33 |2018

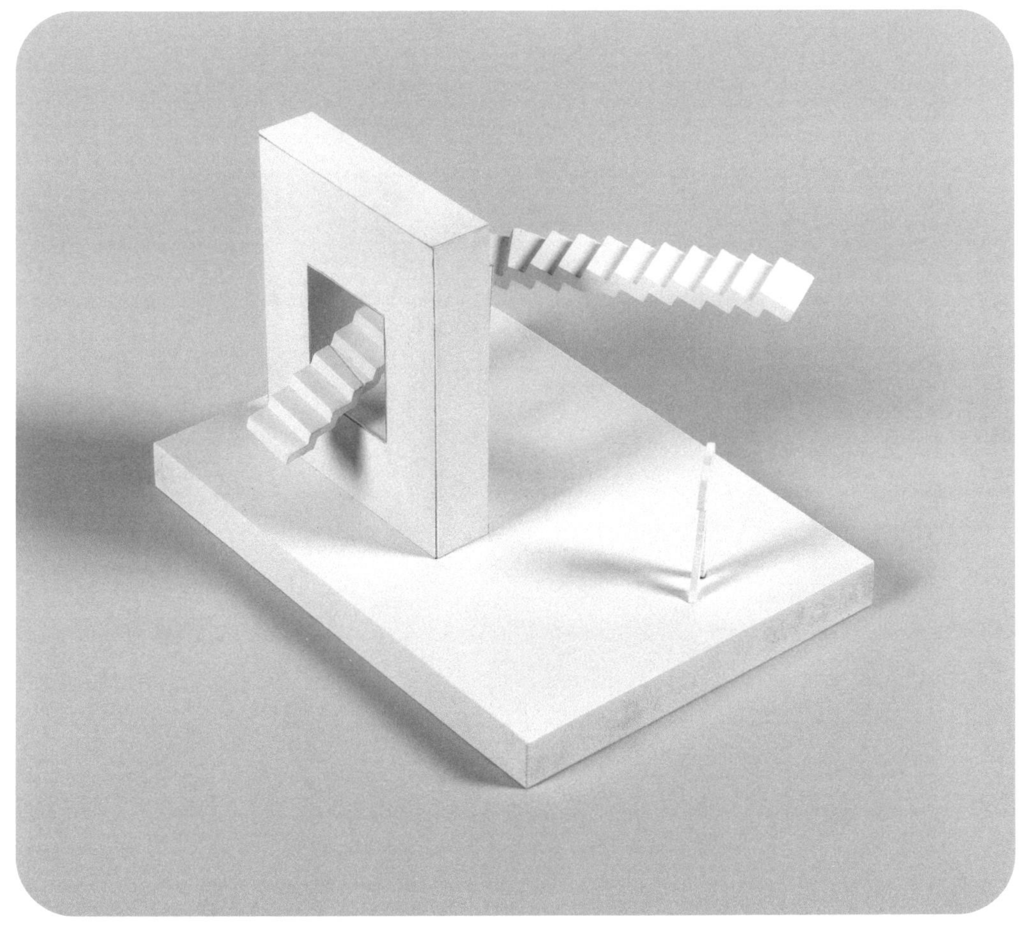

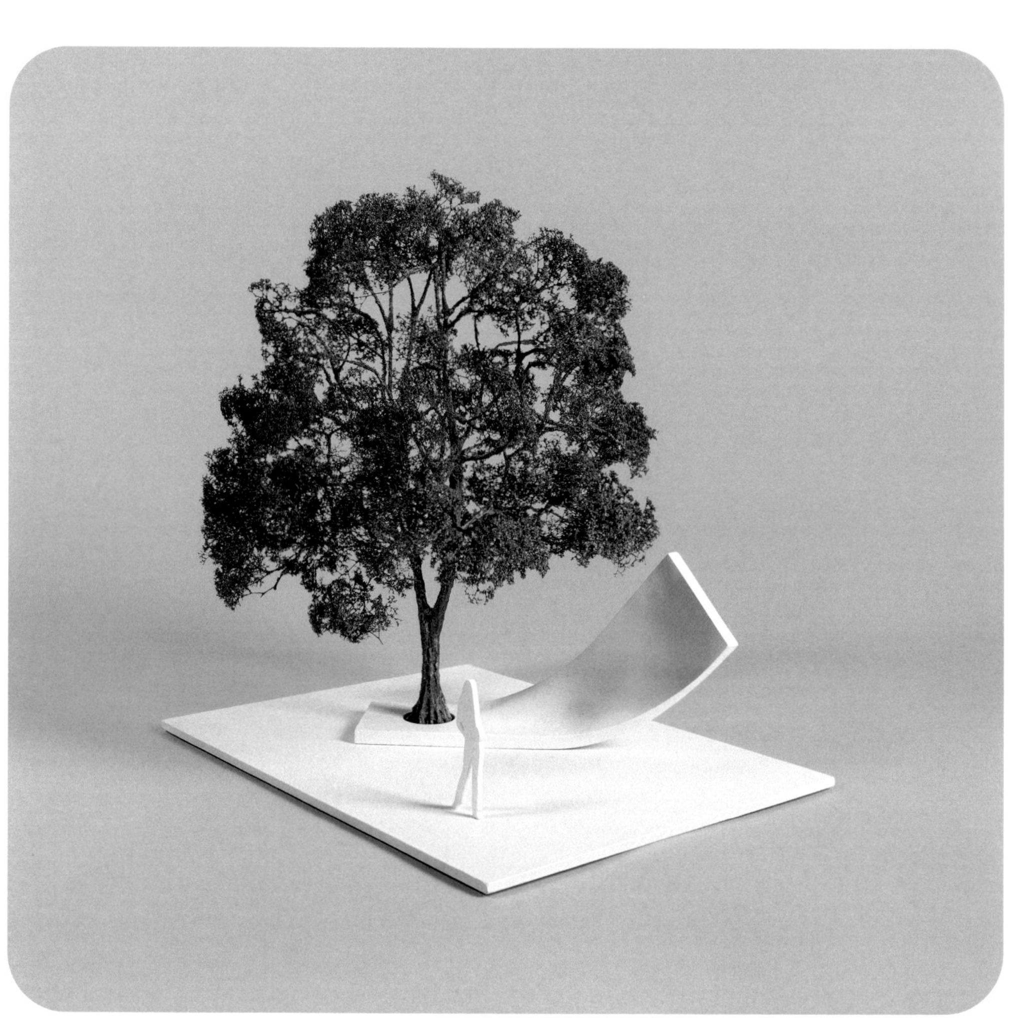

WAVE
1:20 | 2022

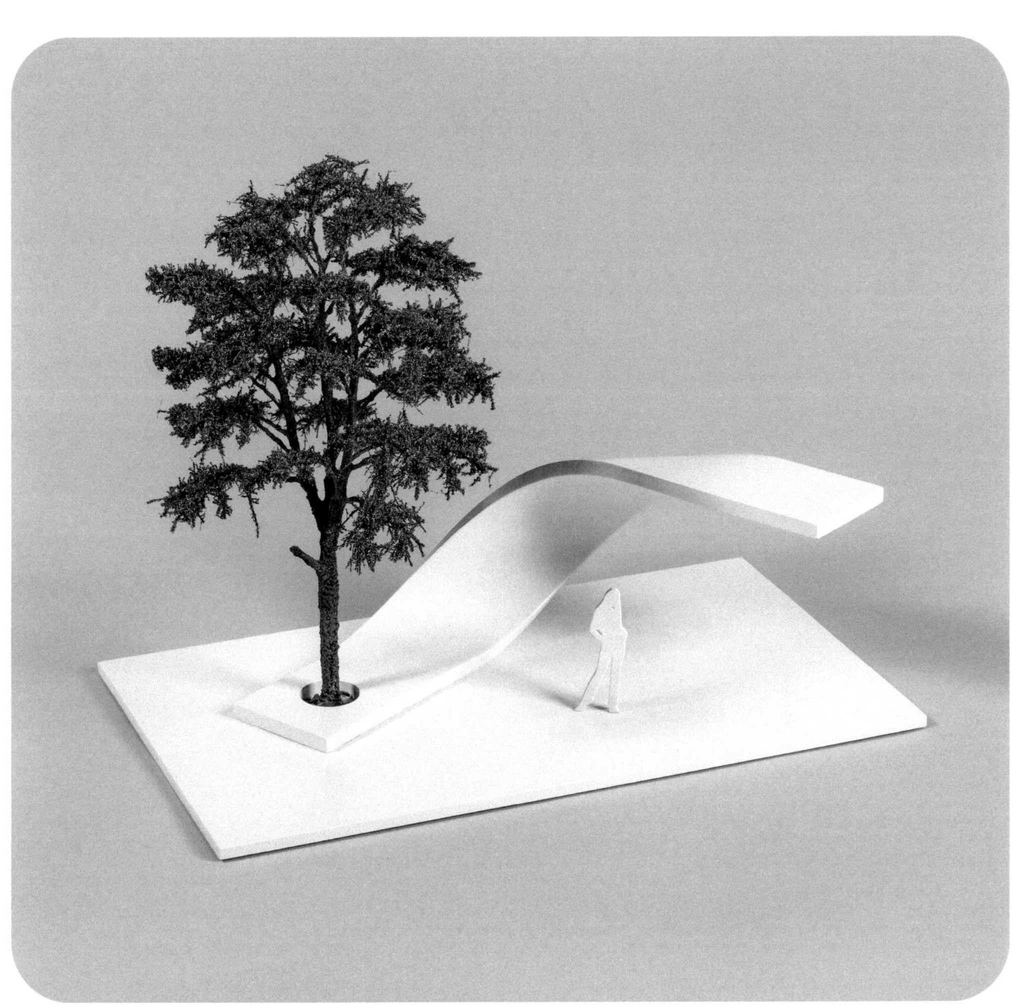

35 SPIRALE
1:25 | 2020

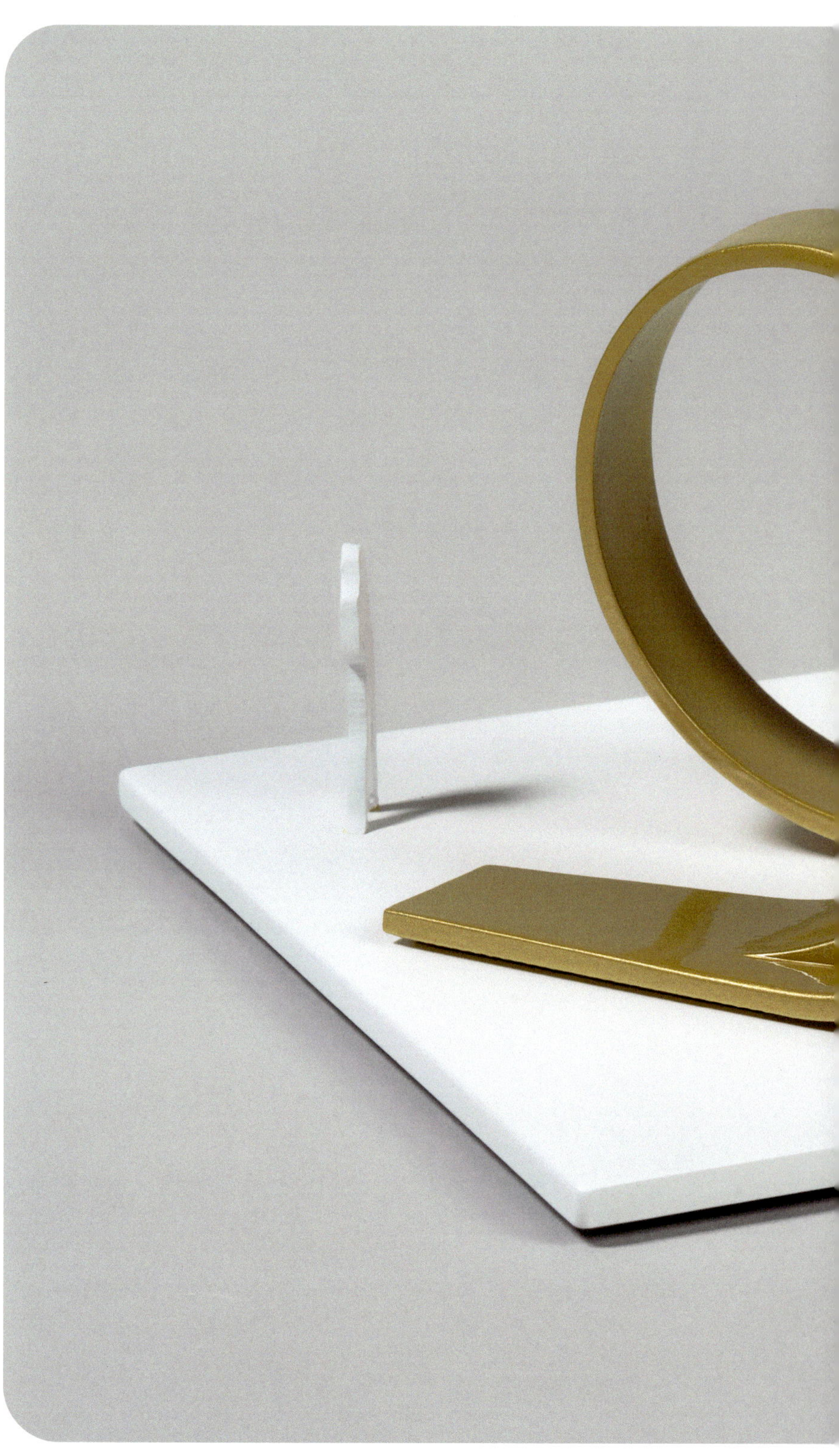

S2
1:40 | 2017

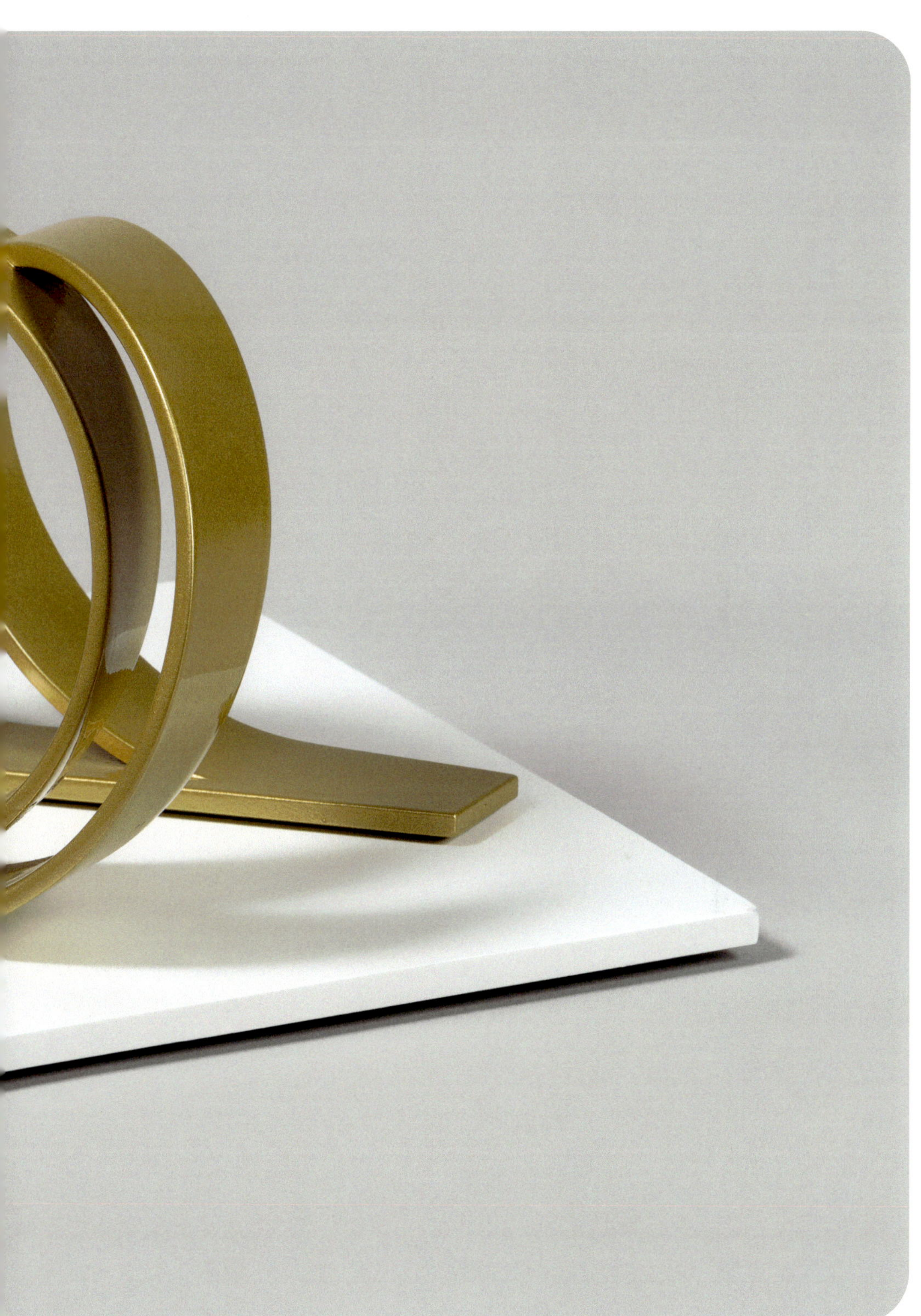

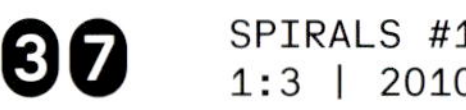

37 SPIRALS #1
1:3 | 2010

38 SPIRALS #1
1:3 | 2010

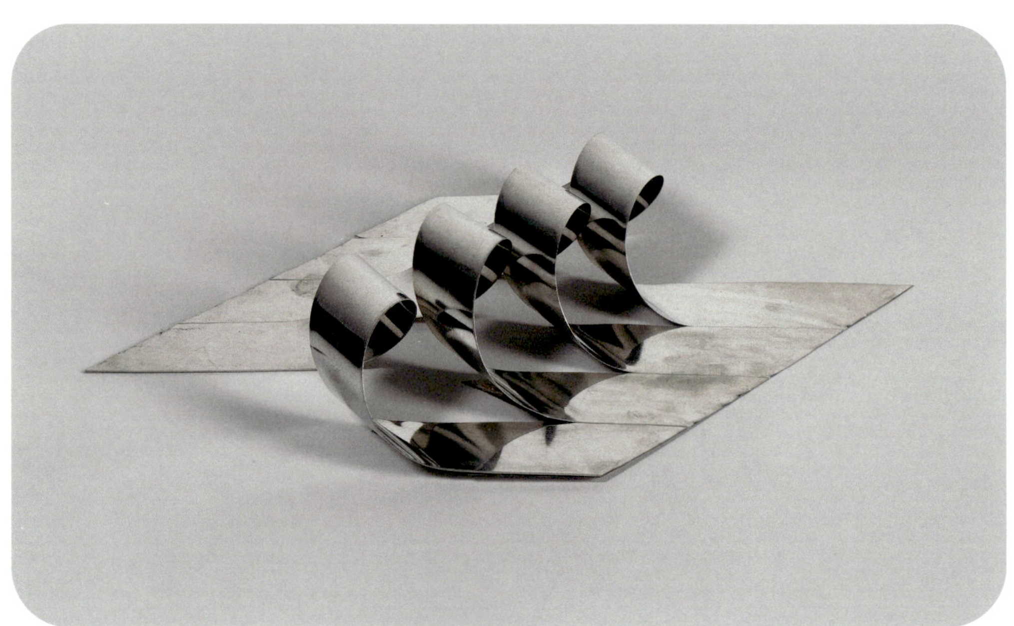

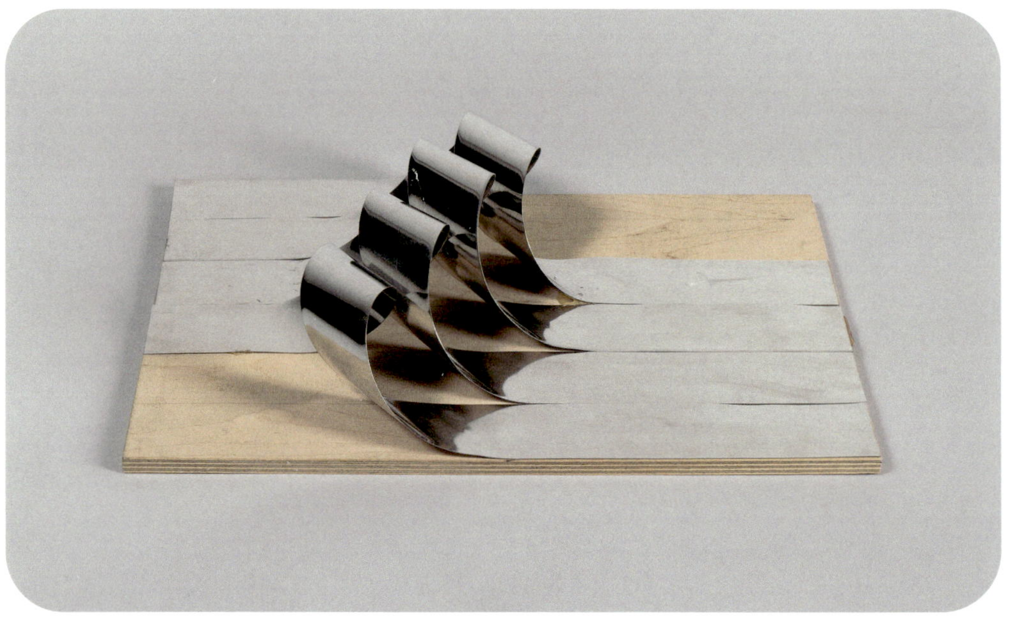

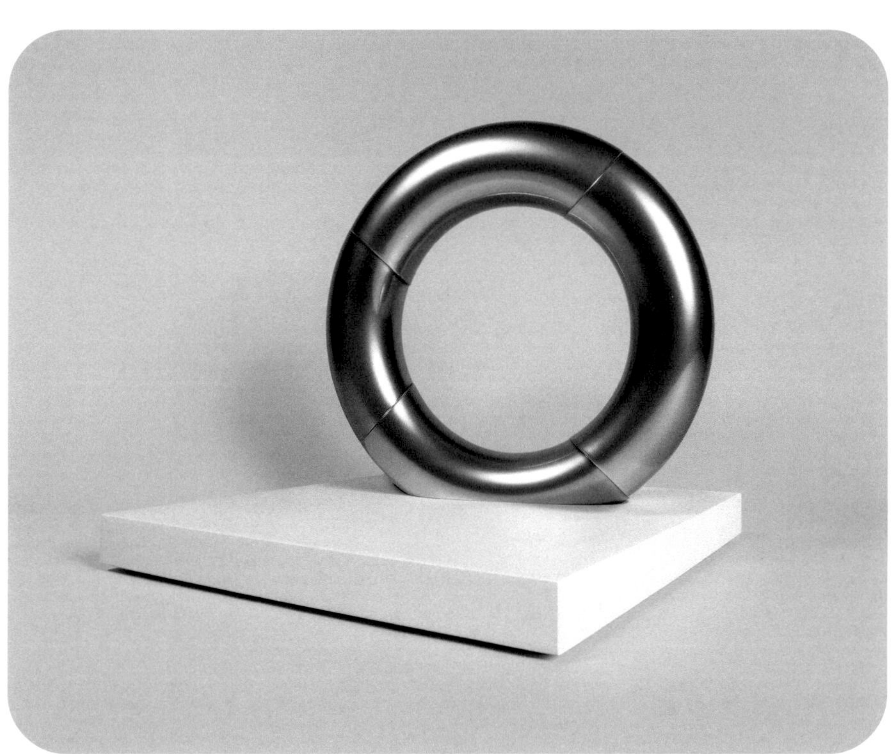

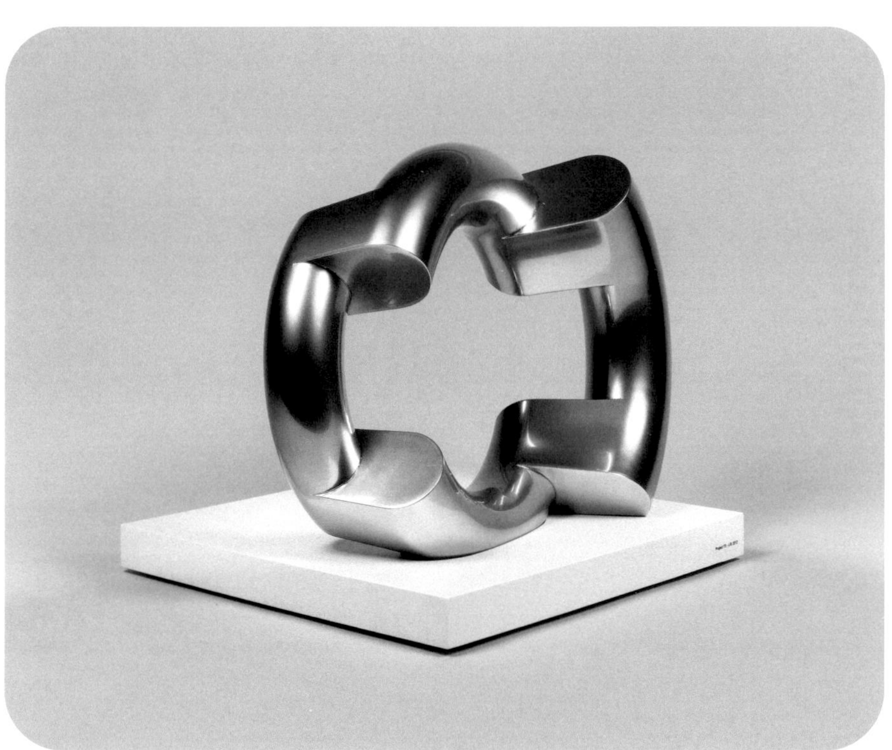

39 T3
1:100 | 2012

40 GOLDEN TABLE
1:60 | 2004

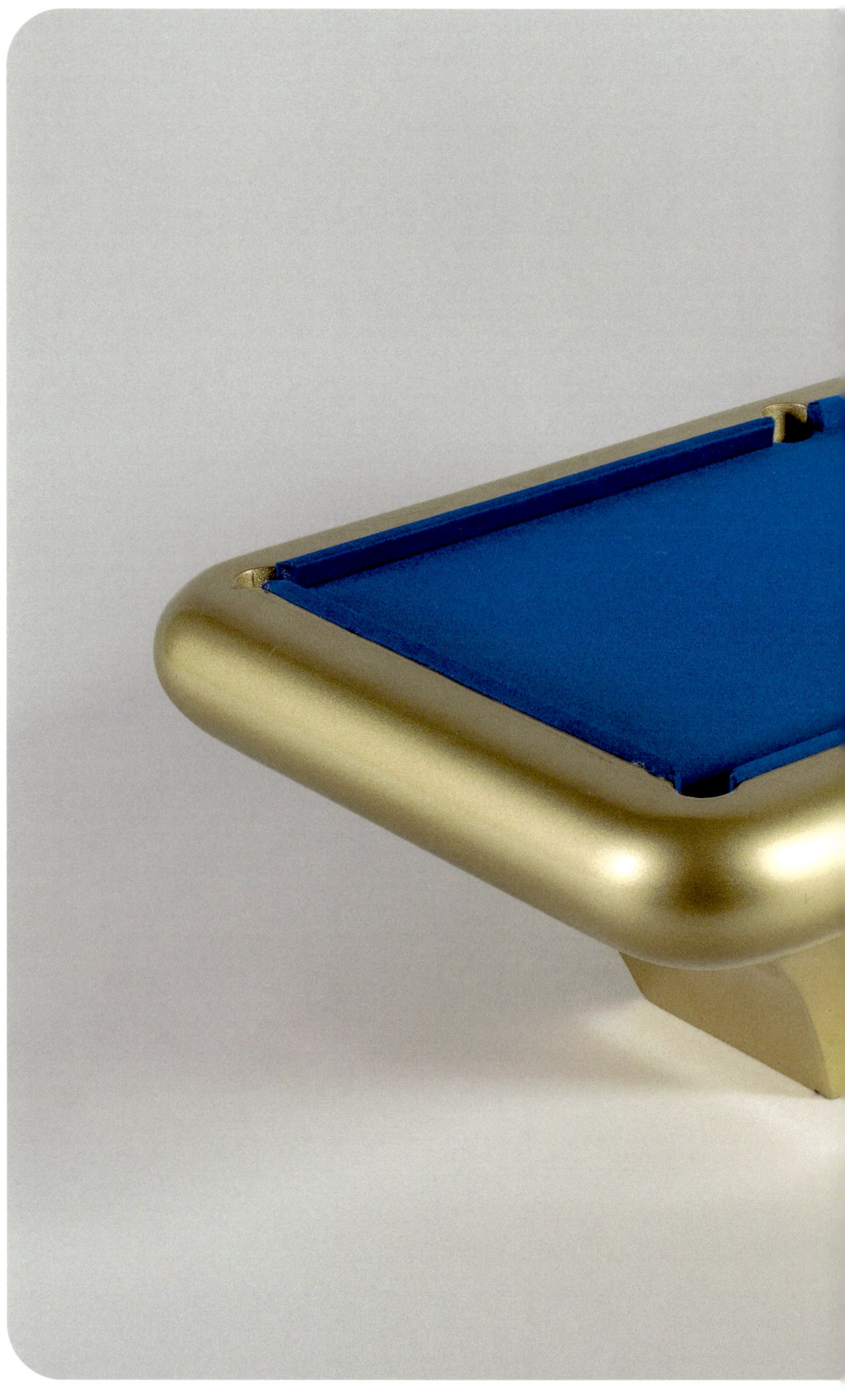

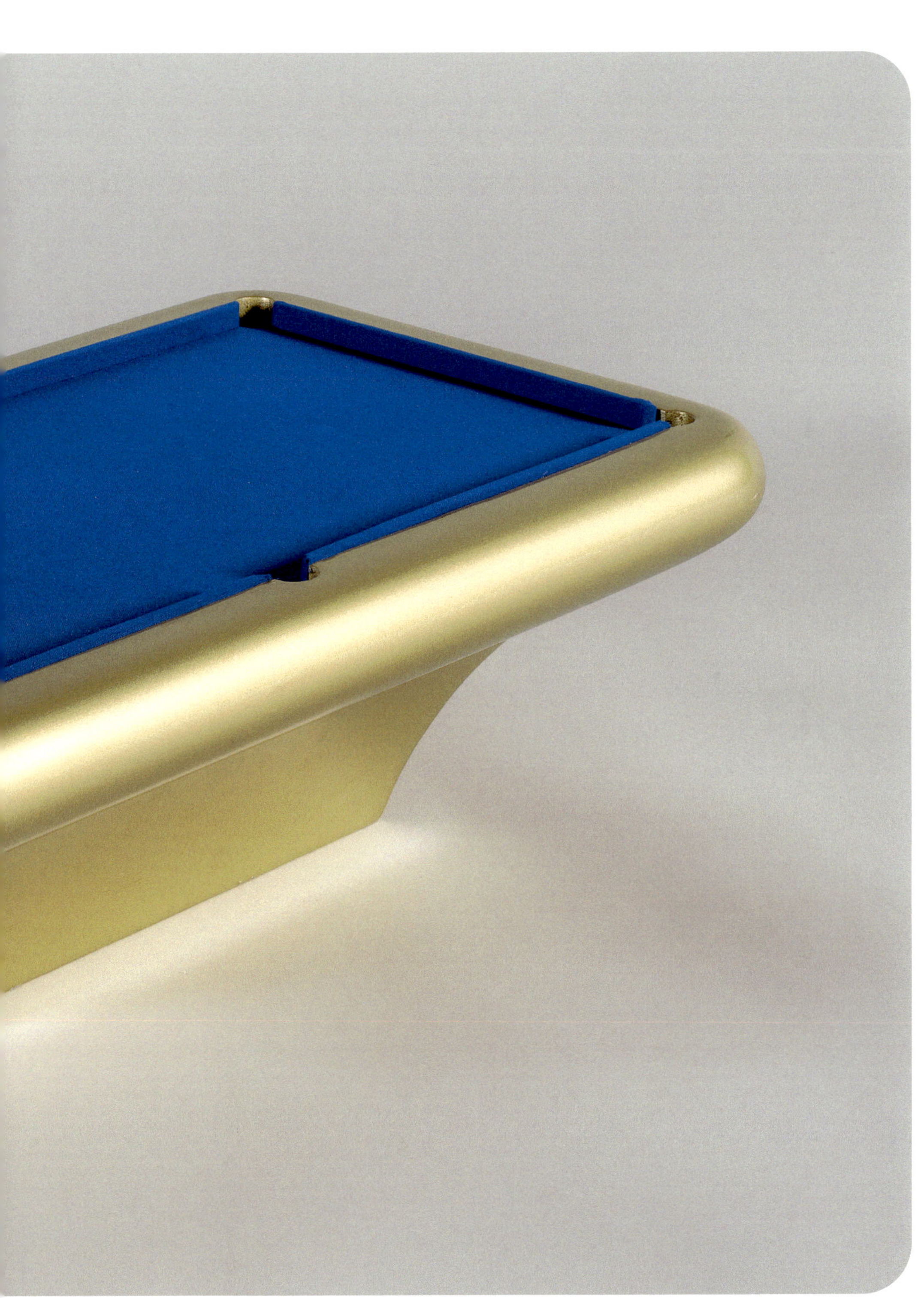

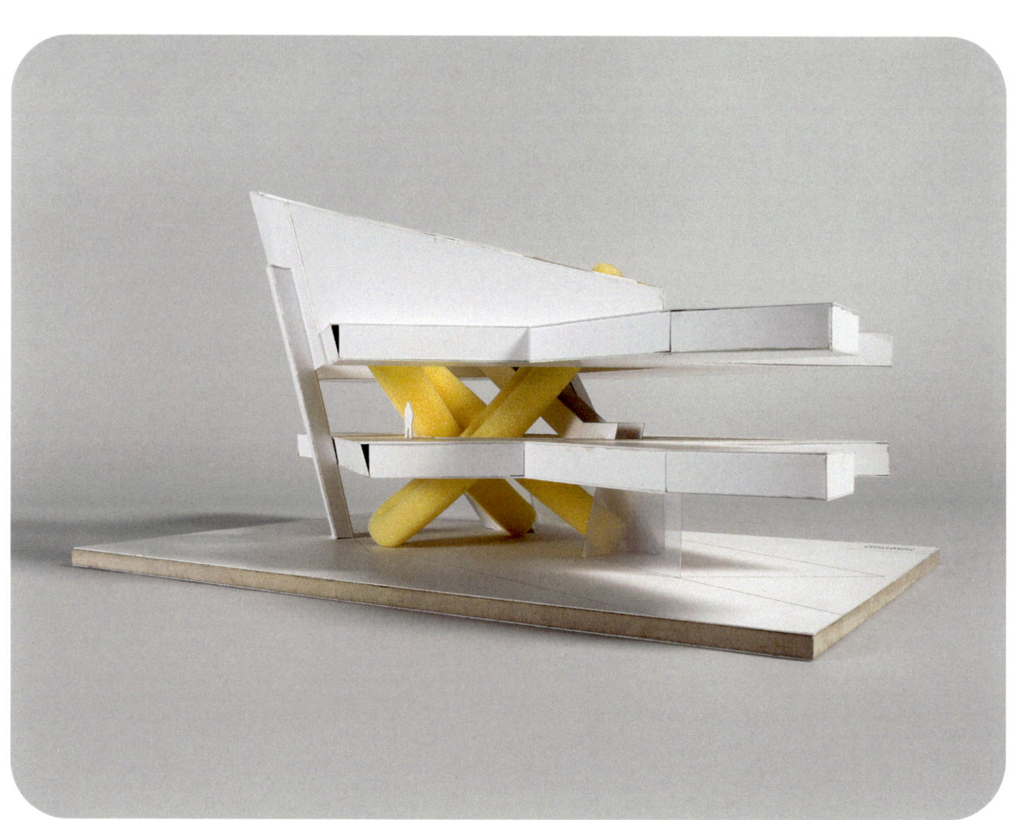

41 COMFORT #6
1:100 | 2009

42 COMFORT #6
1:100 | 2009

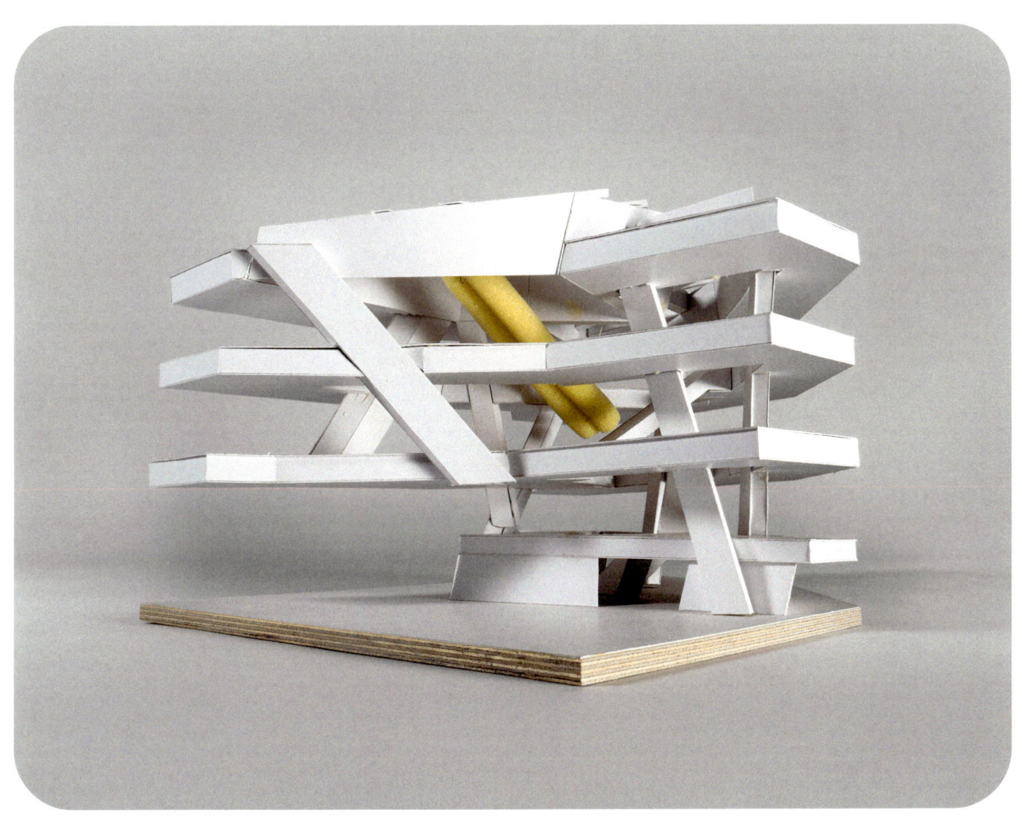

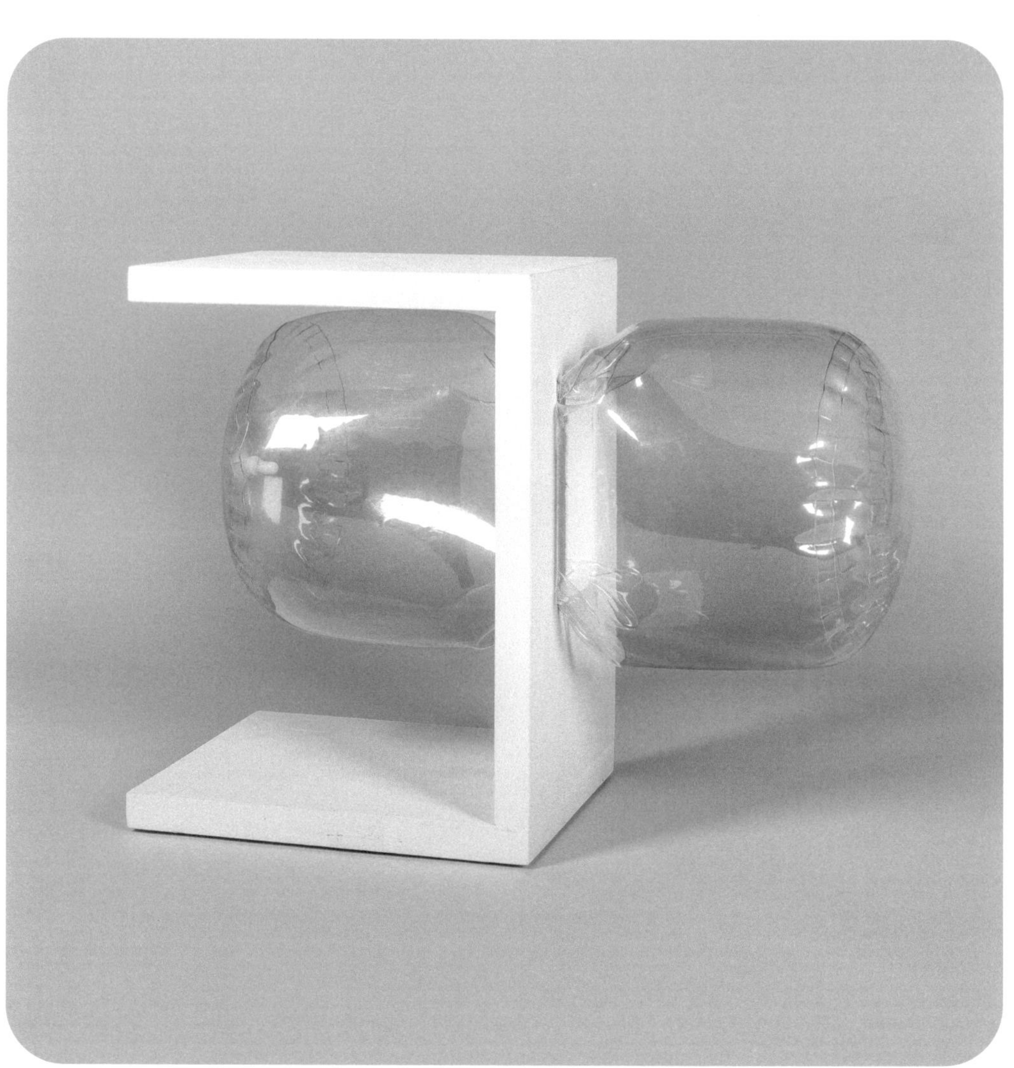

43

COMFORT #3
1:8.6 | 2005

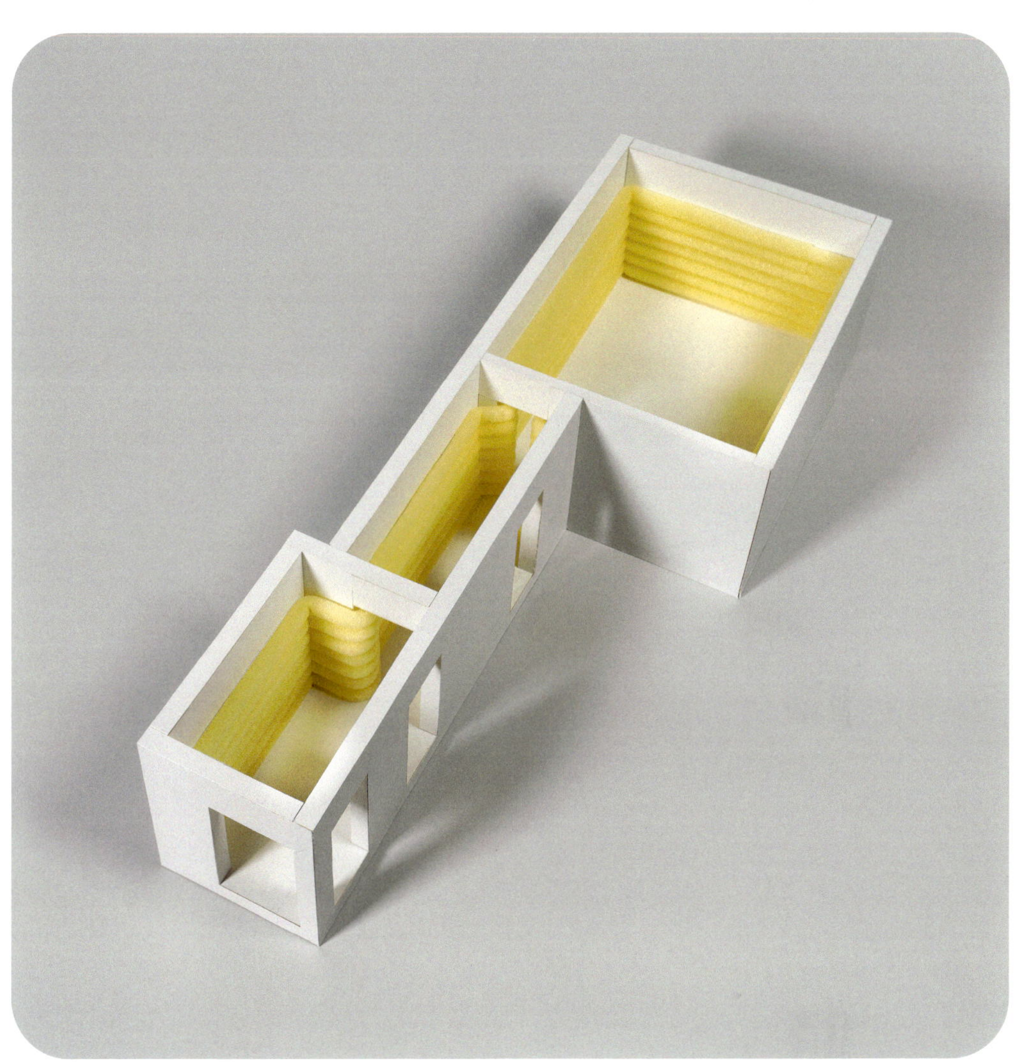

44 COMFORT #8
1:23 | 2010

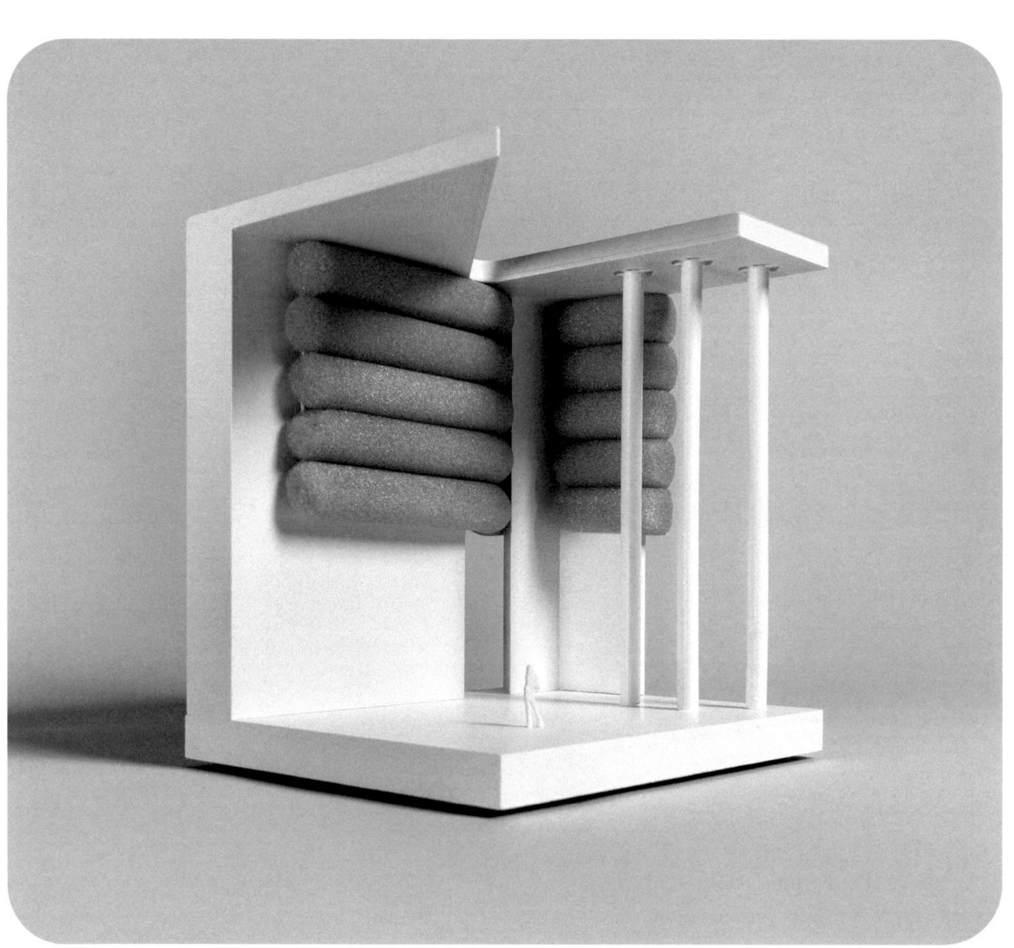

COMFORT #19
1:72 | 2022

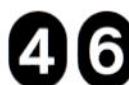

COMFORT #6
1:100 | 2008

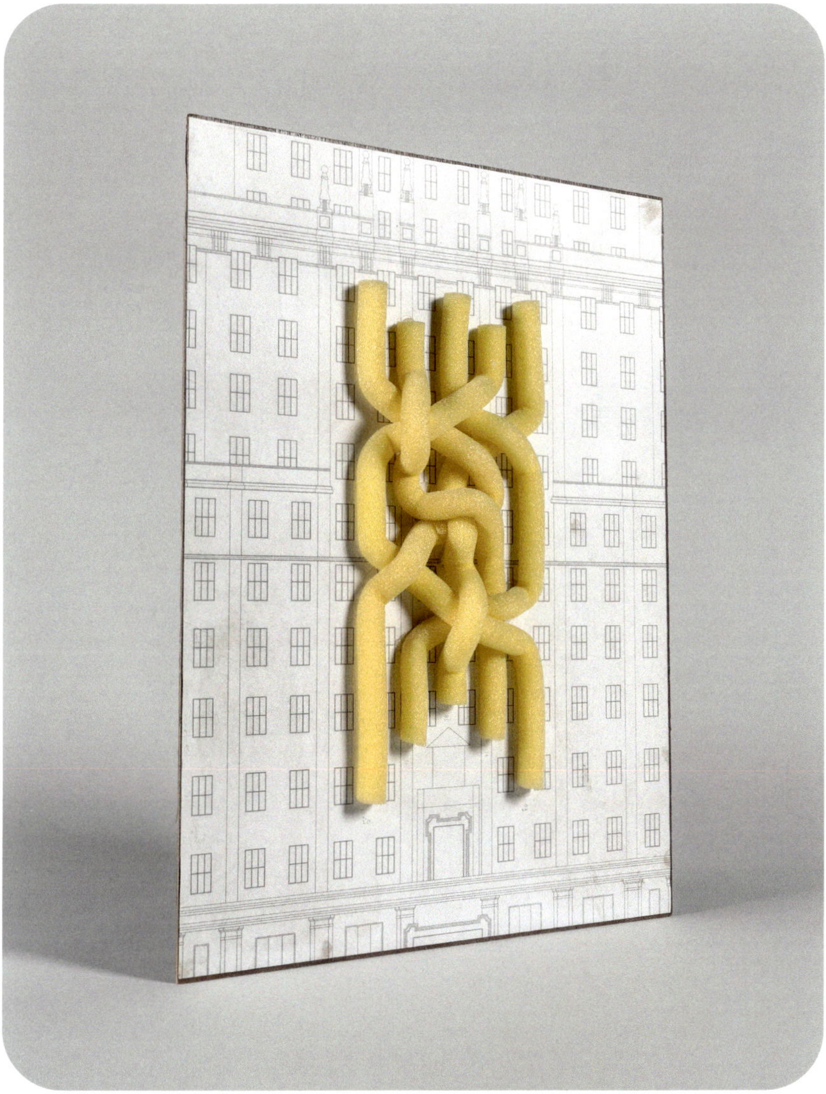

47 BREATHING PILLOWS
1:50 | 1995

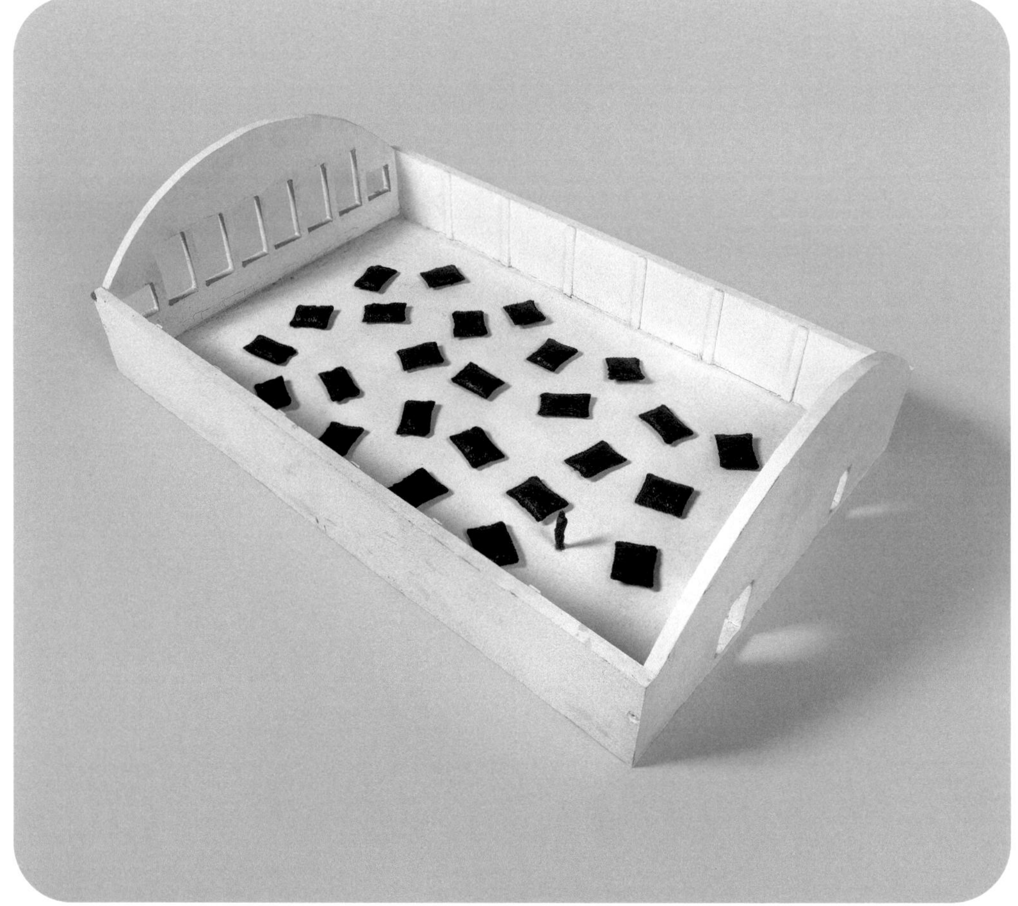

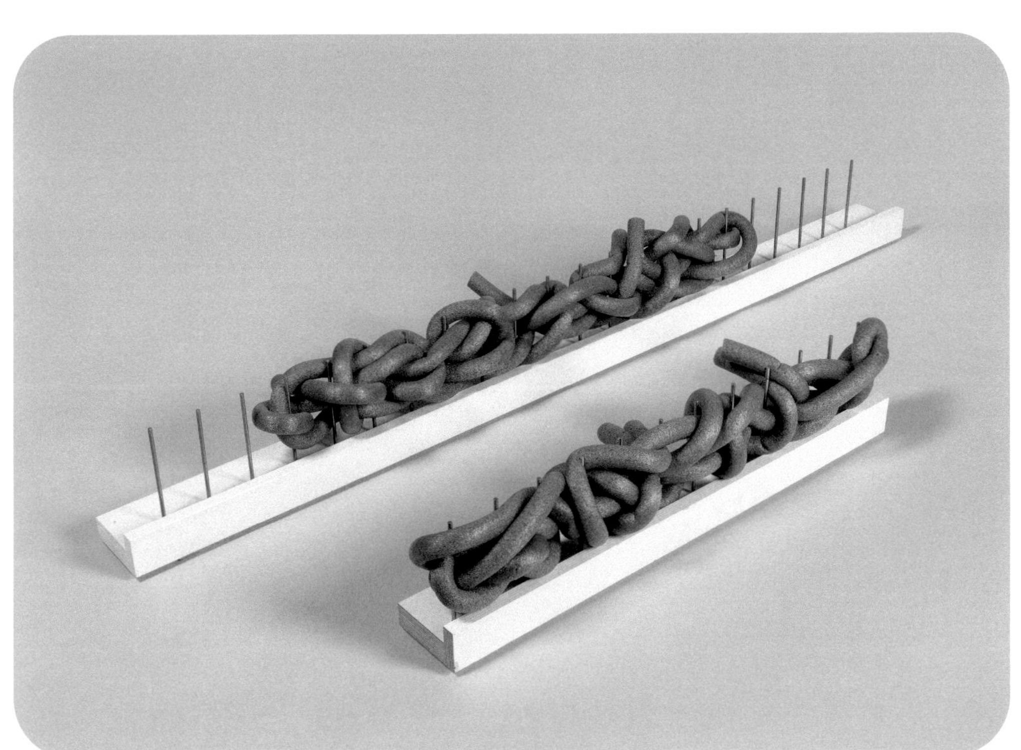

48 COMFORT #4
1:50 | 2015

49 COMFORT #4
1:50 | 2015

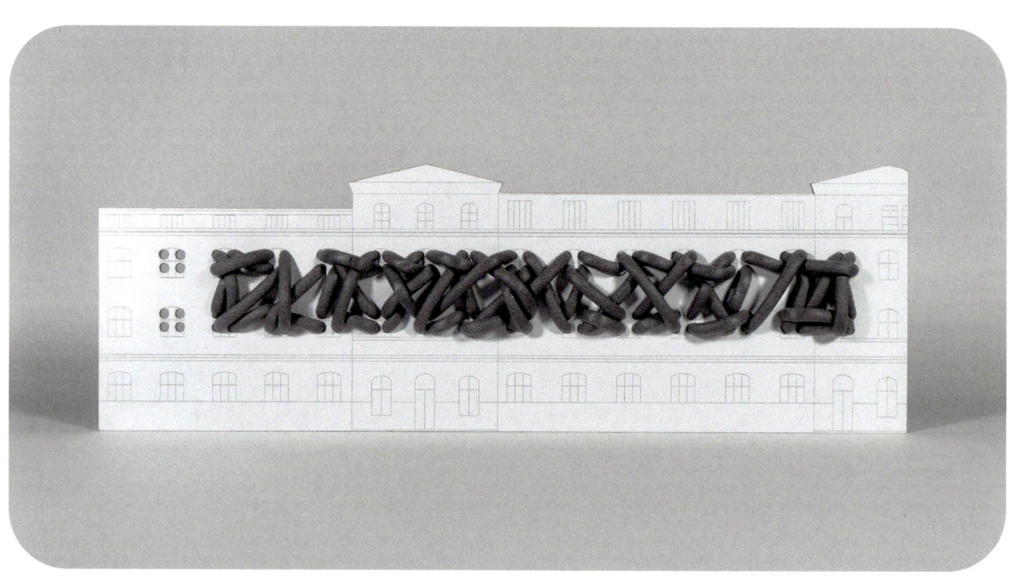

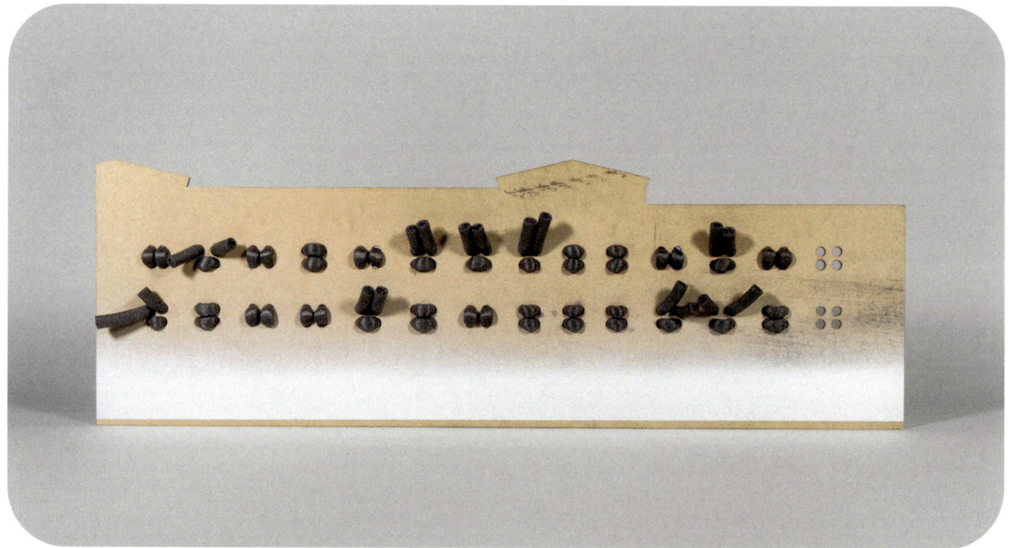

COMFORT #4
1:50 | 2010

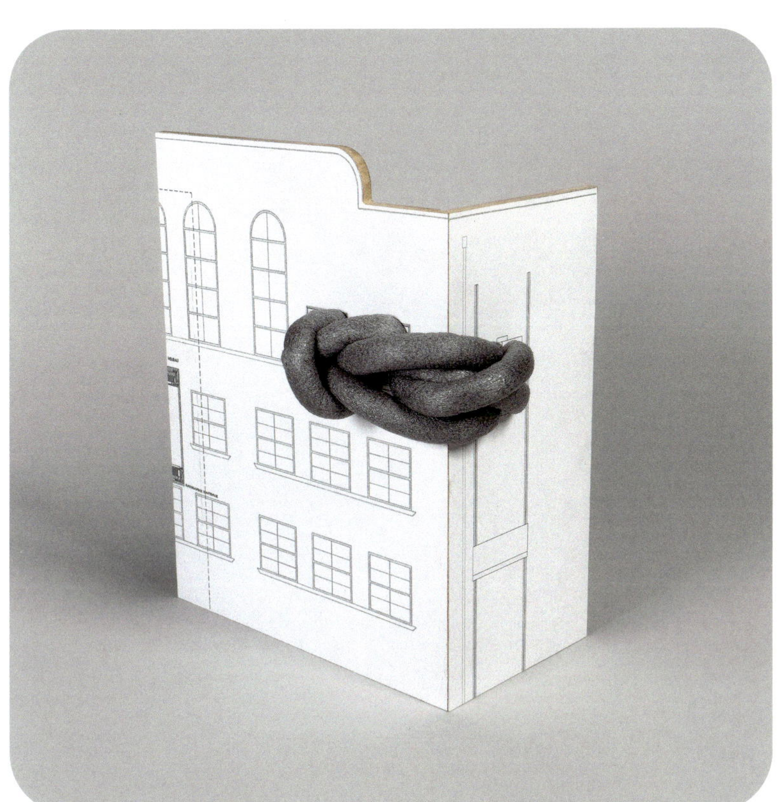

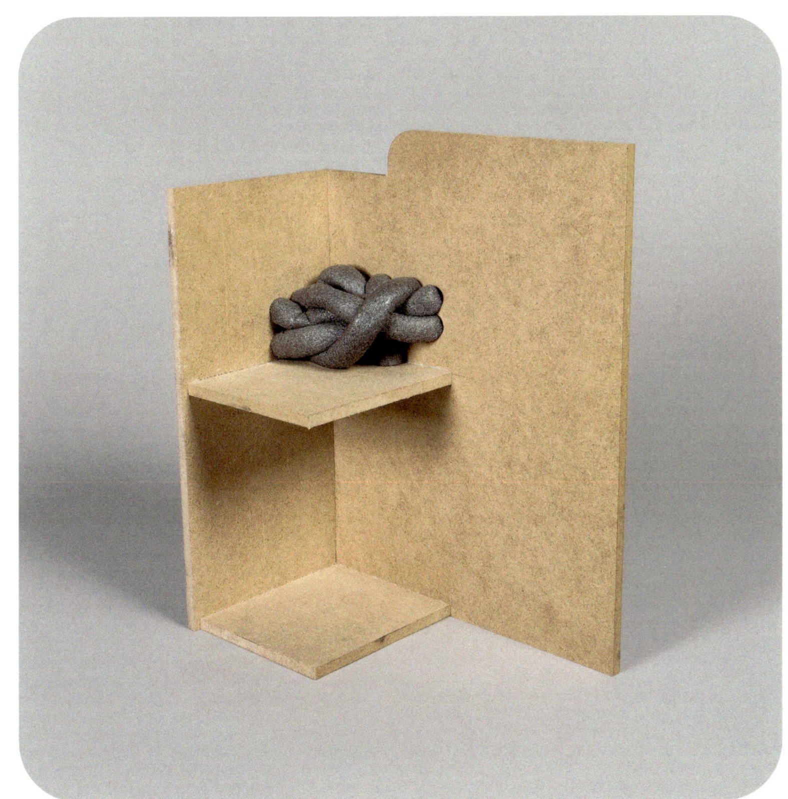

COMFORT #4
1:50 | 2011

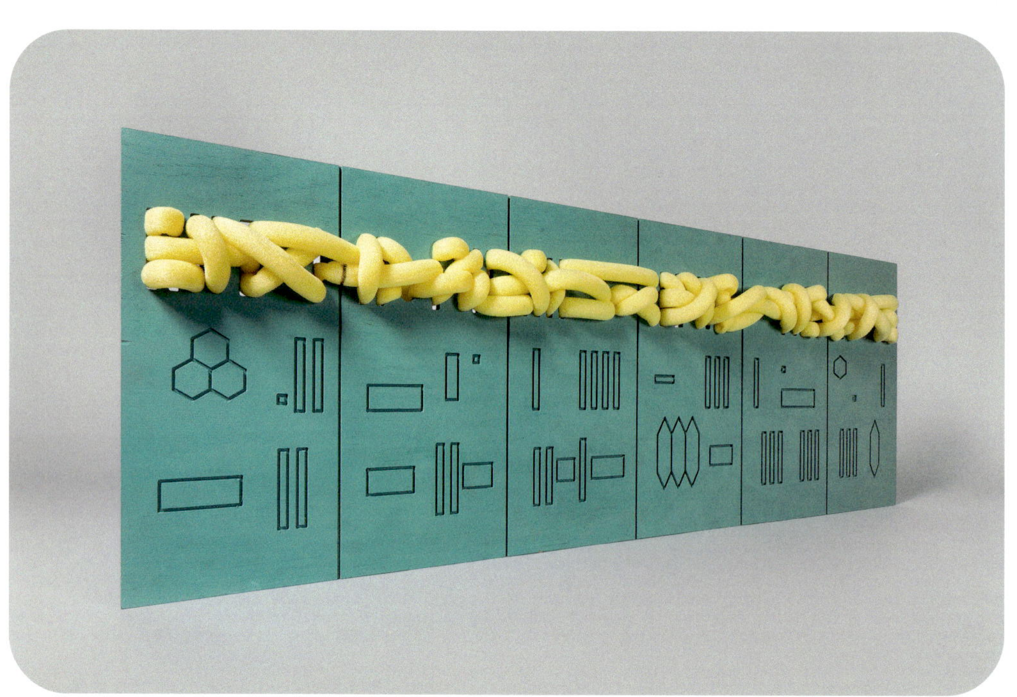

COMFORT #4
1:50 | 2012

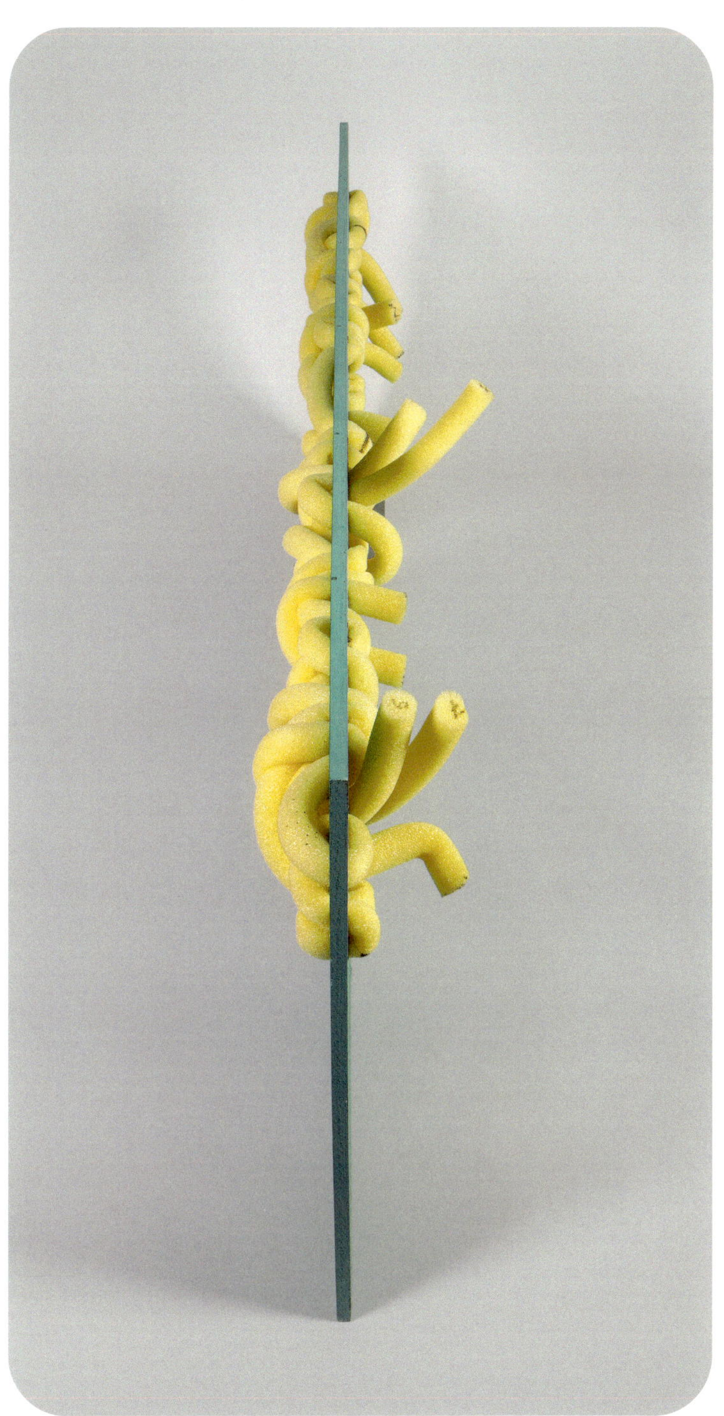

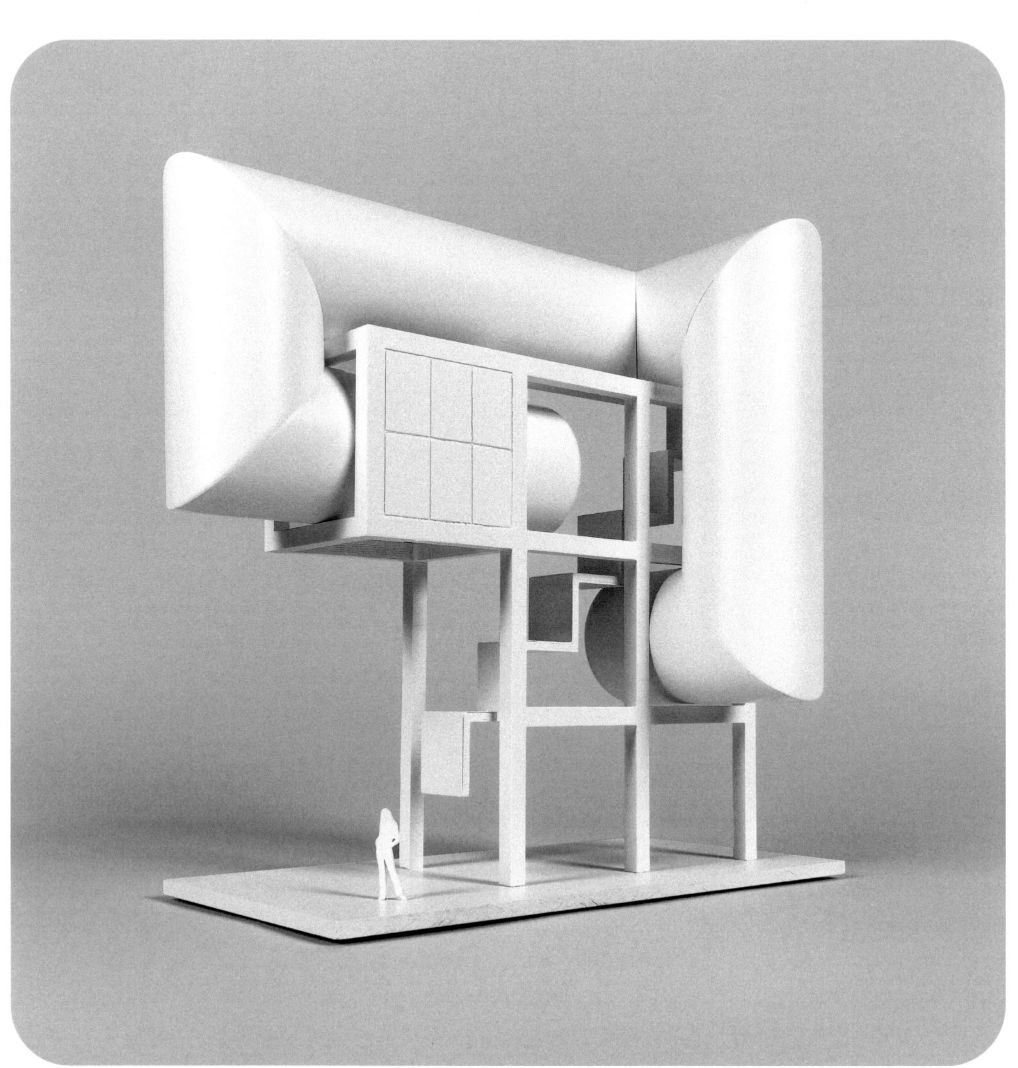

53 COMFORT #20
1:50 | 2022

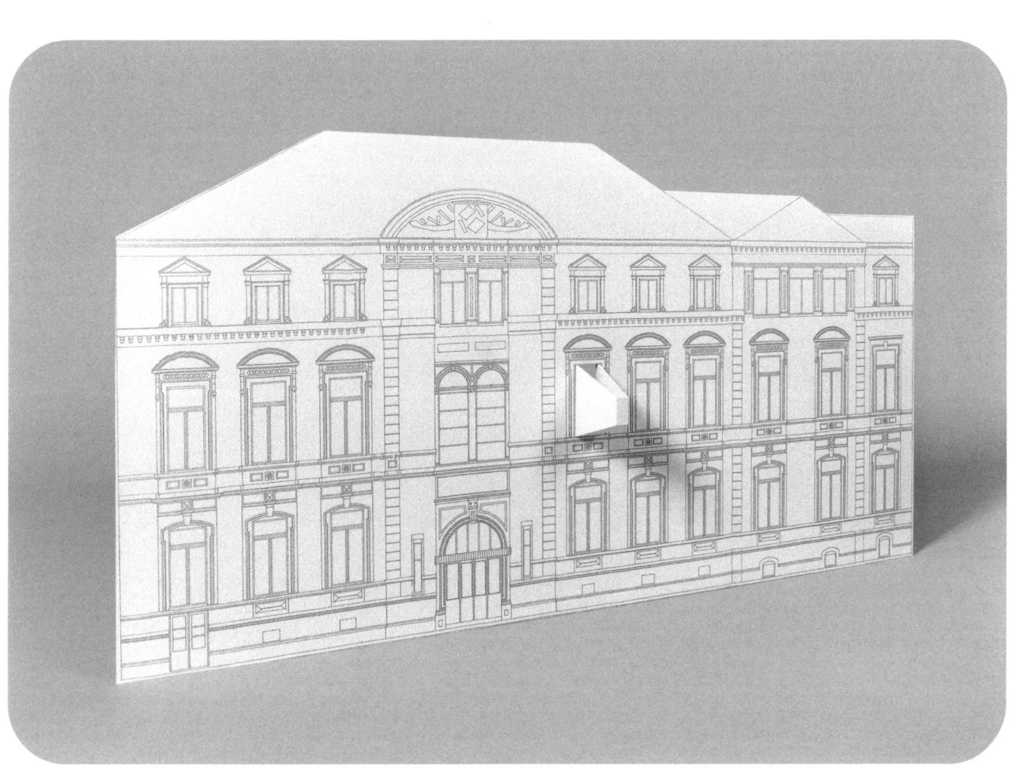

BEAUTIFUL STEPS #10
1:50 | 2014

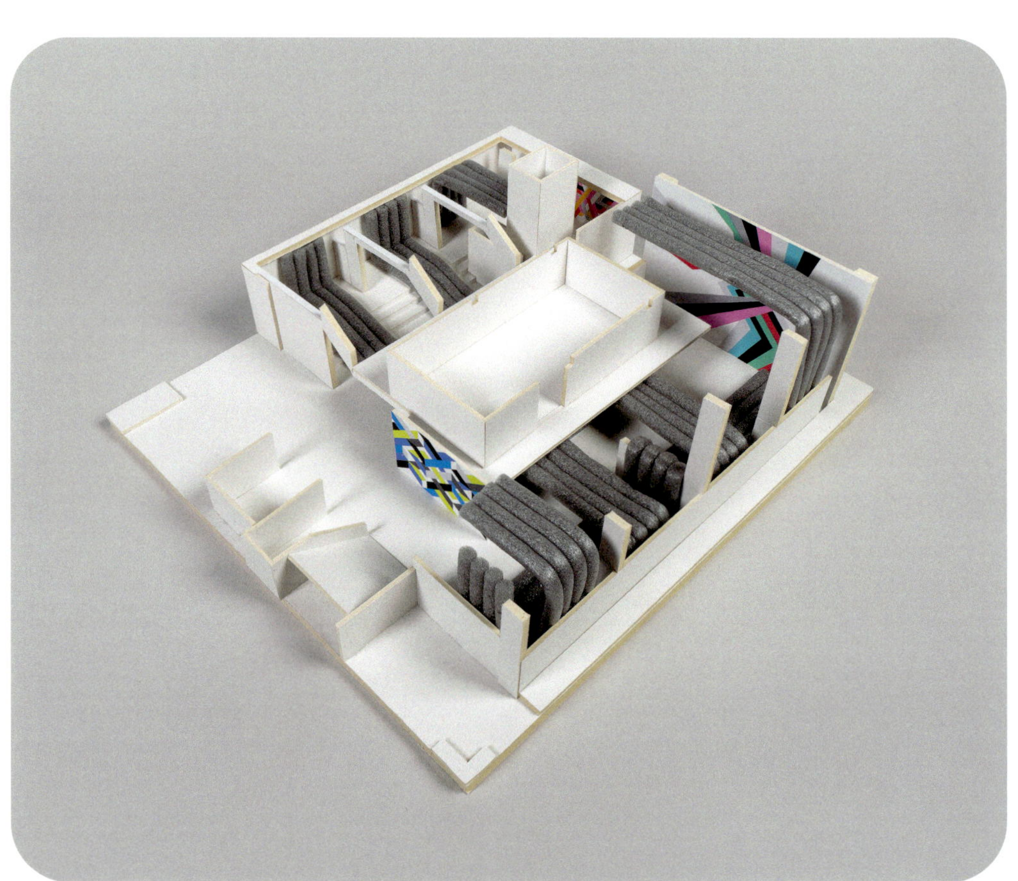

COMFORT #12
1:100 | 2013

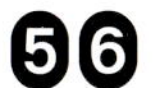

BEAUTIFUL WALL #23
1:20 | 2012

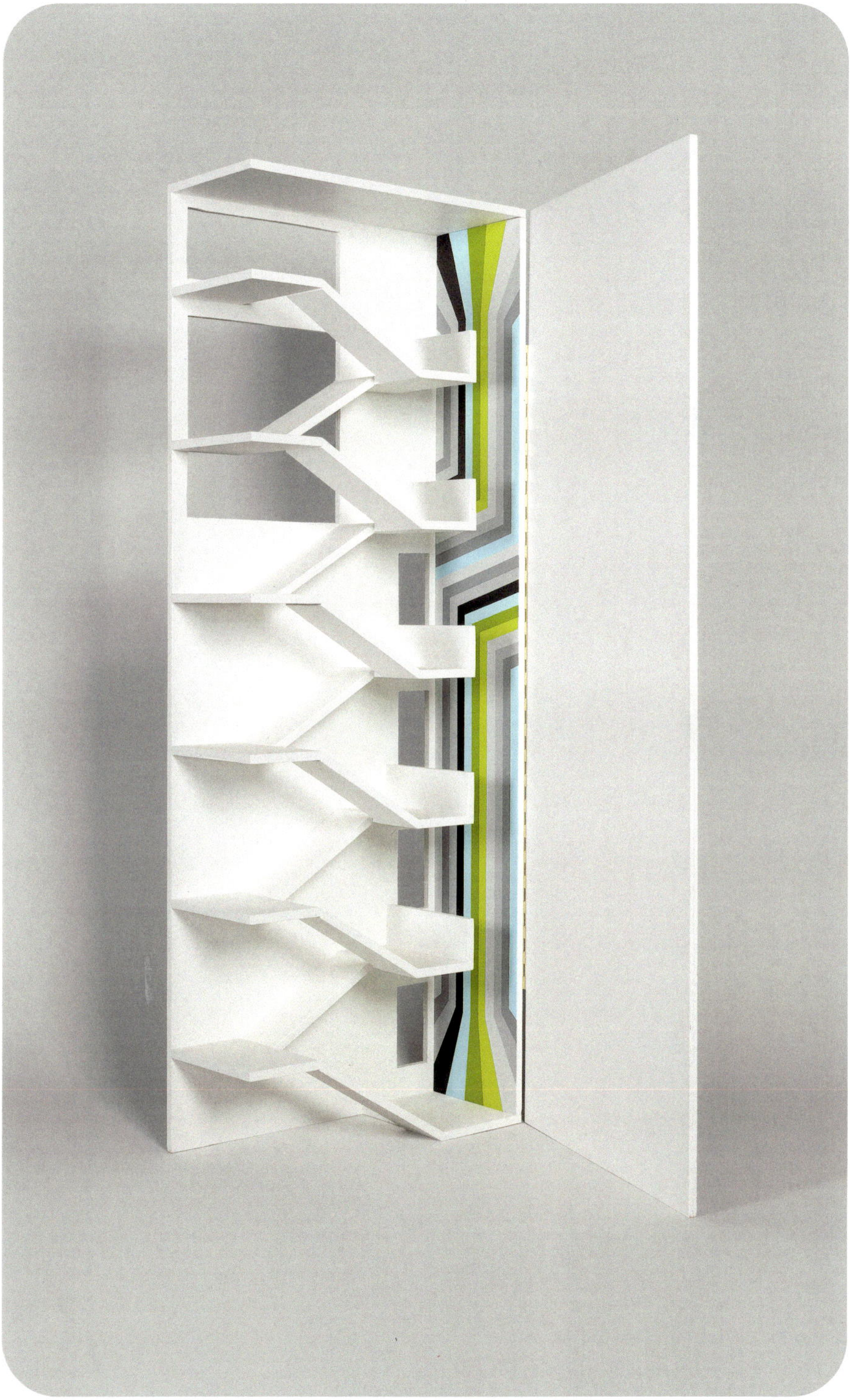

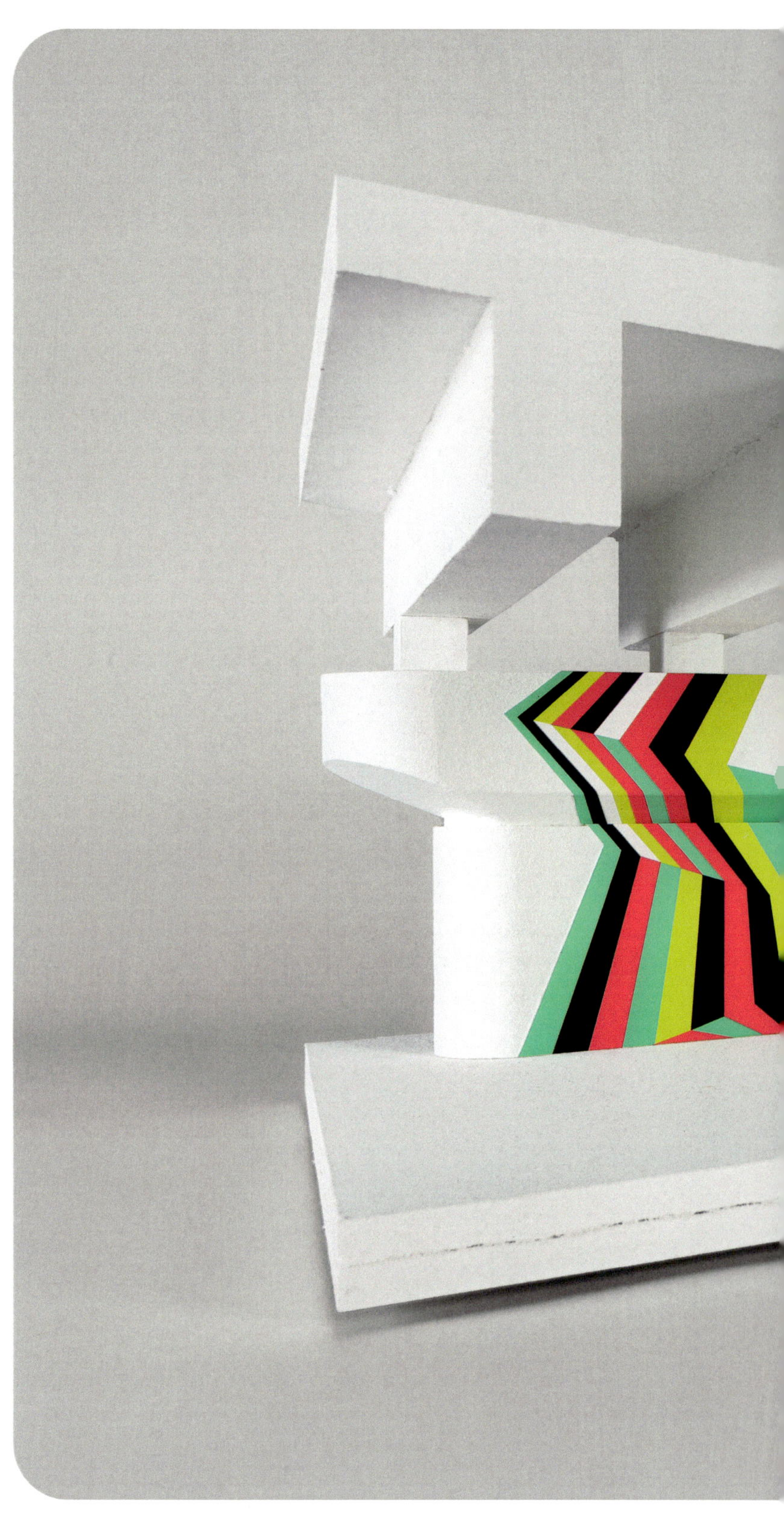

57 BEAUTIFUL BRIDGE #2
1:75 | 2016

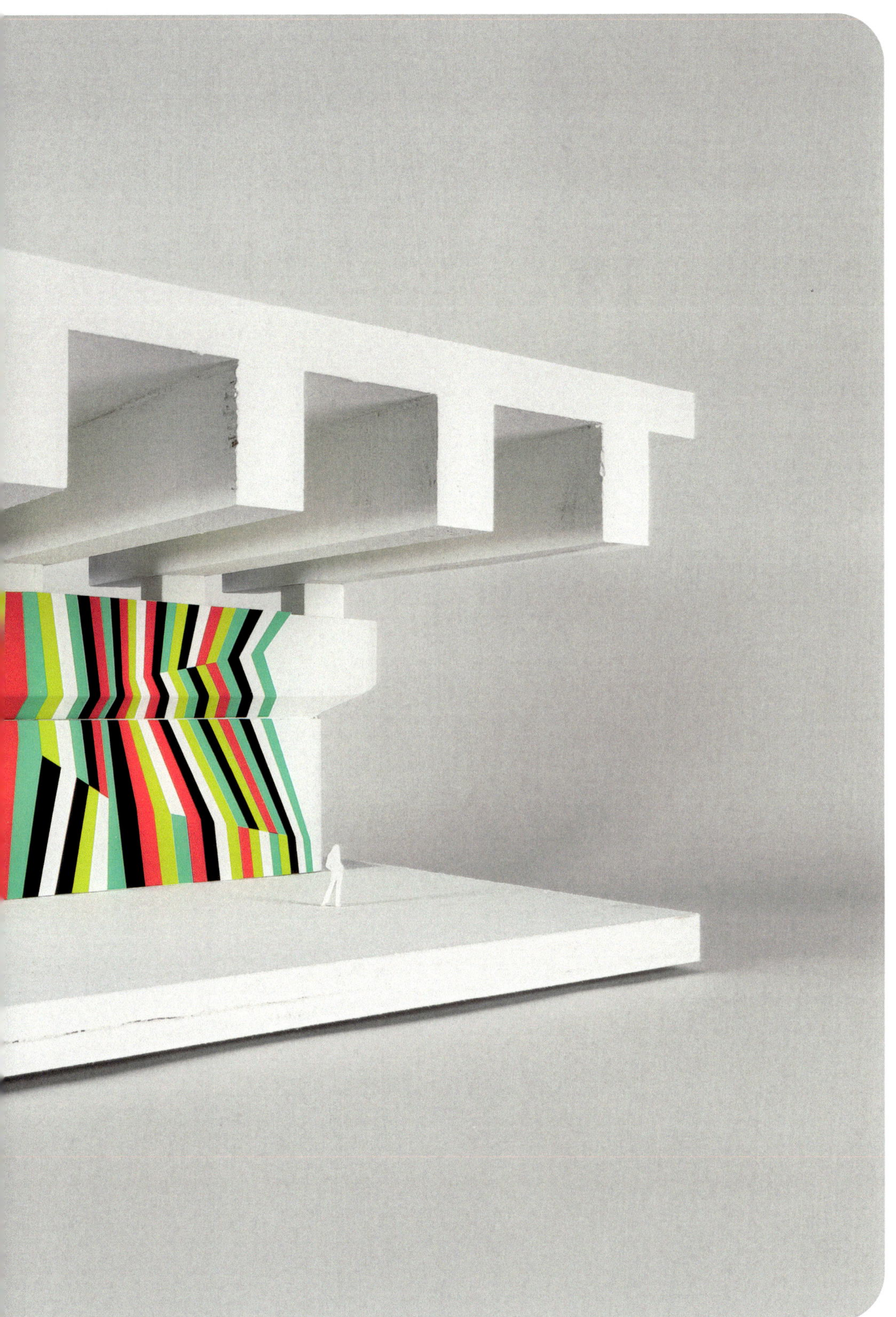

BEAUTIFUL WALLS #14
1:95 | 2005

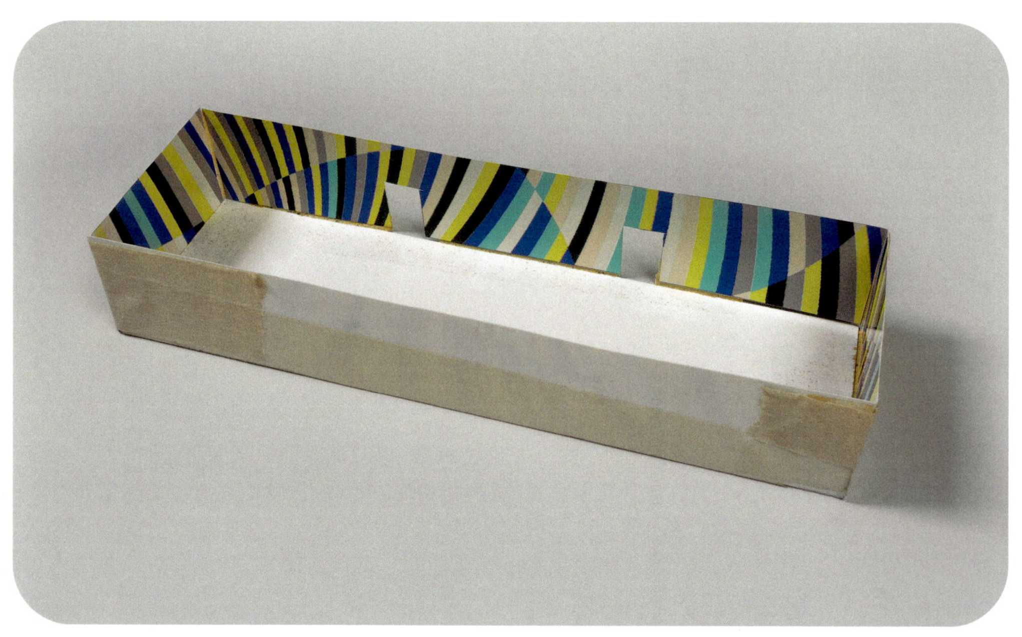

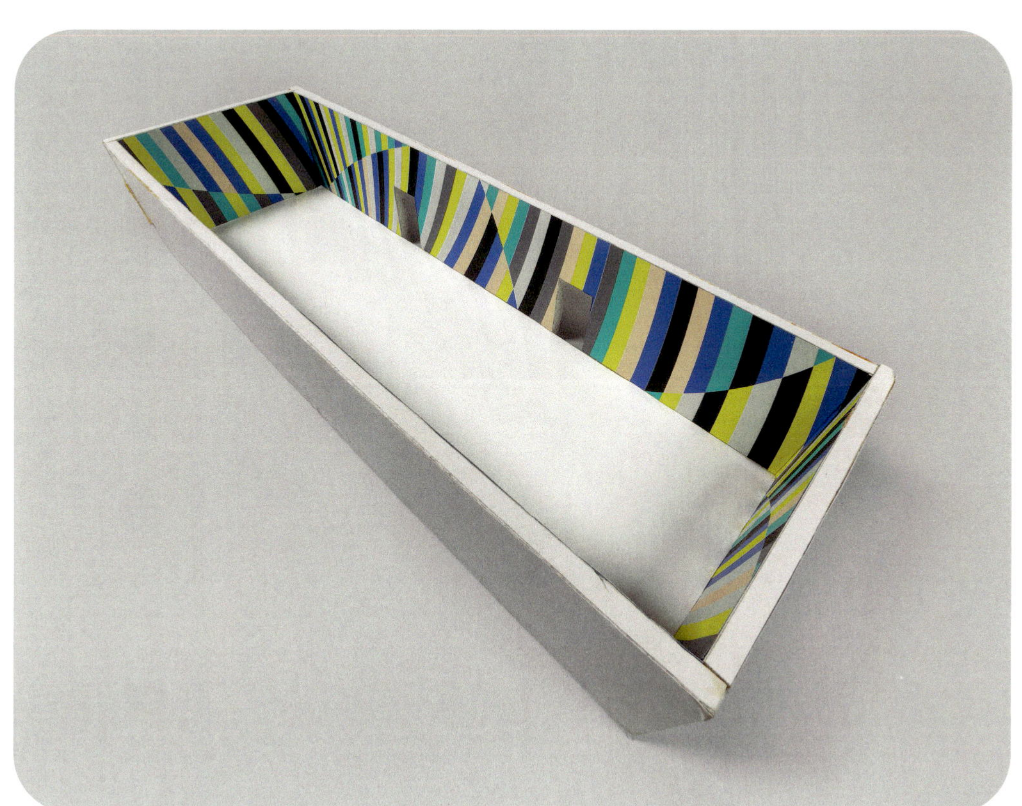

BEAUTIFUL WALLS #14
1:40 | 2005

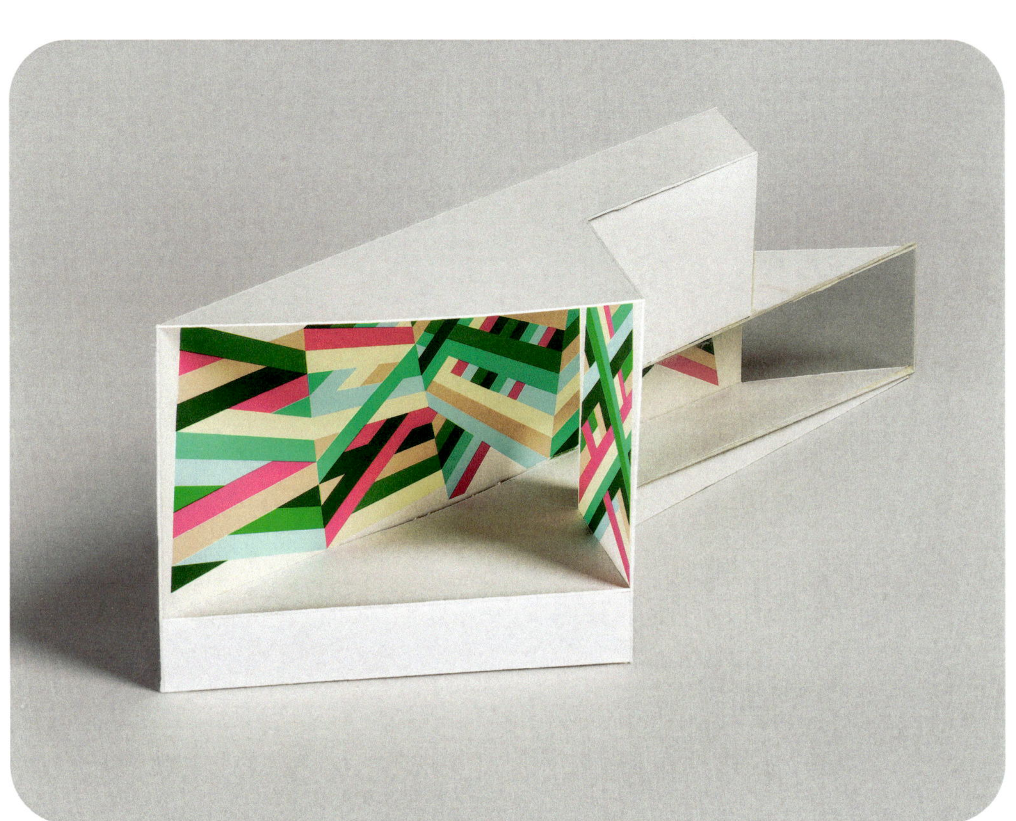

60 BEAUTIFUL ENTRANCE
1:50 | 2010

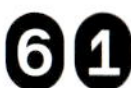

BEAUTIFUL APARTMENT #1
1:100 | 2011

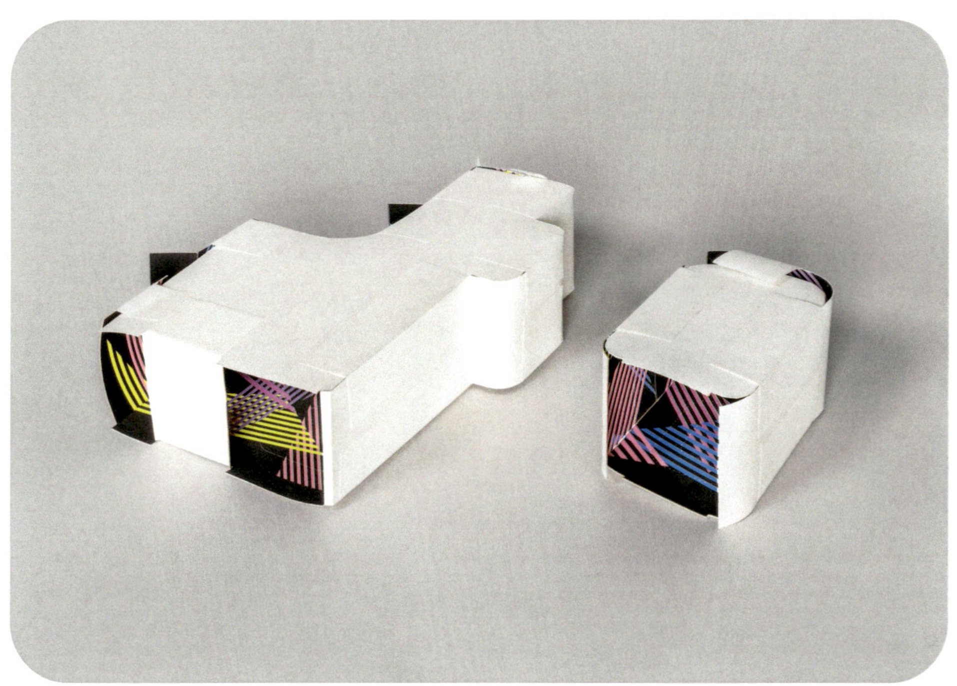

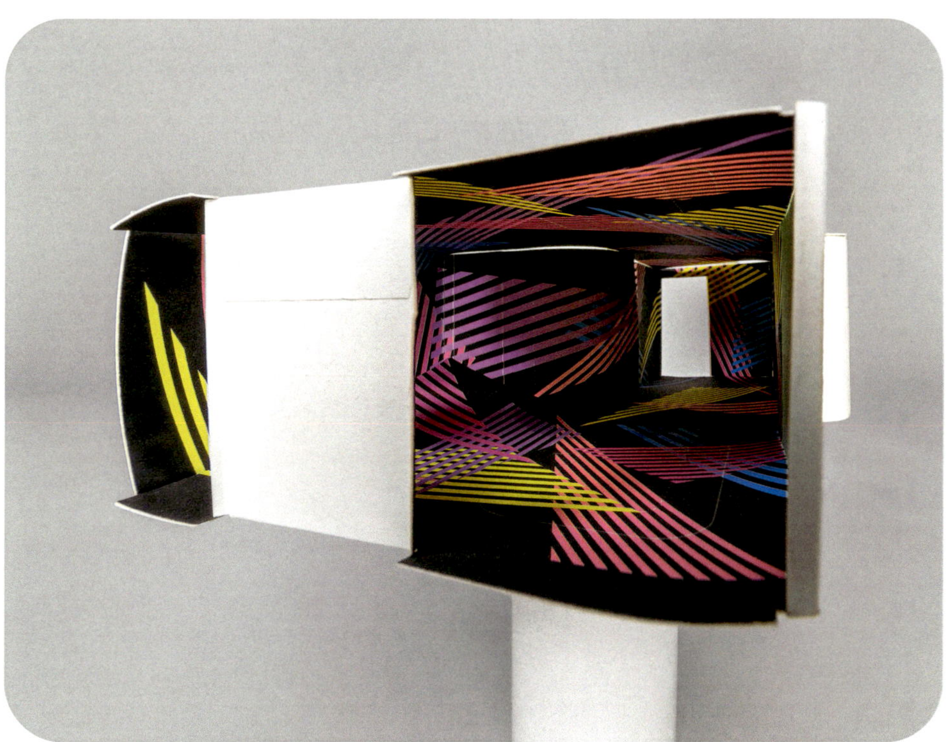

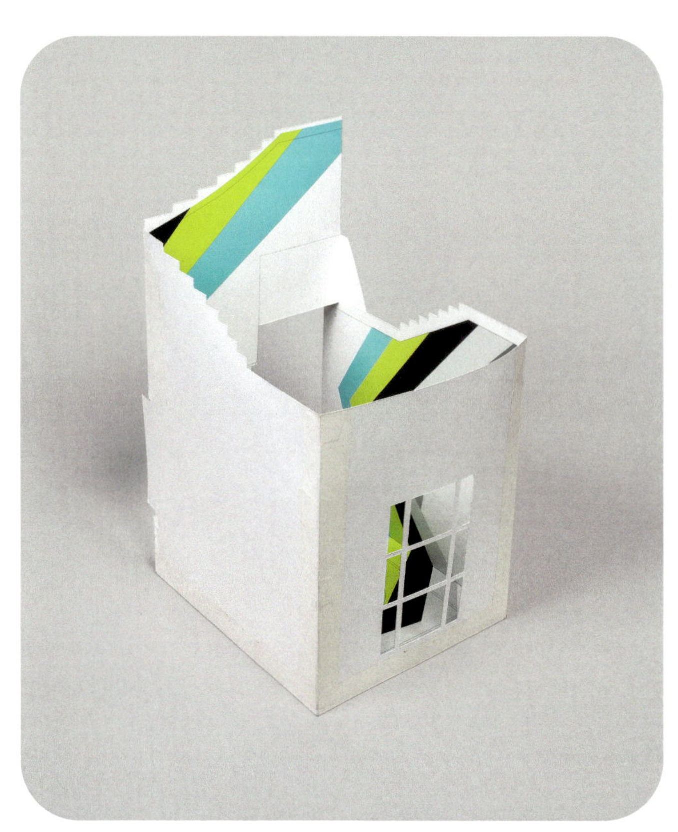

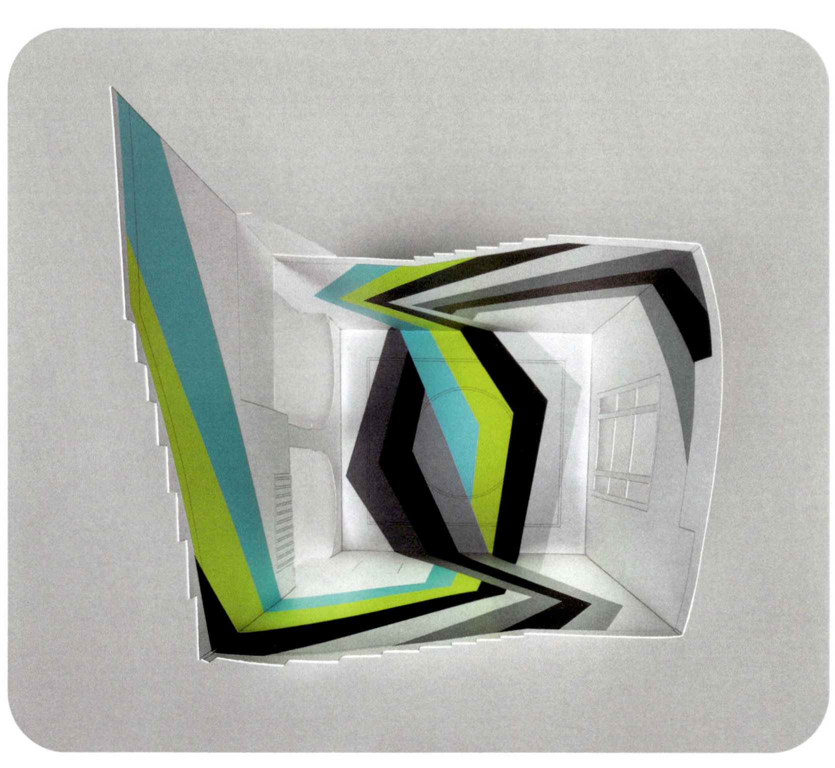

BEAUTIFUL WALLS #22
1:20 | 2012

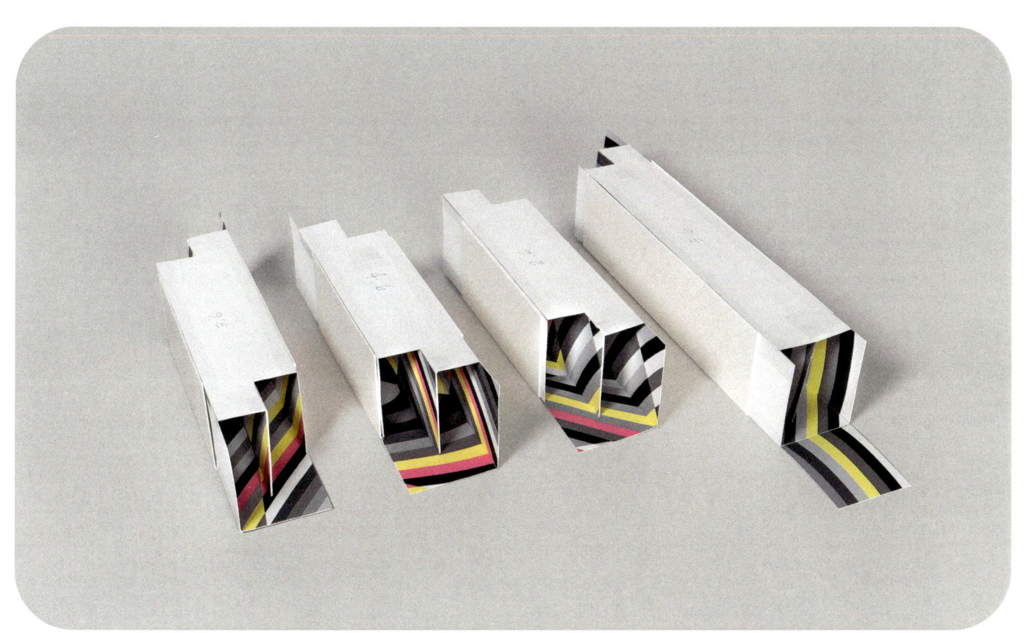

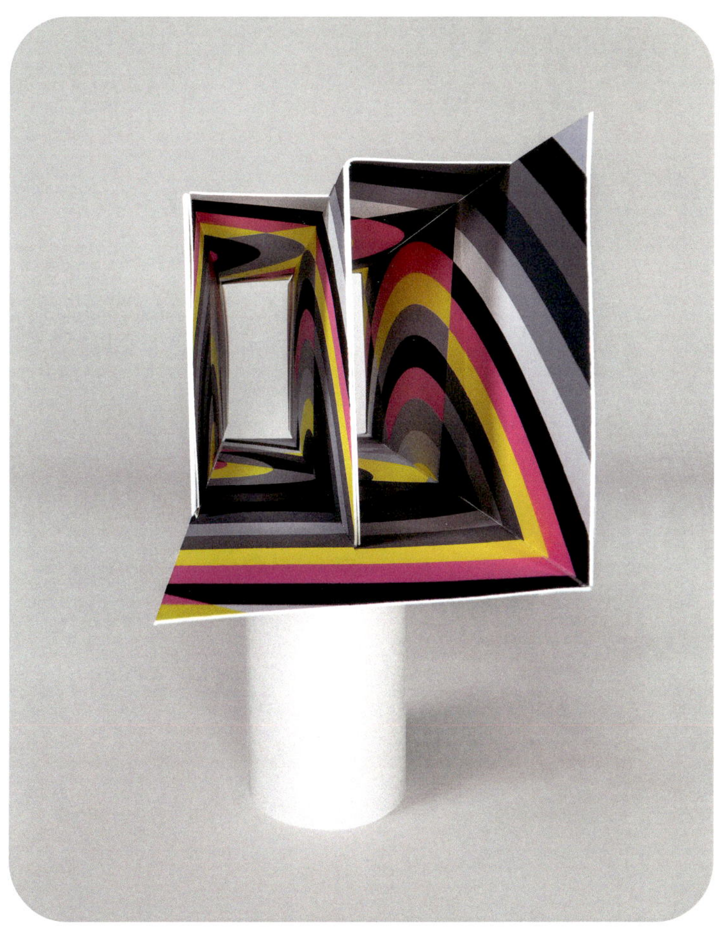

BEAUTIFUL TUBE #6
1:46 | 2019

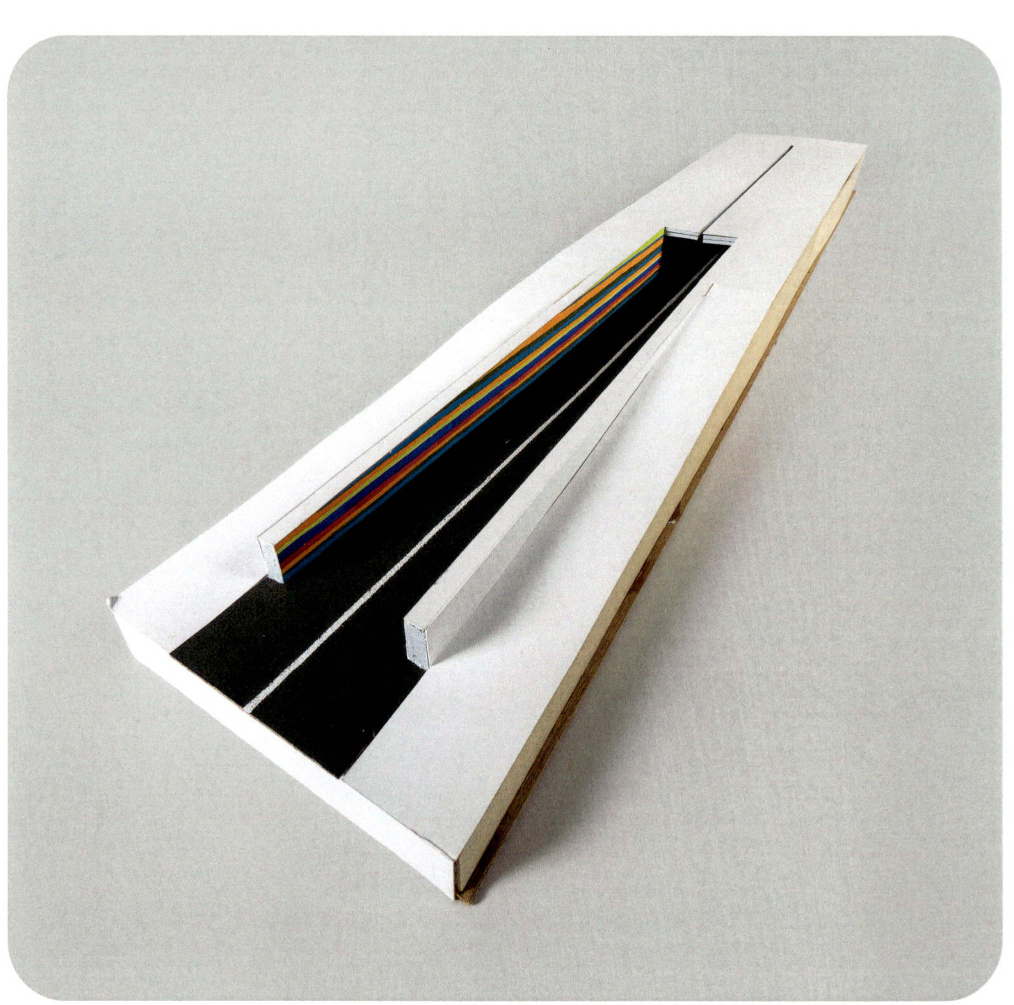

64 TUNNEL MALEREI
1:100 | 2002

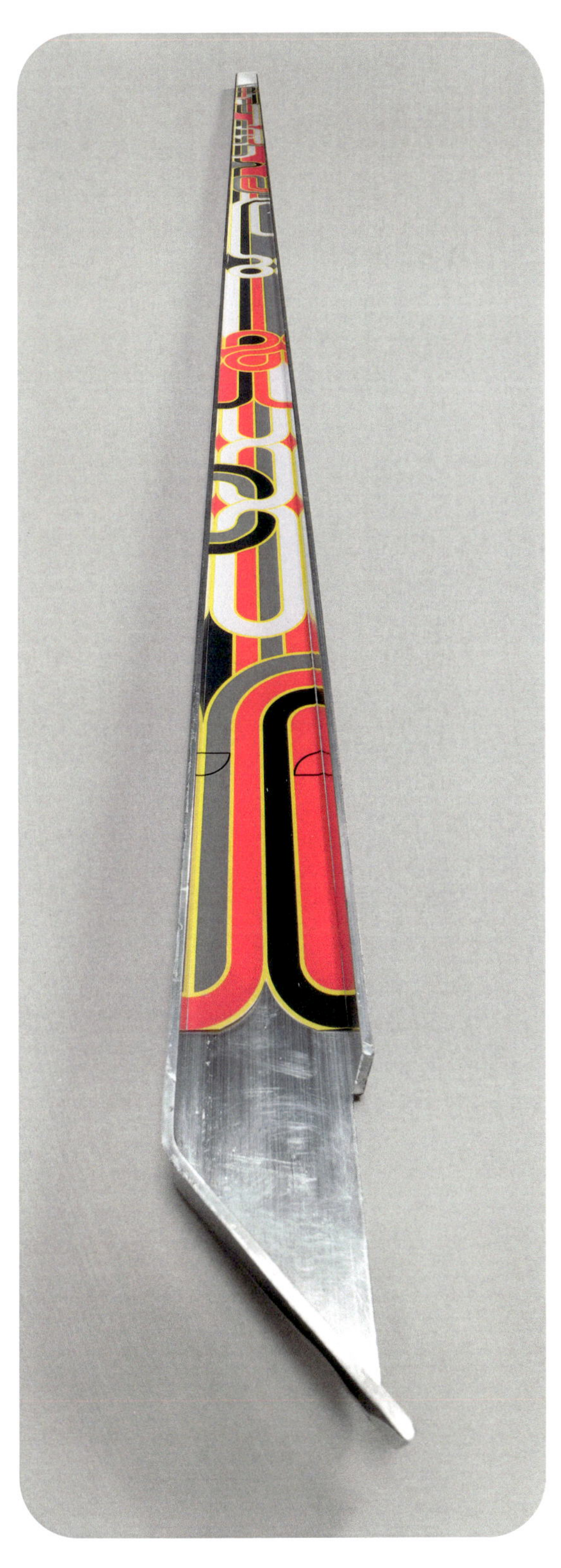

65

STREET PAINTING #3
1:117 | 2012

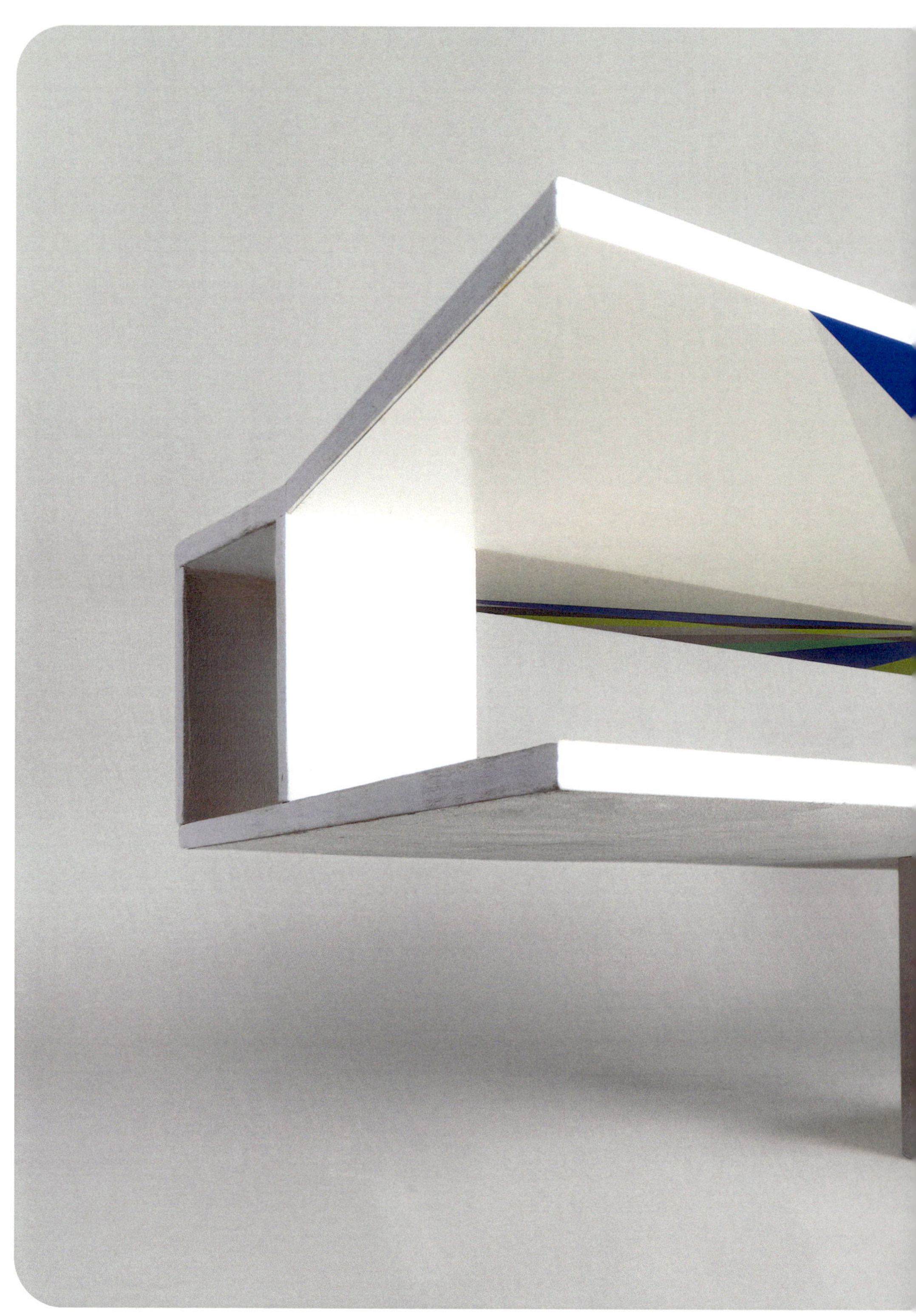

BEAUTIFUL CEILING
1:33 | 2013

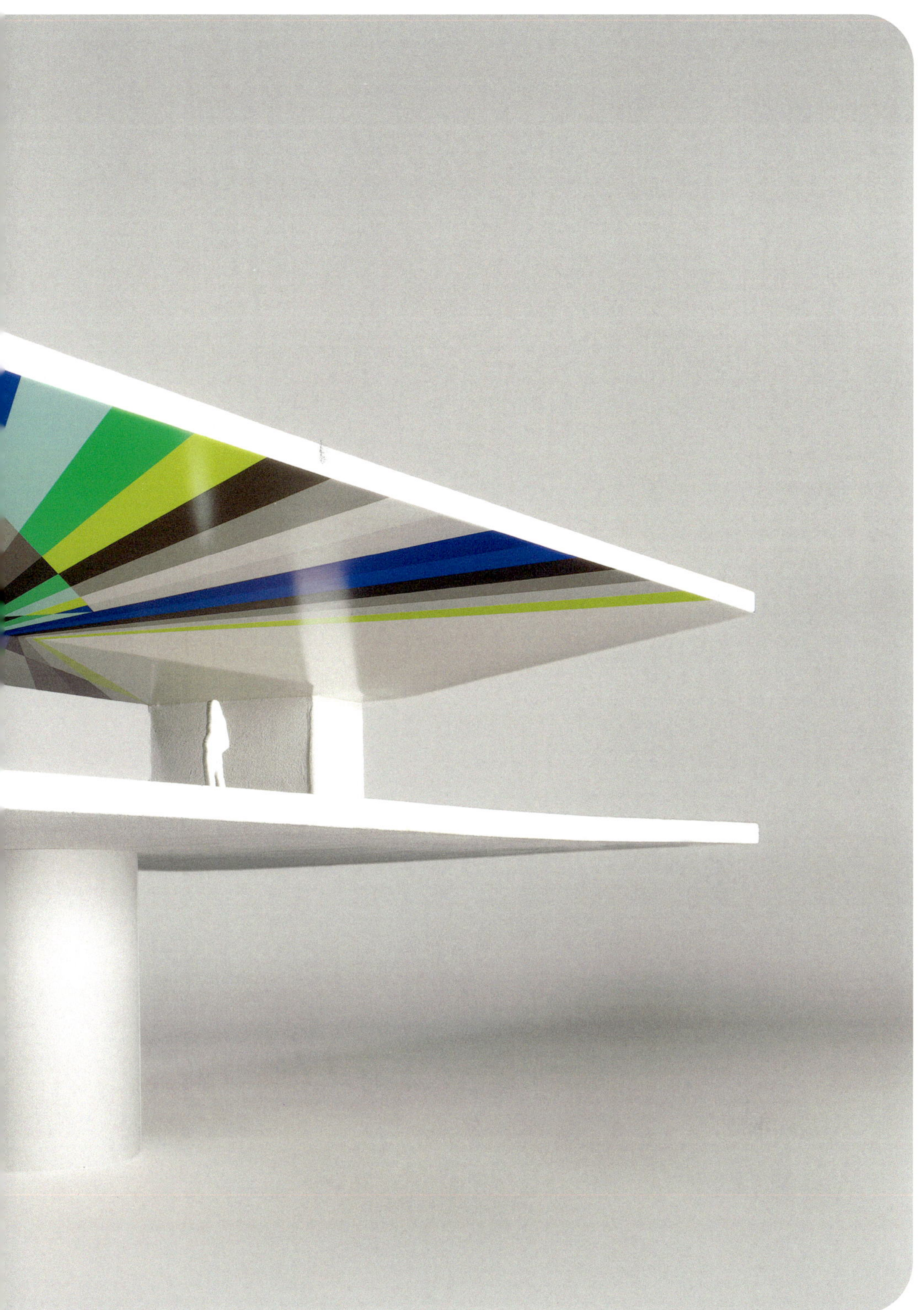

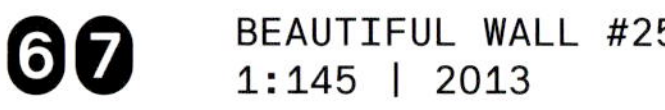

67 BEAUTIFUL WALL #25
1:145 | 2013

68 BEAUTIFUL WALL #25
1:145 | 2013

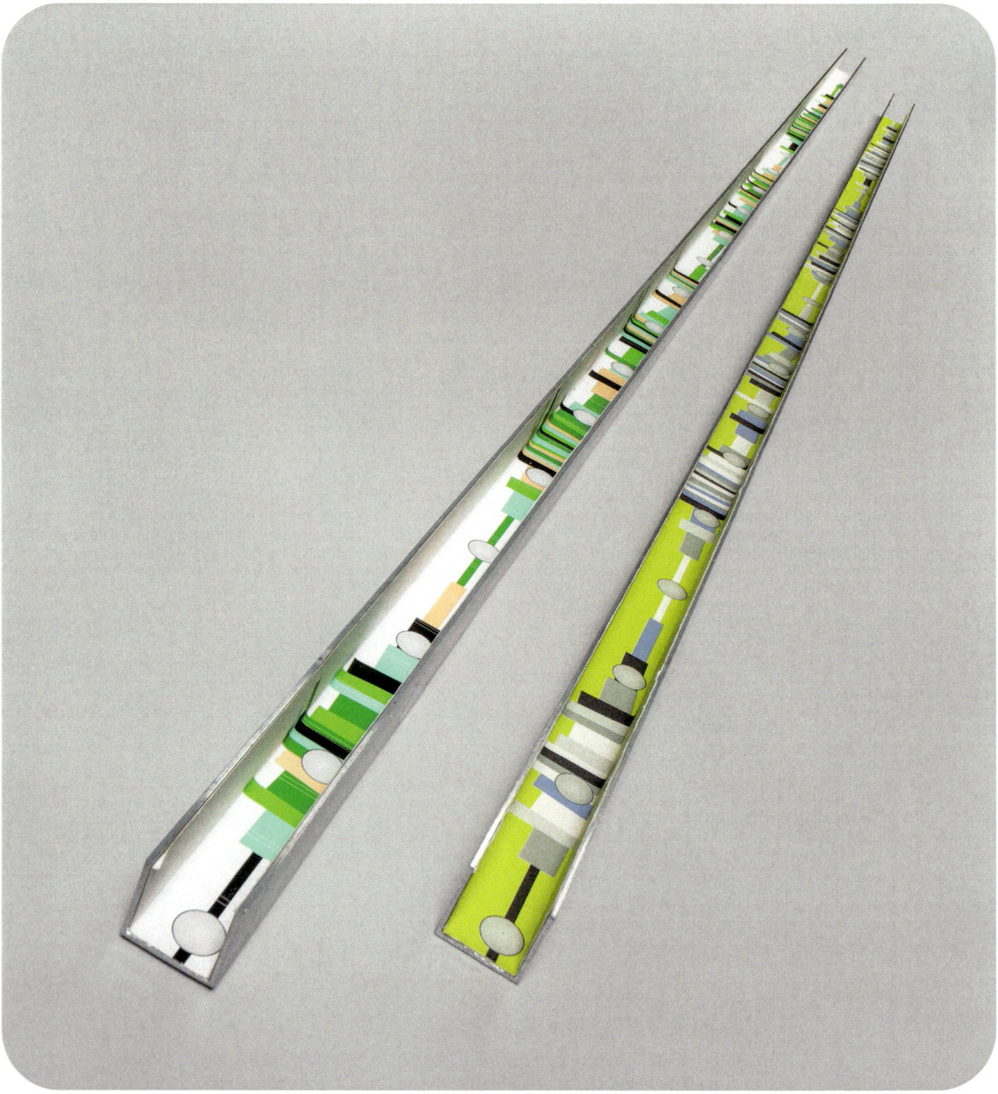

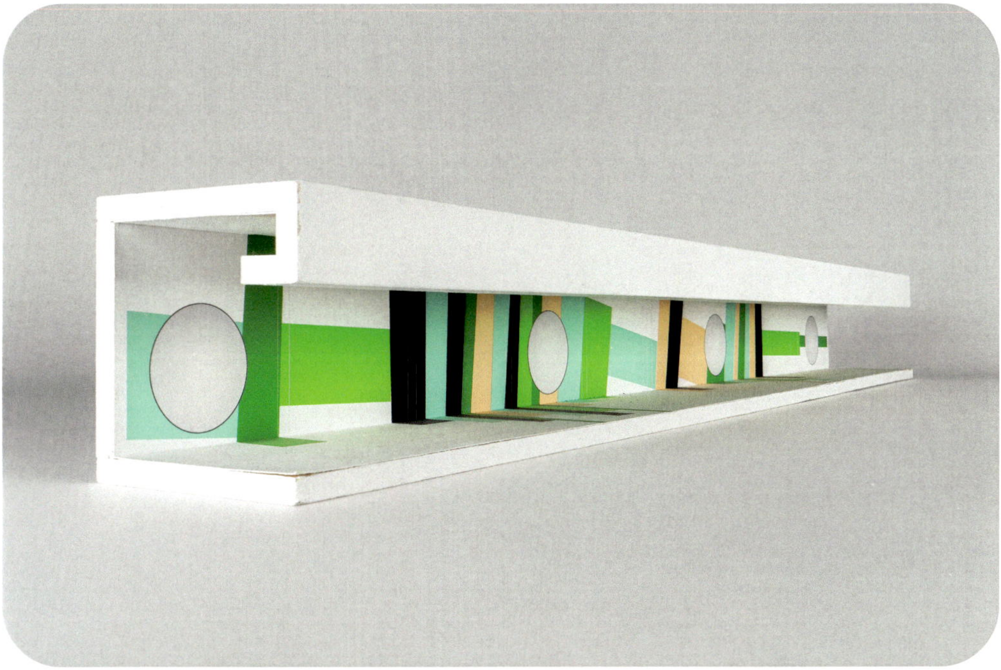

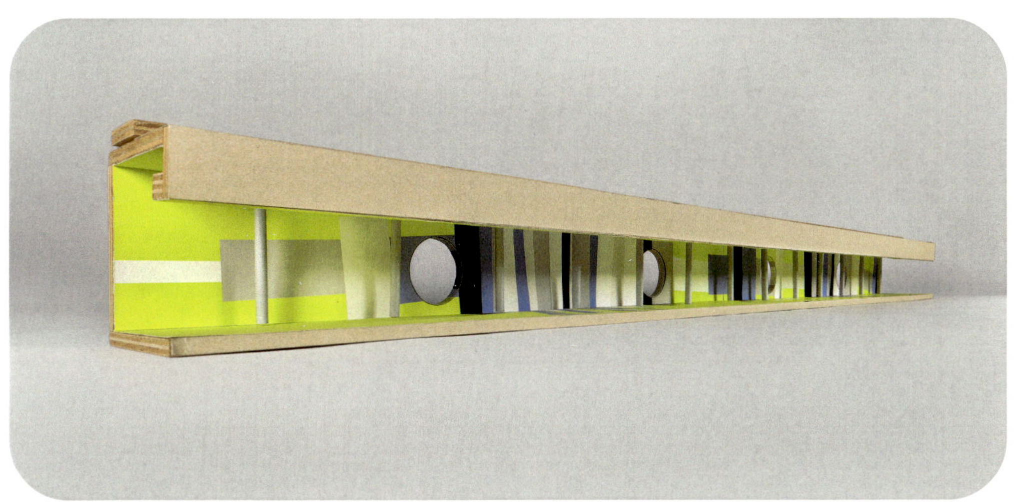

69 BEAUTIFUL WALL #25
1:50 | 2013

70 BEAUTIFUL WALL #25
1:33 | 2013

47. MIGROS ARTIST'S CARRIER BAG
1:40 | 1999

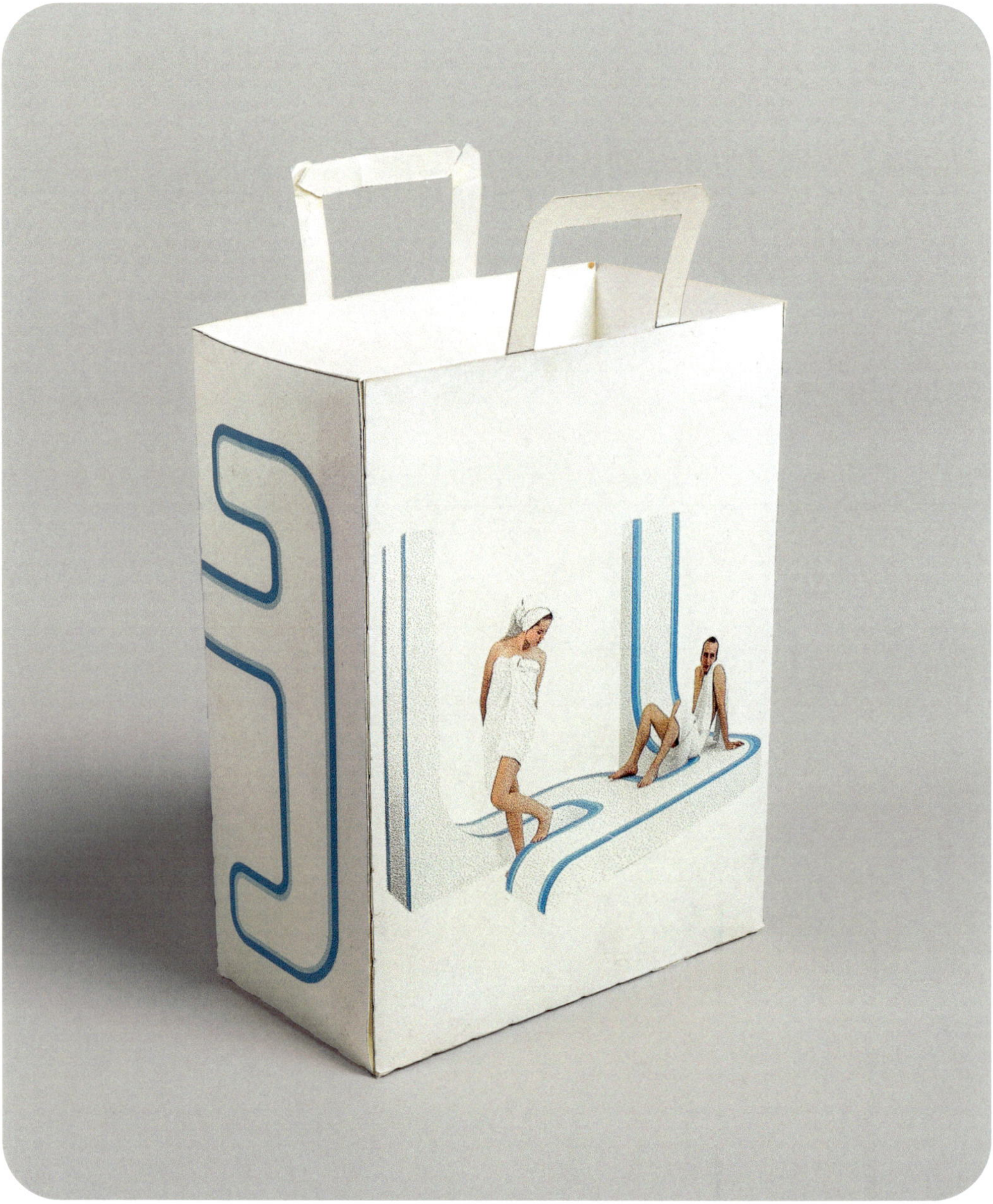

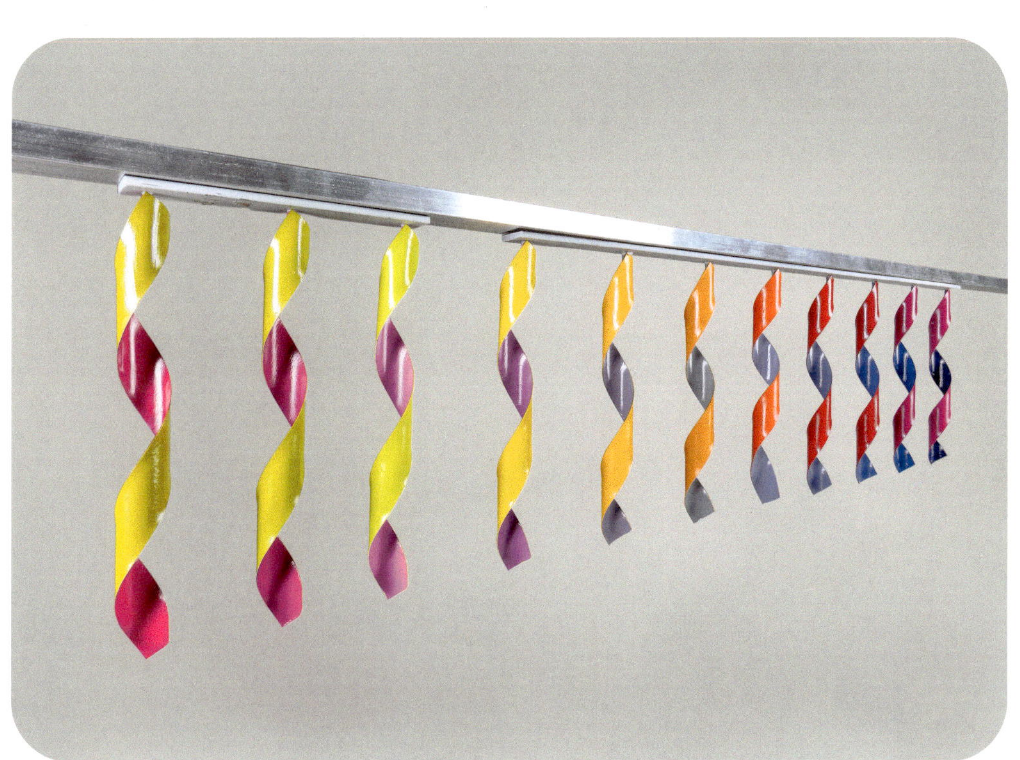

SPIRALS #5
1:50 | T2018

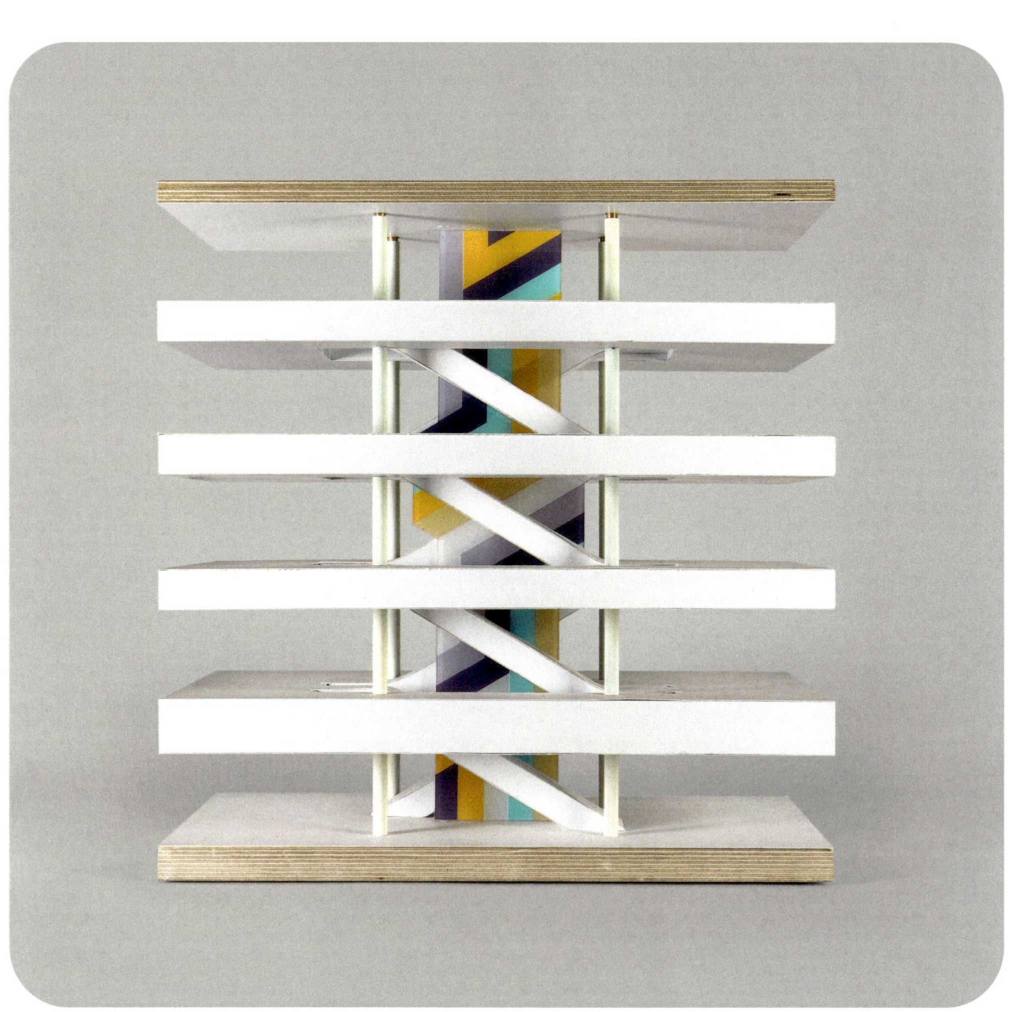

BEAUTIFUL ENTRANCE
1:50 | 2011

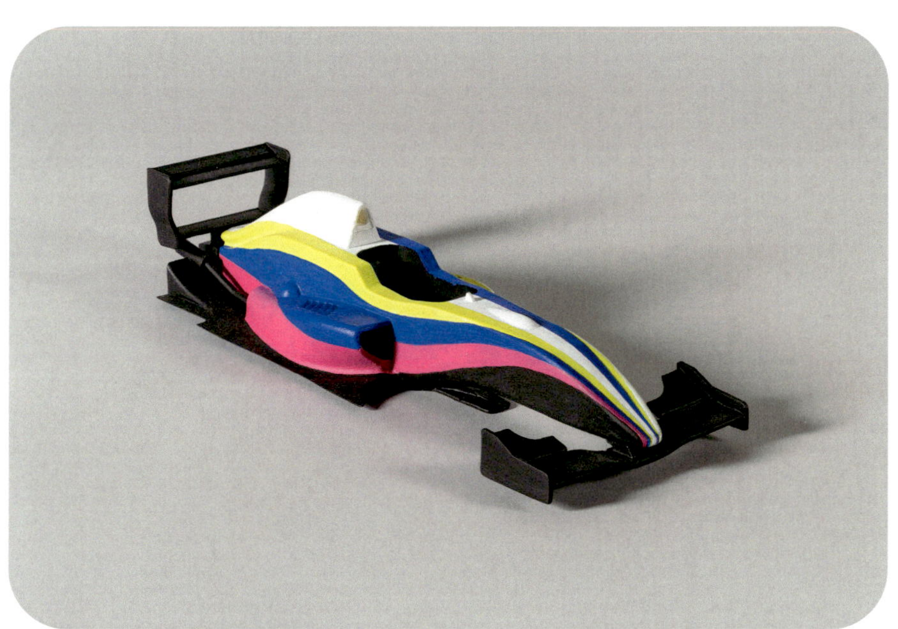

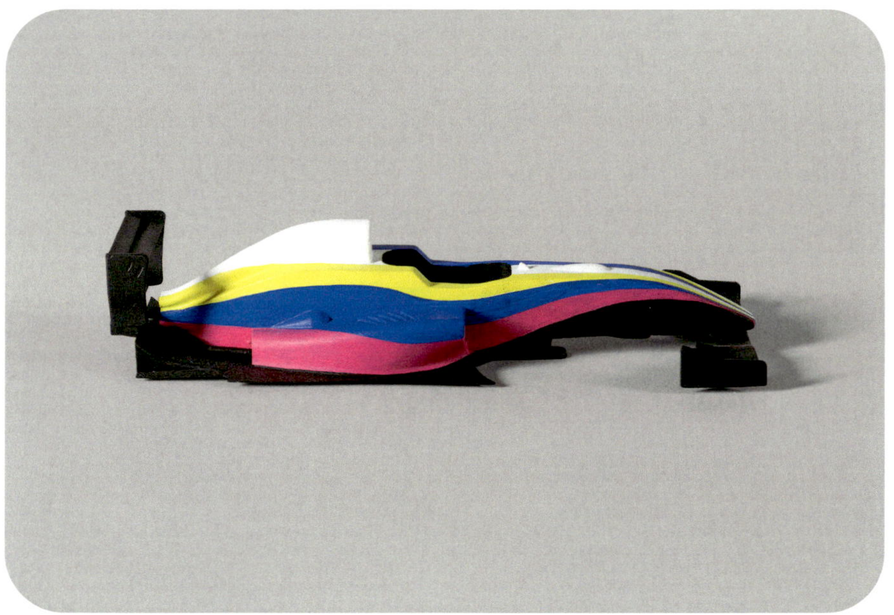

BEAUTIFUL CAR #2
1:15 | 2015

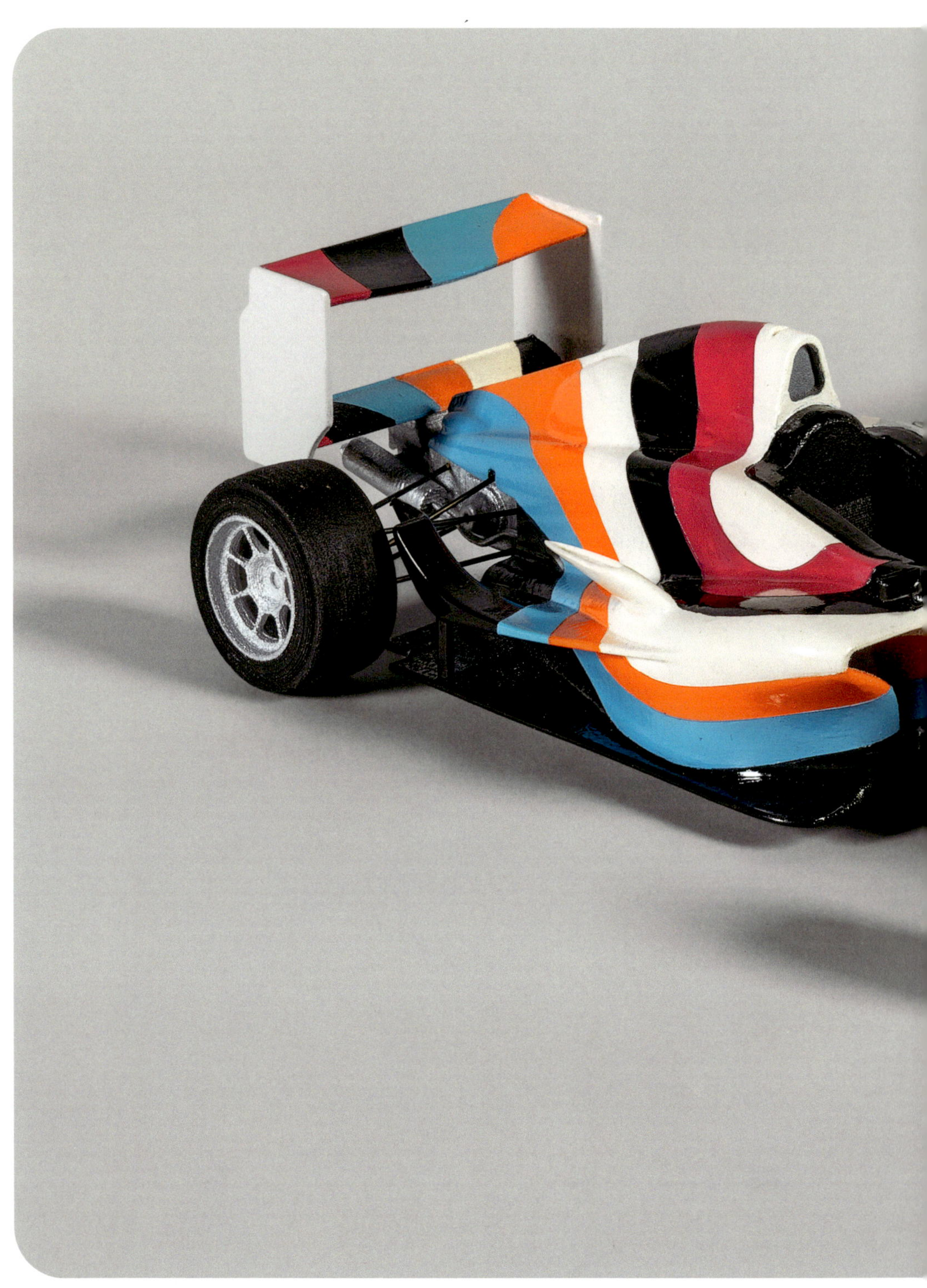

75 BEAUTIFUL CAR #1
1:15 | 2014

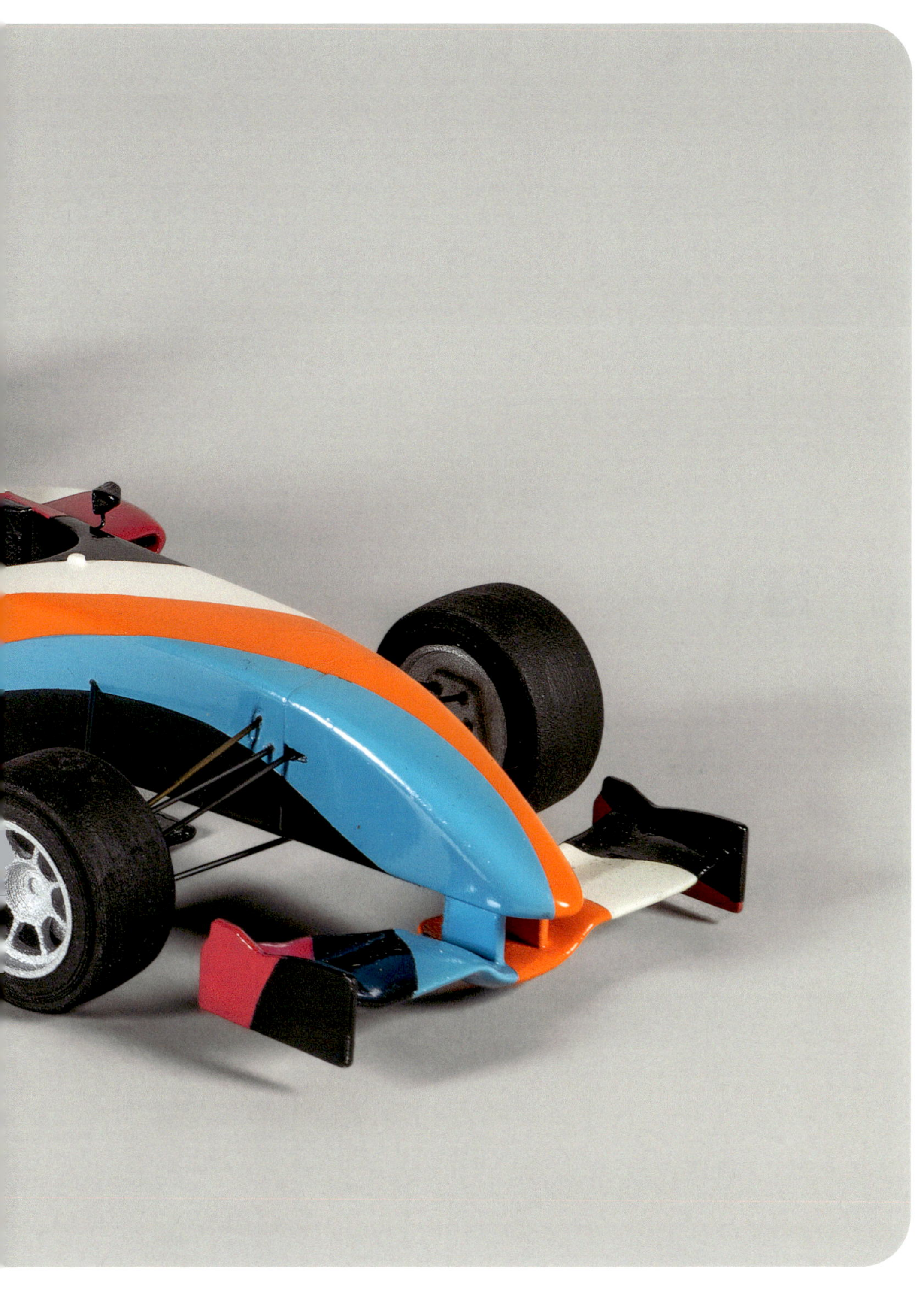

76 REVOLVING STUDIO
1:60 | 2012

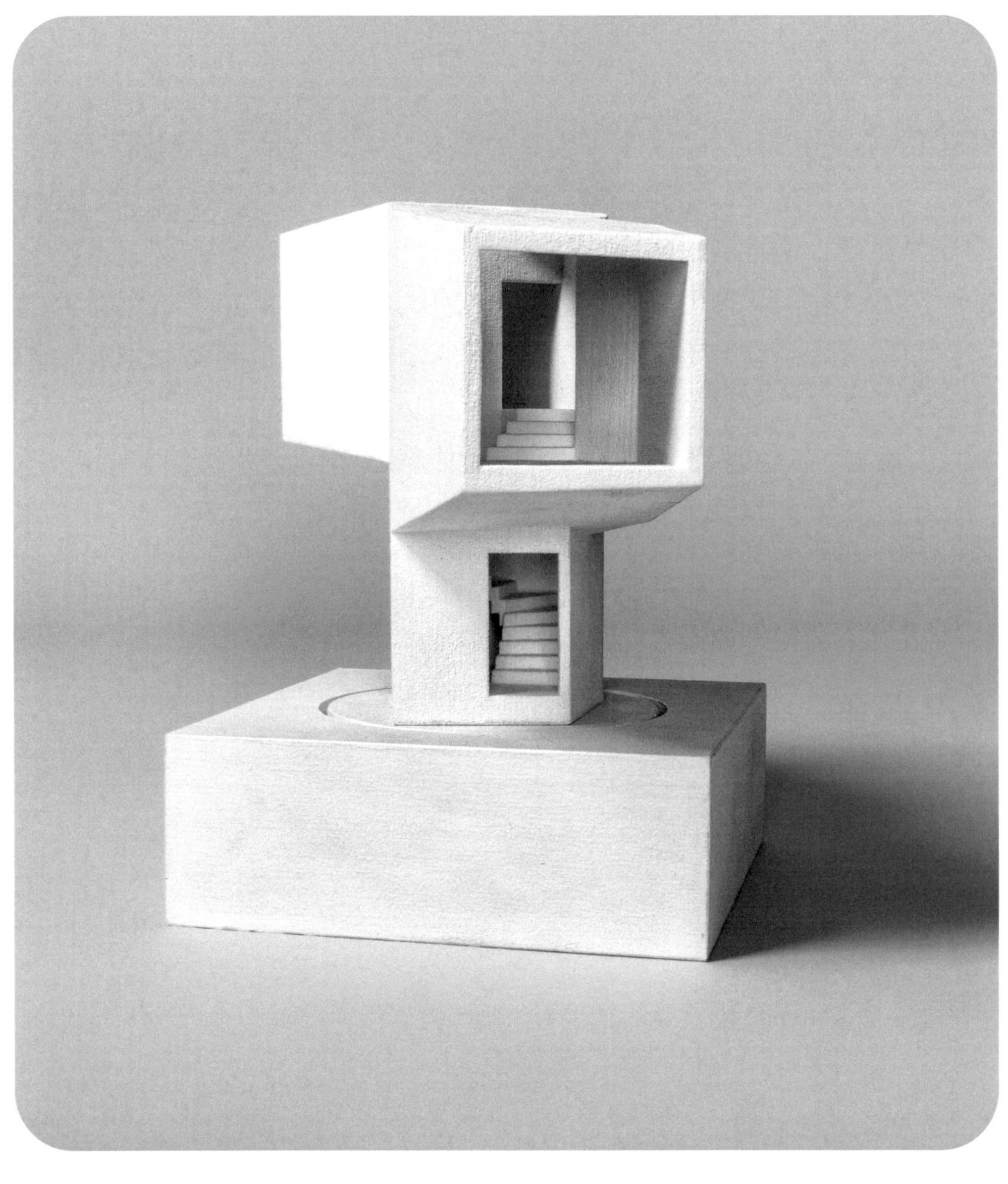

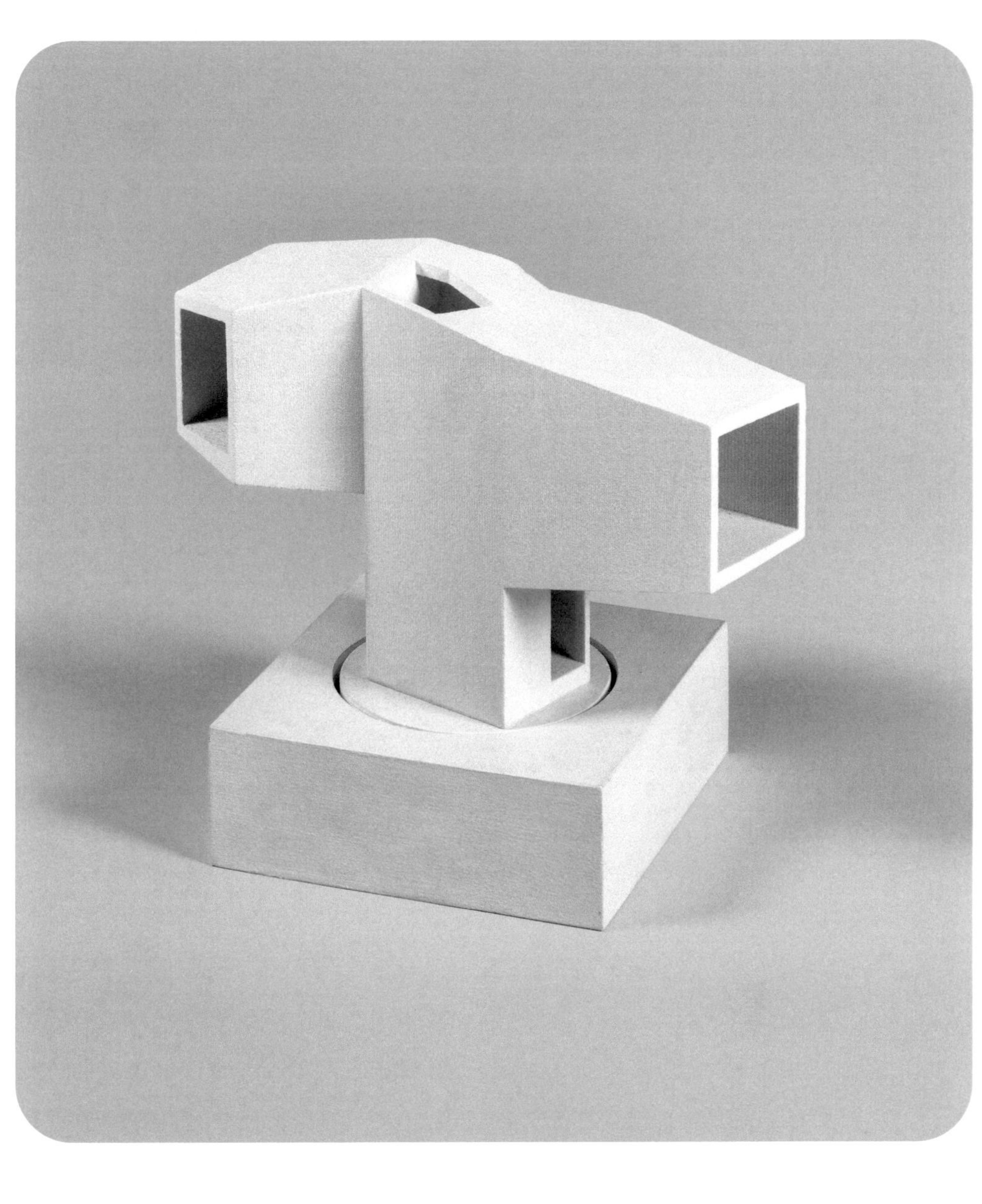

HOTEL EVERLAND
1:50 | 2002

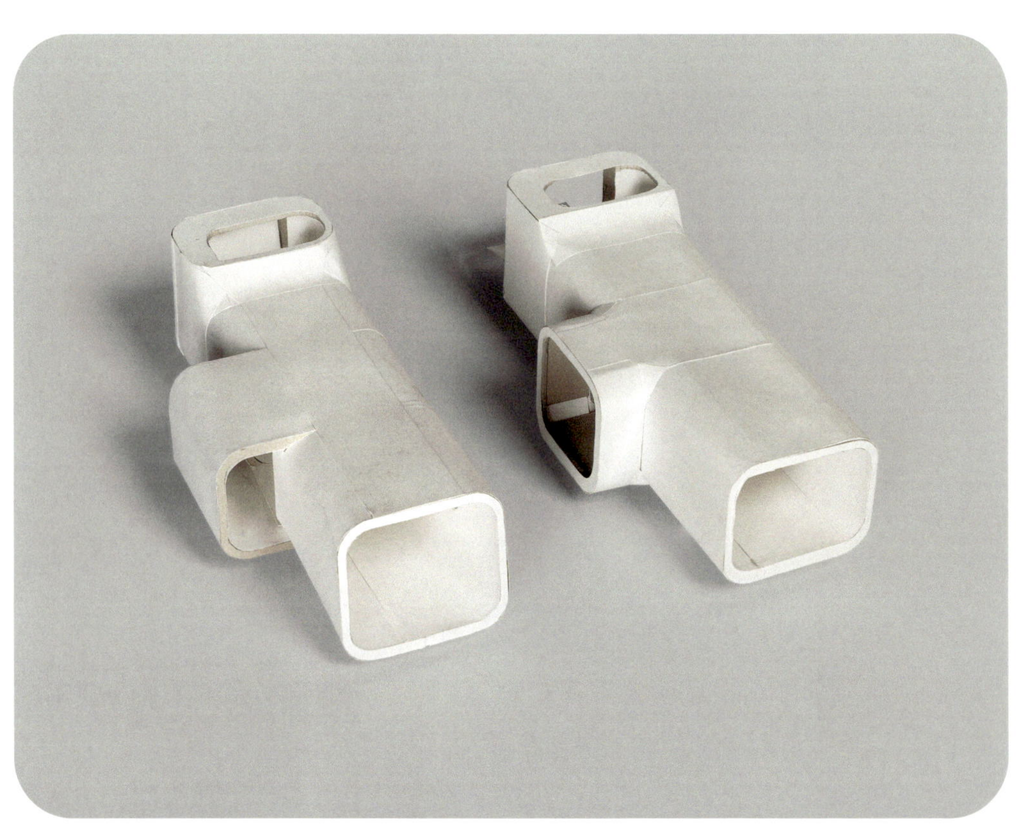

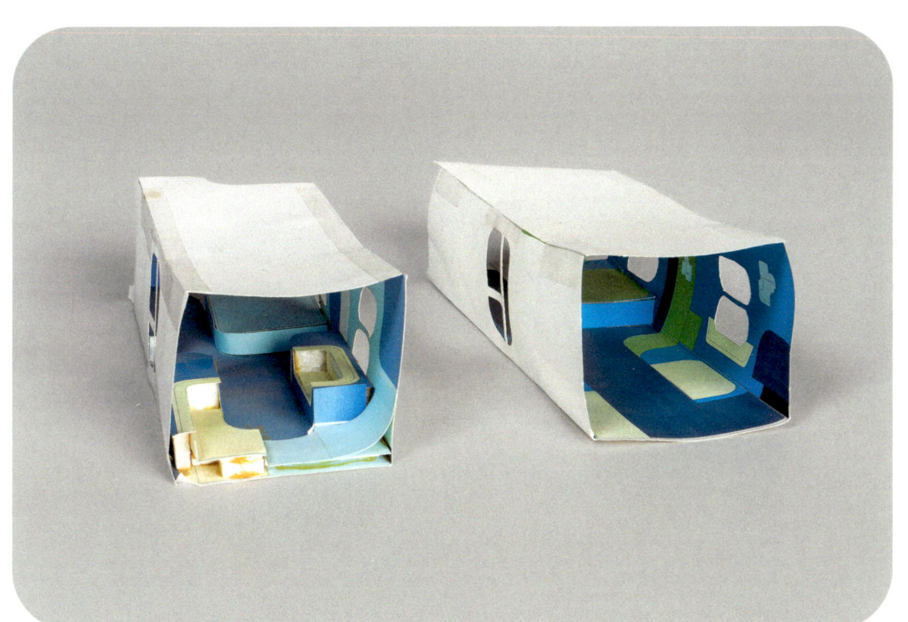

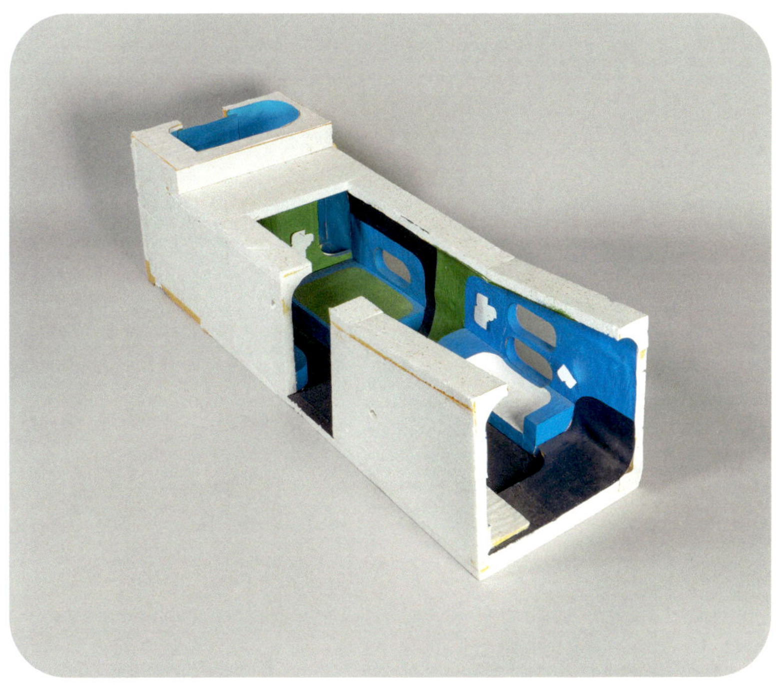

79 80 HOTEL EVERLAND
1:50 | 2002

81 HOTEL EVERLAND
1:10 | 2002

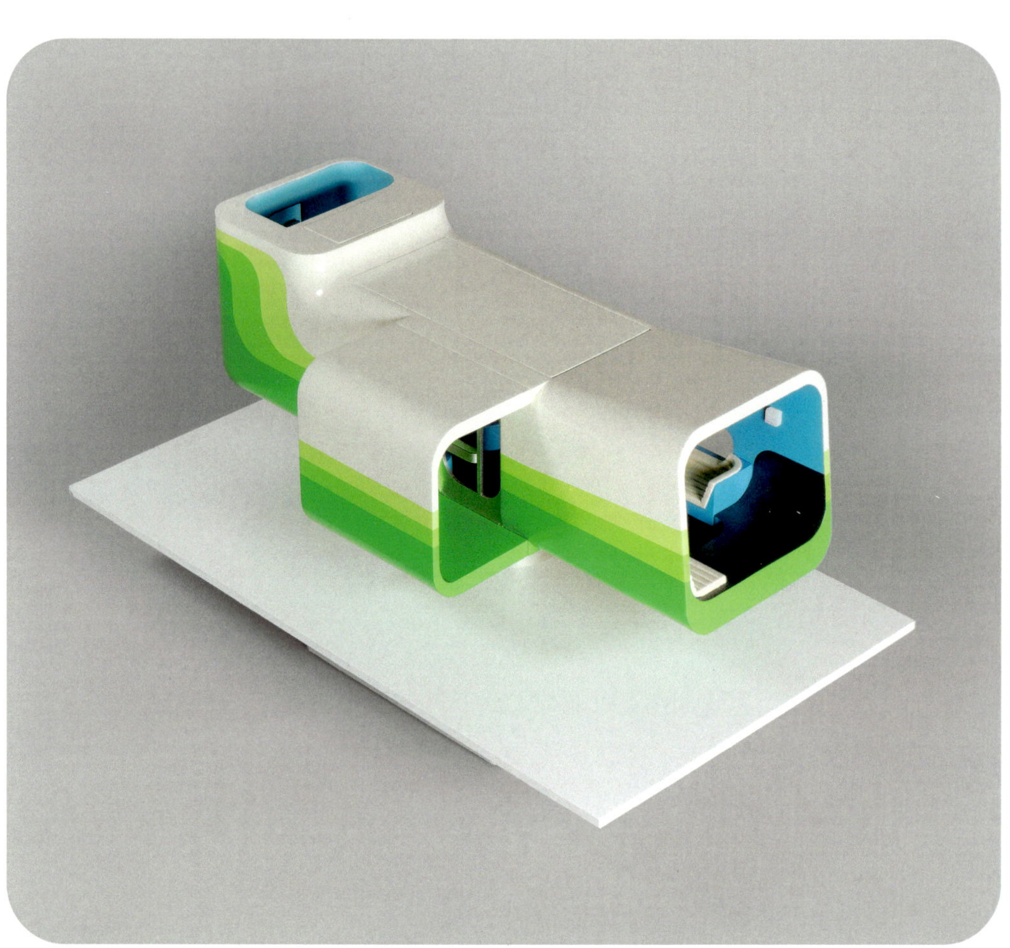

82 HOTEL EVERLAND
1:20 | 2007

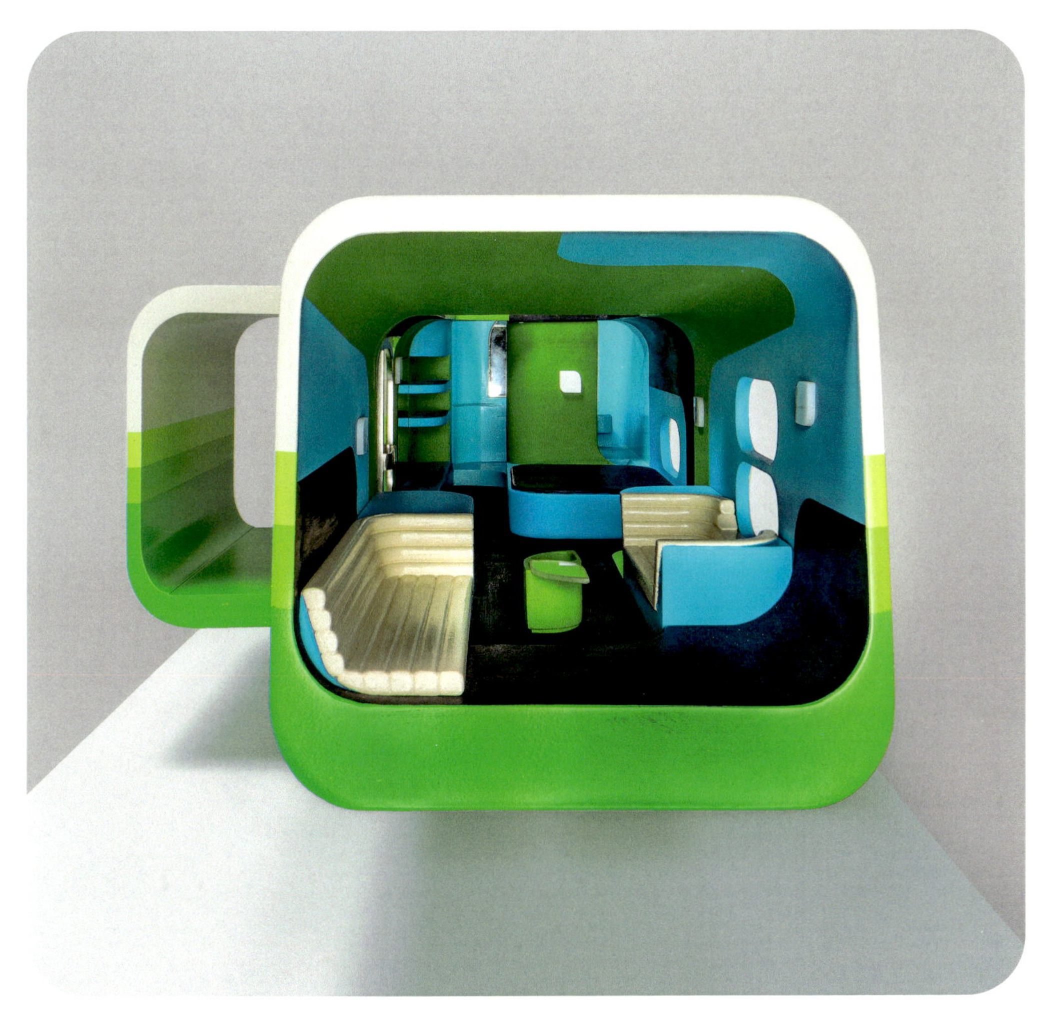

83 WHO'S OUT?
1:20 | 1992

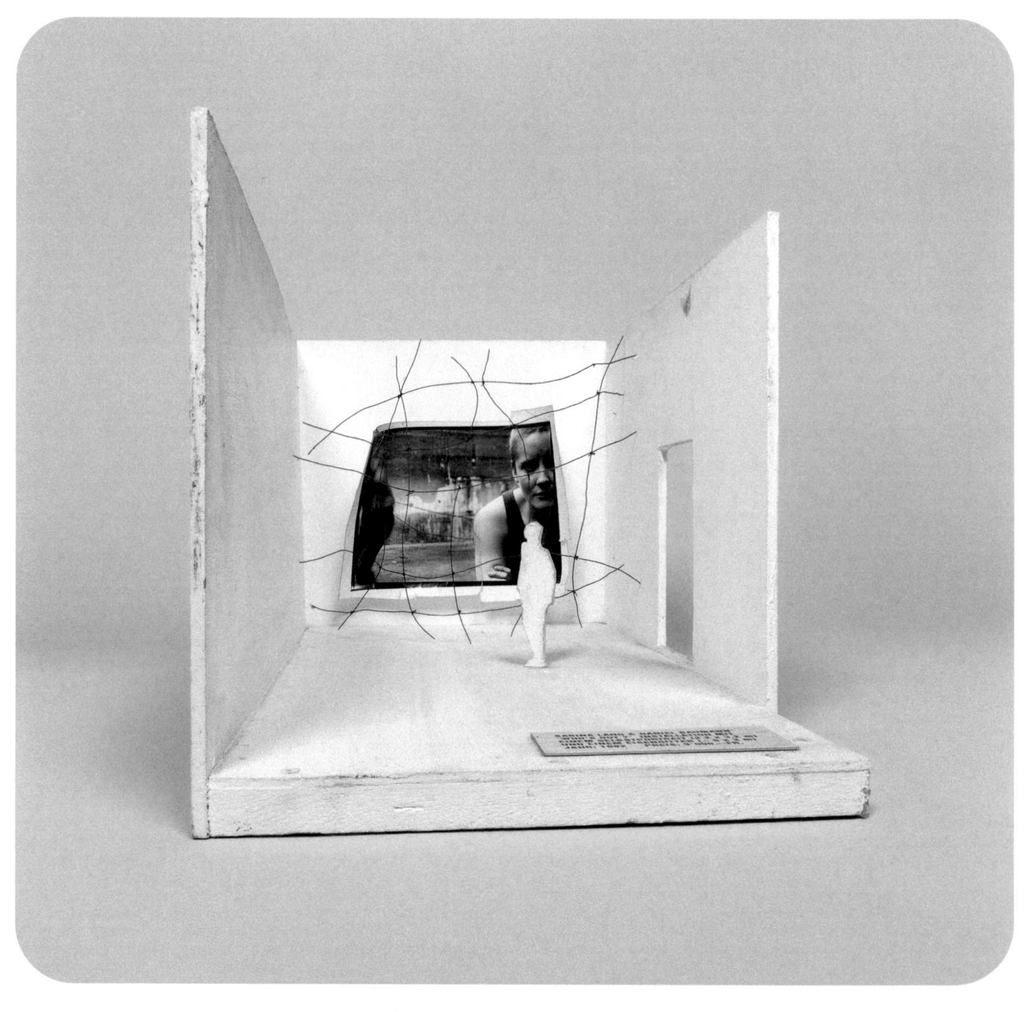

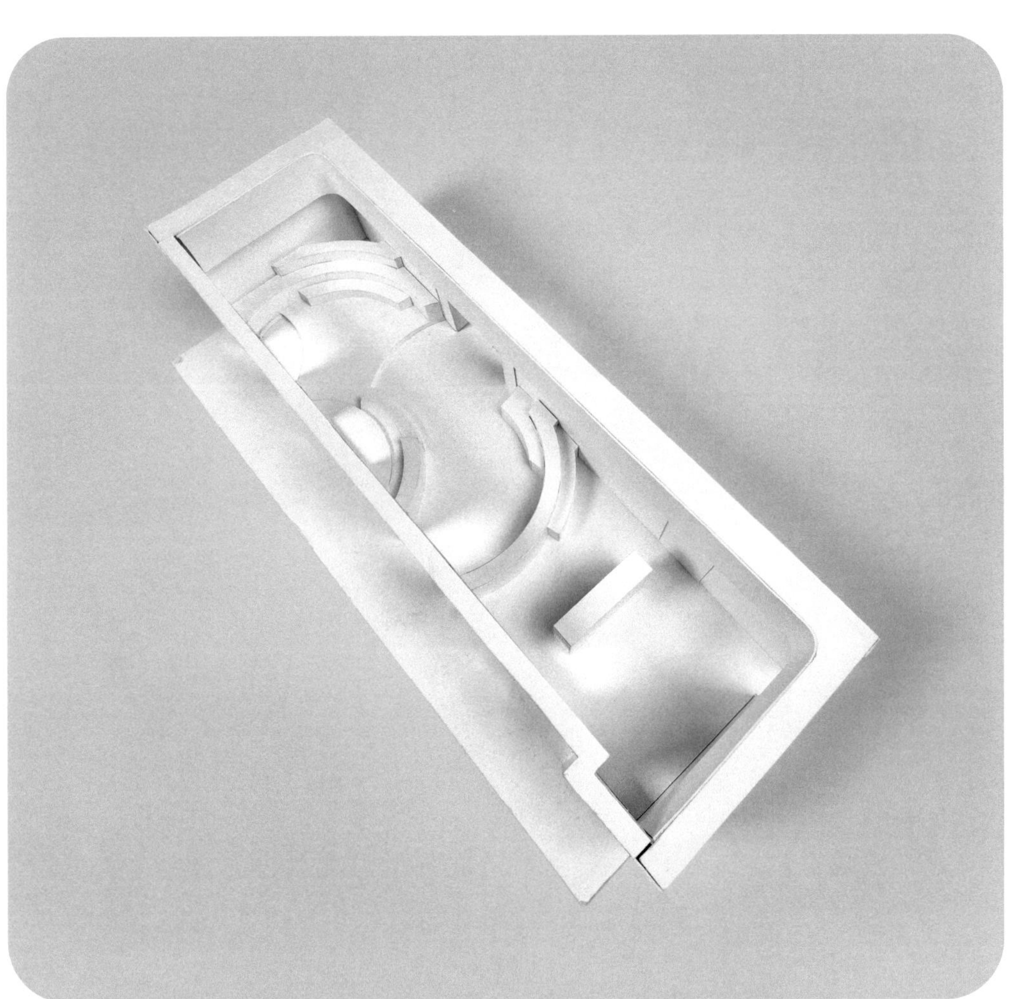

84 LOBBY
1:50 | 2004

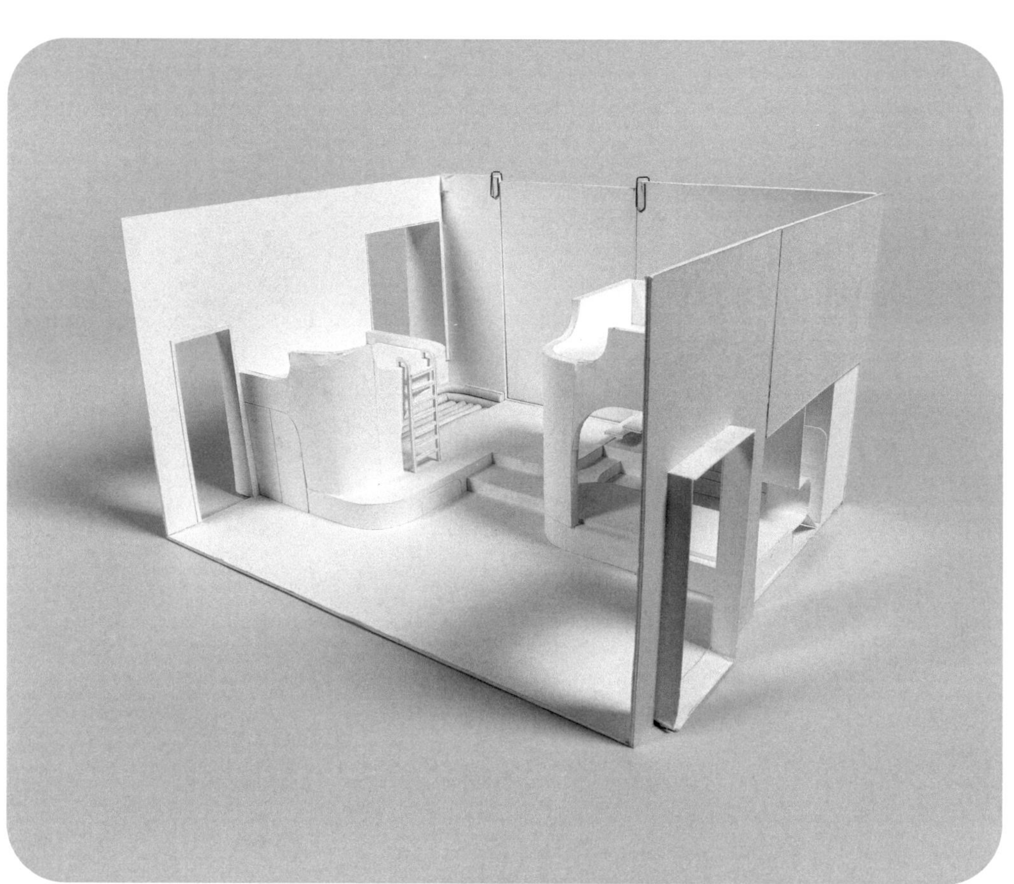

85 CHILDISH BEHAVIOR #4
1:20 | 2004

86 LOUNGE #1
1:25 | 2003

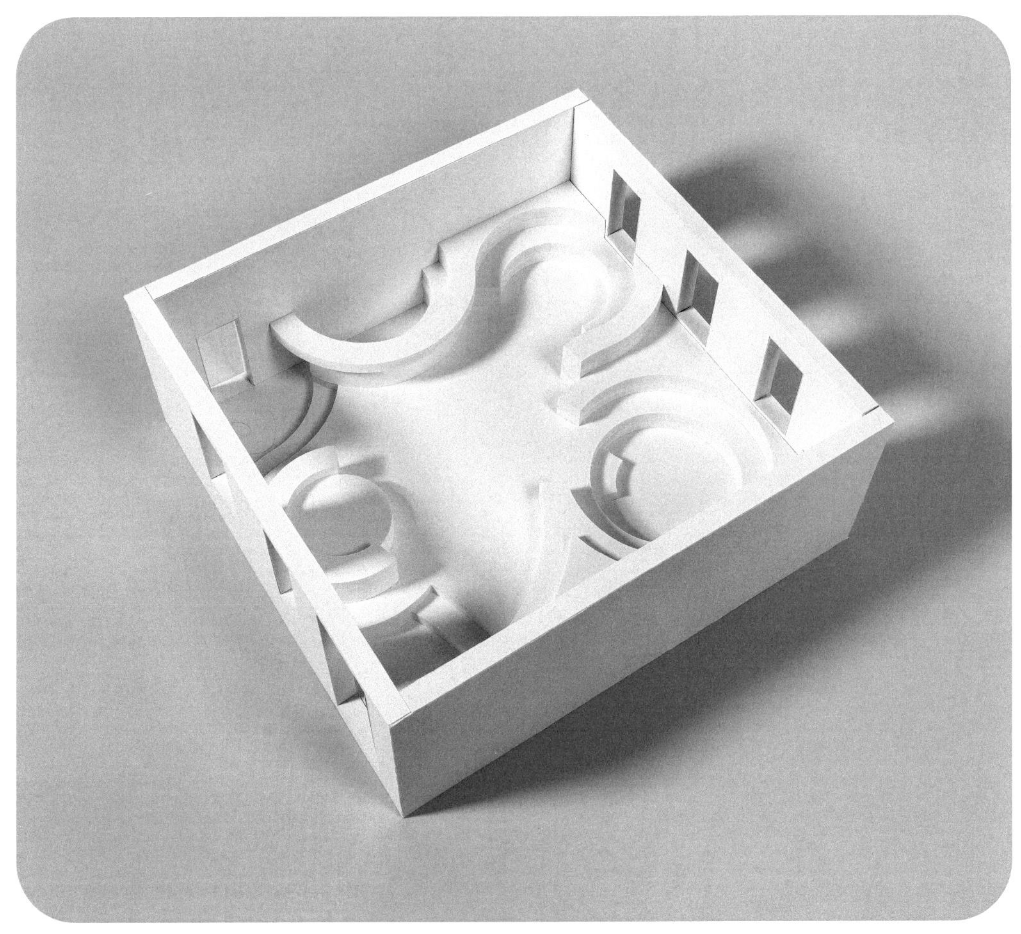

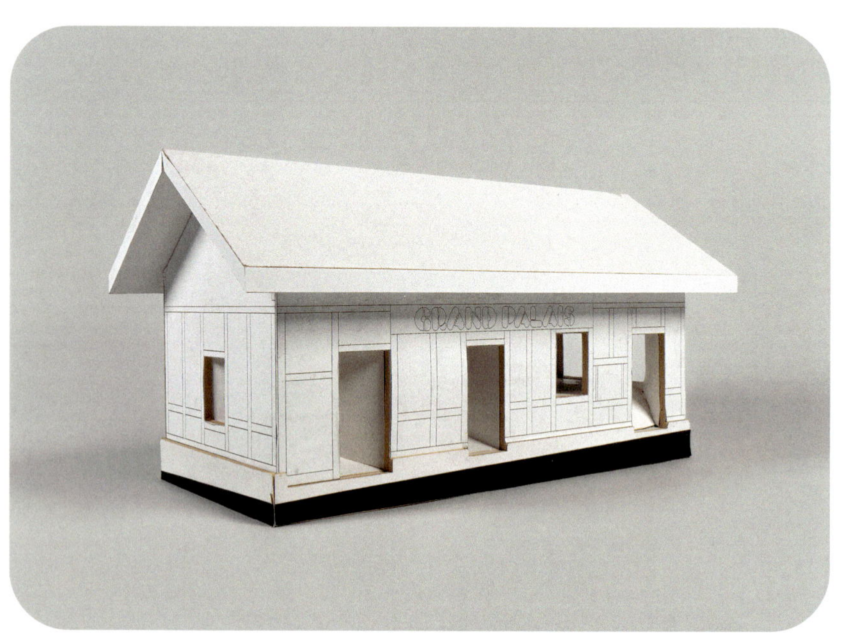

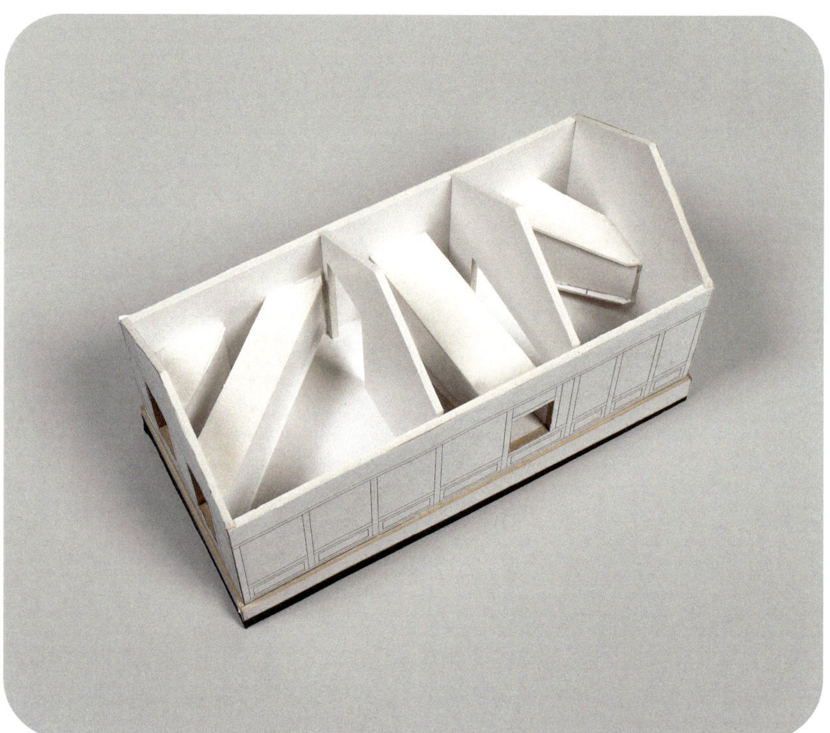

87

OPEN
1:33 | 2012

88 BEAUTIFUL CURTAIN #2
1:10 | 2015

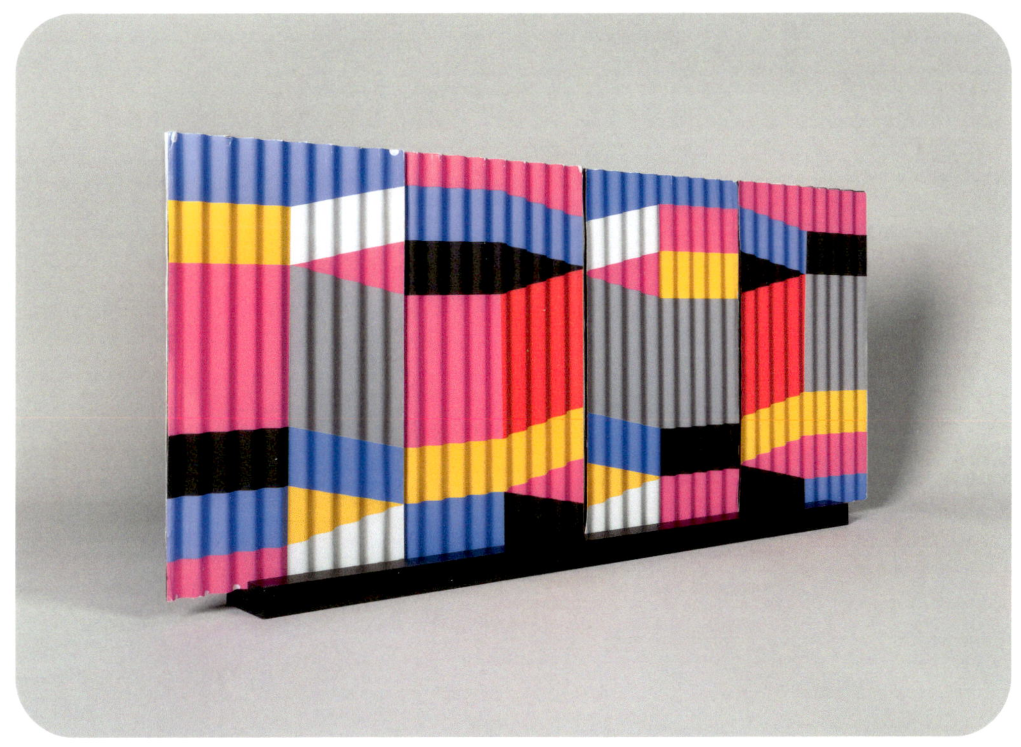

MODULE #4
1:25 | 2016

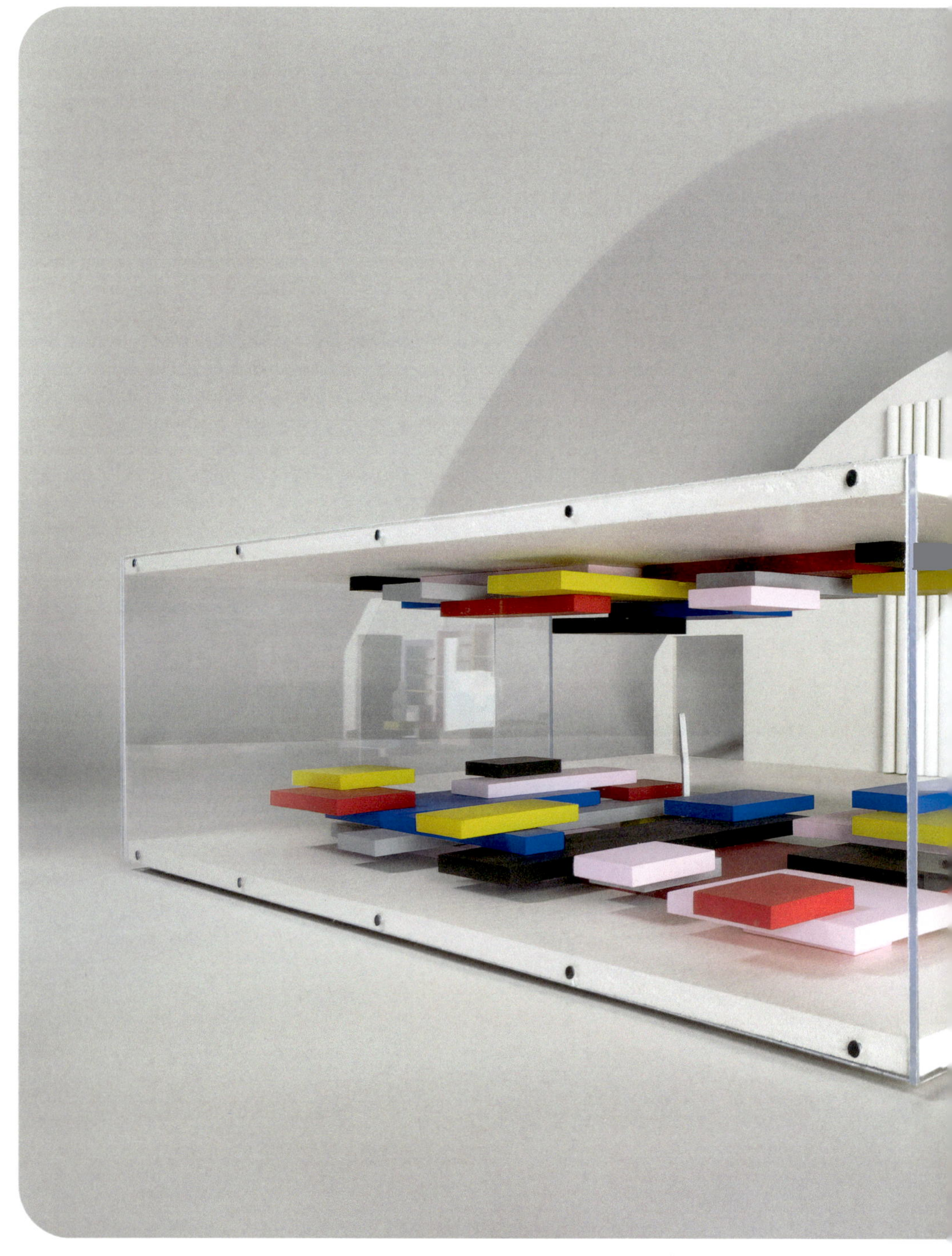

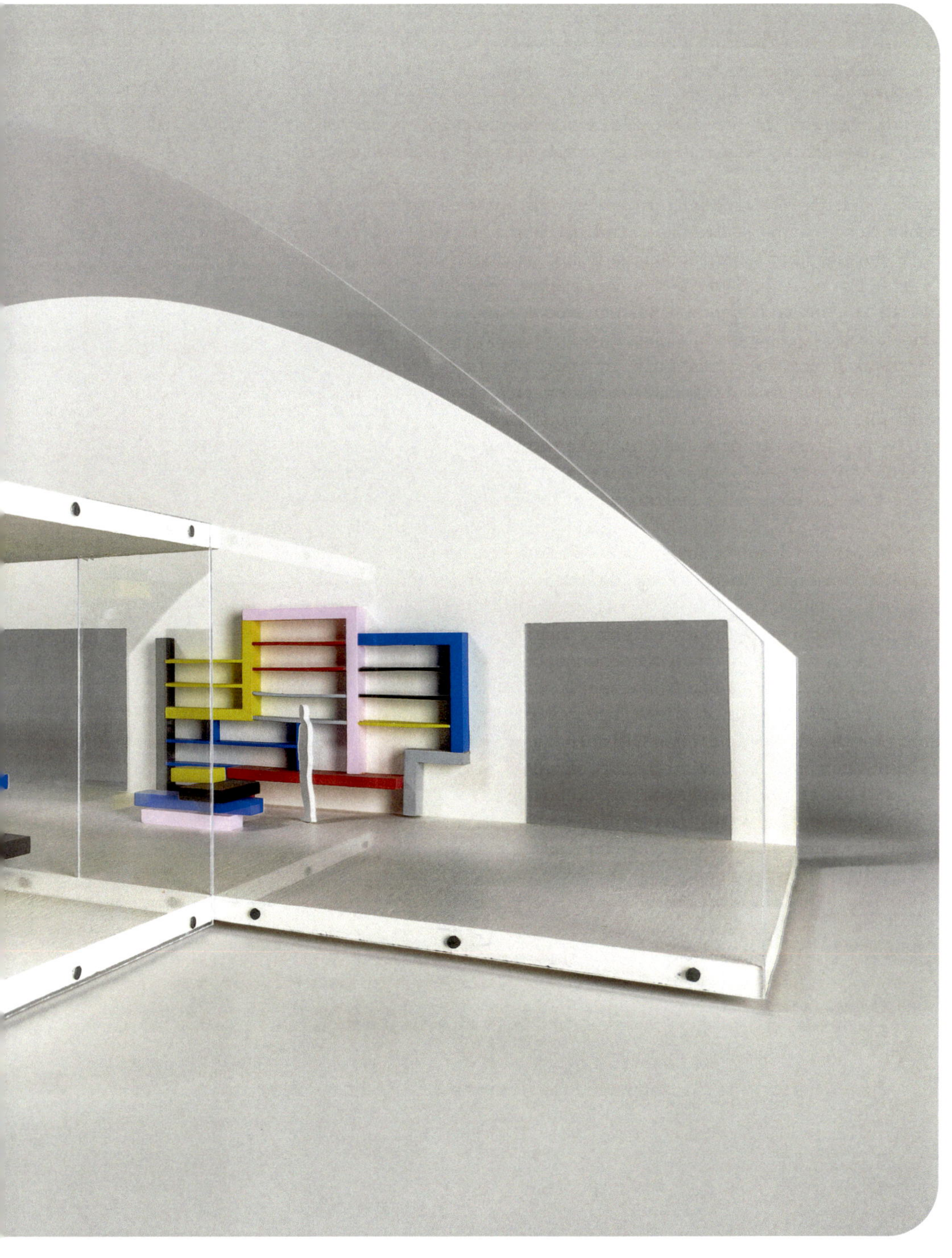

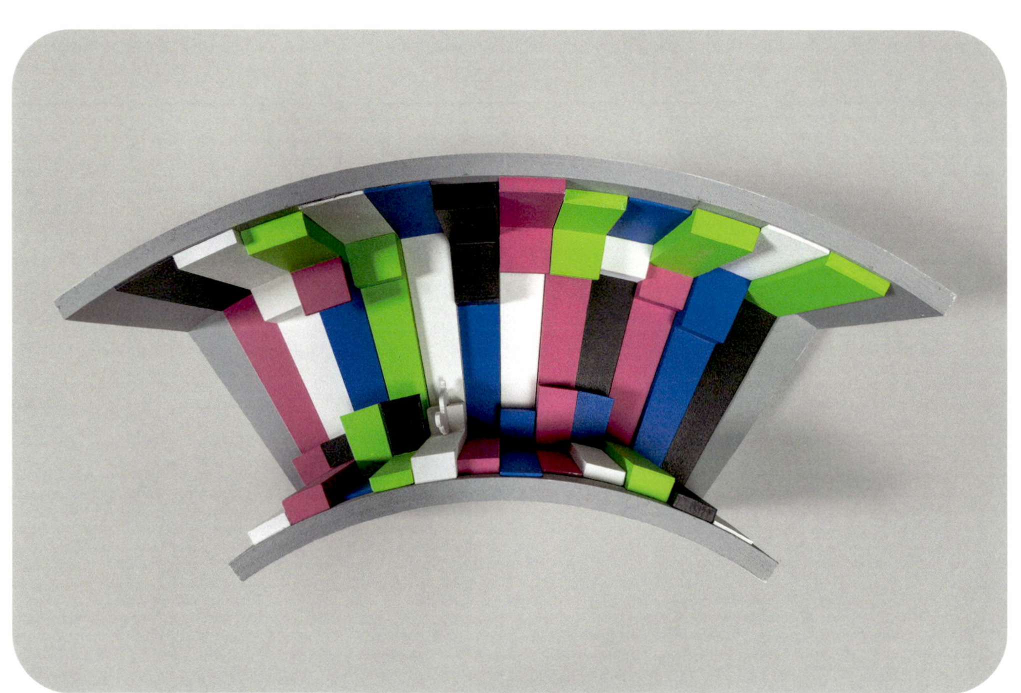

BEAUTIFUL TUBE #1
1:20 | 2011

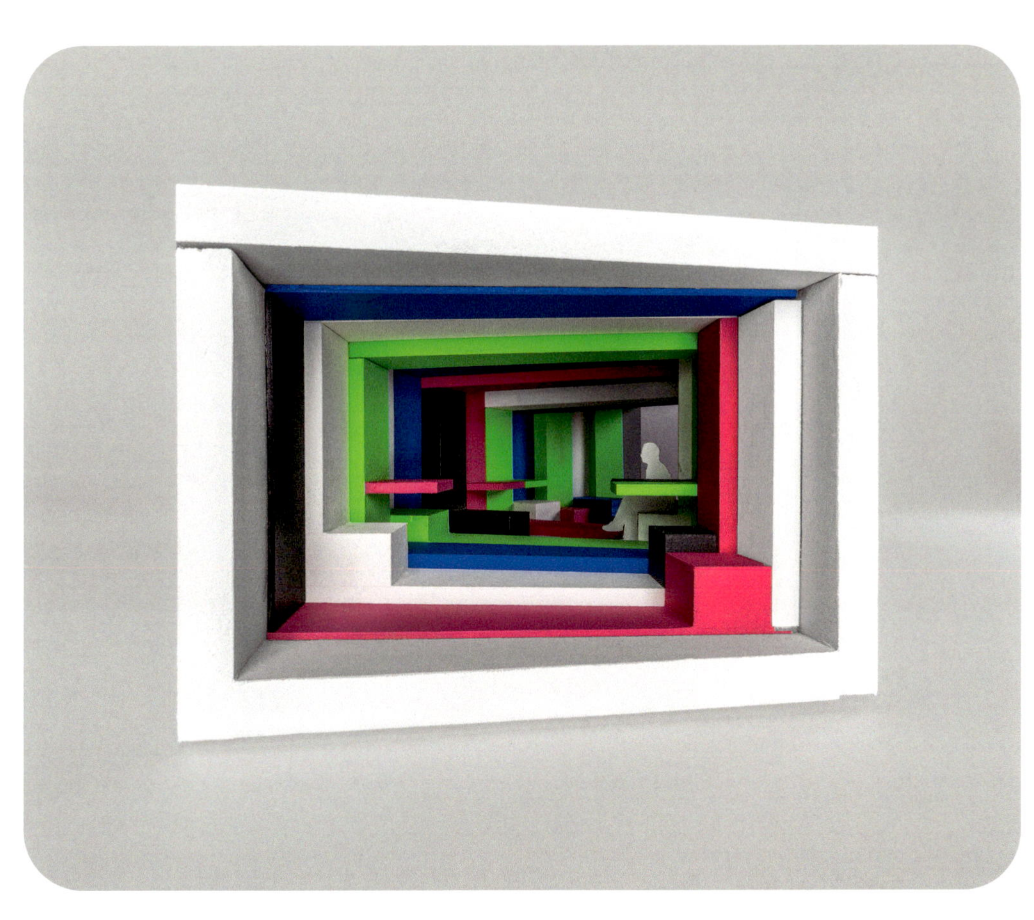

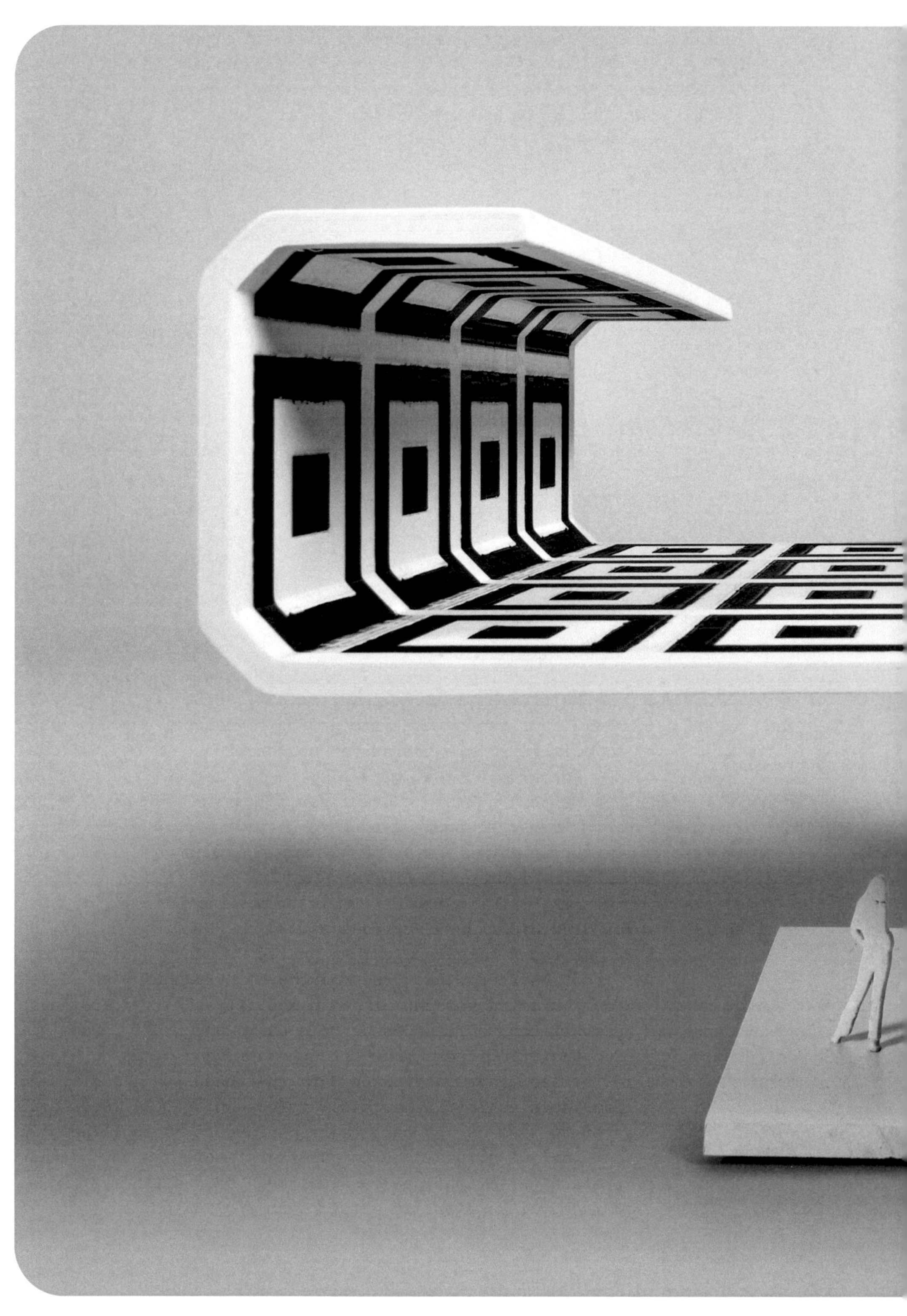

MODULE #5 (KUNSTHALLE BAR)
1:50 | 2018

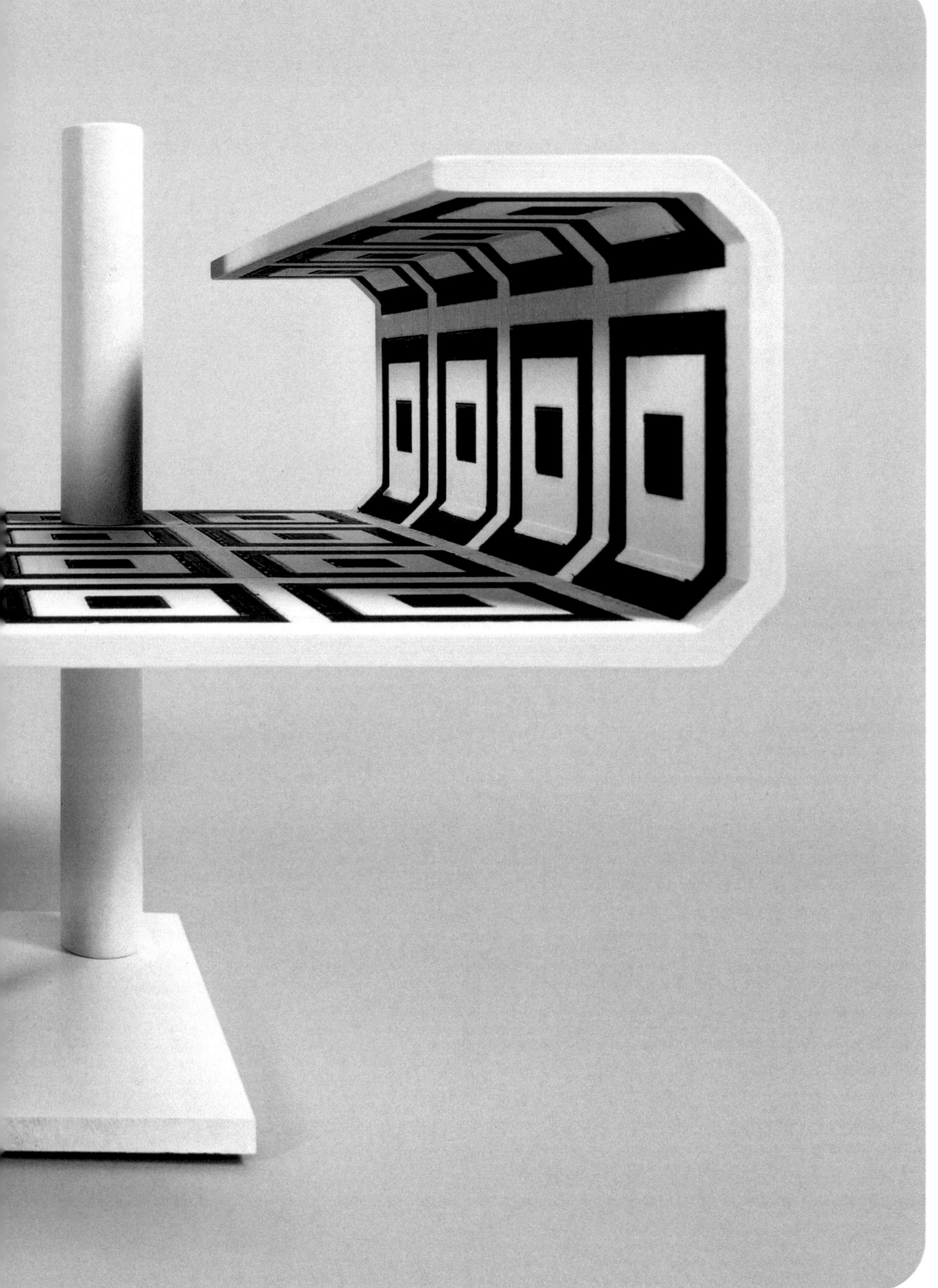

DISCOVERING MAGNIFICENCE IN MINIATURE

LILIA GLANZMANN AND DAVID GLANZMANN IN CONVERSATION WITH SABINA LANG AND DANIEL BAUMANN

Lilia (LG) ◀ All of your models are stored on a rolling stack. You've now taken 96 of them out of your compactus storage unit. When did you complete your first model?

Sabina (SL) ▶ WHO'S OUT was created for an application to take part in the 1992 Christmas exhibition at the Kunstmuseum Thun – an installation with a black-and-white self-portrait measuring 3.2 by 2.2 metres, with a iron lattice measuring 5 by 3 metres spanned in front of it in the room. We weren't able to show a finished object as a reference but had to demonstrate that the idea would work, so we built a model.

Daniel (DB) ▶ There weren't any image-editing programmes or 3D tools for us to use back then, whereas model making was something we were attached to and with which we were familiar. I trained as a structural draughtsman and Sabina grew up with parents who were architects. Building models was something we both liked doing at the time, and still do.

David (DG) ◀ As a whole, all the finished models from the last 32 years make up an extraordinary collection. Why did you keep hold of them all?

DB ▶ It's true we haven't thrown a single one of them away. In general we archive everything, even our very first email!

SL ▶ That's right, everything gets saved, even old bills! But we don't do it for the sake of archiving; we actually often go back and reference these materials, extract information that we need to work.

As opposed to architecture, our works are more transient; they disappear again. In model form they remain intact as miniatures, and the three-dimensionality of a model shows aspects that photographic documentation can't preserve as such.

DB ▶ For a long time we had the models on shelves, scattered somewhere in a cellar or stored in the studio. The oldest models still bear the scars – they had to endure a lot! But we ourselves had never thought about staging an exhibition with them.

LG ◀ In model making the key thing is the reason it's built – to sketch something out, to test something or to present something. What type of models are yours?

SL ▶ They're working, presentation or exhibition models, whereby the fewest belong to the last category. One of them was created for the HOTEL EVERLAND in Paris. The visitors weren't allowed up on the roof anymore after 6 o'clock in the evening because there were already guests in their hotel room. But the Palais du Tokyo stayed open late, so we built a model for the palace entrance hall, with lights and all the details, so that people could still get a realistic impression of the work.

The presentation models make up the largest category: they're very differently elaborated – it's always a question of who we're presenting them to. For discussions with curators, they're usually rather more abstract, but more detailed for competitions so that they can be understood without explanations. Our working models are produced pragmatically; their purpose is that we can take them along with us when the exhibition is installed and can distil information from them.

DB ▶ Like for instance the model for the installation BEAUTIFUL TUBE #6 in the gallery of the Galeries Lafayette [A.▀]. In this case the model helped us to check whether the carpet was laid in the right place.

LG ◀ Have you made models for all of your projects?

SL ▶ No, not by any stretch of the imagination. When there's a need to discuss an idea with other people, plans or visualisations will also do. But in terms of spatial understanding a model is always very helpful, especially, for example, for our inflatable structures, which are difficult to show on a computer.

DB ▶ The models always stay with us. Over time we also realised that they're often the only thing that physically remains from the ephemeral works. In terms of execution, not much has changed, apart obviously from 3D printing, which allows even highly complex models to be produced a lot faster.

DG ◀ Sometimes models stay as small utopias. Are there examples like this in your collection?

DB ▶ A good example in this respect is REVOLVING STUDIO for the Christoph Merian Stiftung at the Dreispitz Areal in Basel. Unfortunately the project was never realised, but nevertheless it's still our dream to one day build a revolving house. There are often also ideas that get continuously picked up again and altered until they can finally be realised. That's how BEAUTIFUL VIEW #1 in Nanterre close to Paris came about [F.▀]. The sculpture is now 22 metres high, but originally we developed the first idea for an over-40-metre version for a football training pitch close to Zurich. The height symbolises the upper rows of seating in the Basle stadium – essentially a mark of the ultimate achievement to strive for in Swiss football at the time.

DG ◀ As opposed to your small models, your works are gigantic, which can be already seen from your first model. What is it that fascinates you about sheer size?

SL ▶ Some of our very early works involved the realisation of projections for concerts in the attic of the Reitschule in Bern: using overhead and slide projectors, we saturated the whole space with images.

DB ▶ The idea there was about seizing hold of something, the intoxication, which was magnified the more of them there were. We've never been interested in reduction and reticence. And coming across gigantically was also a provocation.
SL ▶ Our rule was always about what we could still carry, rolled up, by train. You can also see that in the techniques we still use today, like tubes or wall paintings, which we can inflate or mount in situ.

DG ◀ What were the '90s like as the start of your joint work?
SL ▶ We wanted to make art. To start with we were active in and around the Reithalle; collectives were a topic, and the Reithalle provided an opportunity to try things out, even if visual art wasn't really all that accepted. The important thing for us was the "go-ahead-and-do-it" aspect.
DB ▶ I exhibited my photographs in the Reithalle. That's where we met each other.
SL ▶ Daniel had long hair and I had none at all!
DB ▶ We were active in alternative art spaces – in the Kunstmausoleum in Biel or the Kunsthaus Oerlikon in Zurich. We were simply looking to get involved in these kinds of places and were able to acquire our first experiences of exhibiting with them. One formative place for us then became the Kunsthalle Bern, where we visited almost all of the exhibitions, joined the opening receptions, and so got to know the art scene. But most of our art friends in Bern were ten years older, which is why early on we turned to Zurich and tried to connect with a younger scene in other Swiss cities, or in France or the Netherlands.

LG ◀ Why the double name?
SL ▶ Right at the beginning we did solo exhibitions: Daniel with his photos and me my paintings under the title "Blutige Hände" (Bloody Hands), likewise in the Reithalle. We experimented with a lot of things. Then came this chance to exhibit in Leipzig in the former spaces of the Eigen + Art gallery. We travelled up there, and for the first time showed our works together.
DB ▶ We got annoyed when everyone asked "What's by you?" or "And what did you do?" People used to break our concept down into individualised bits. From then on we decided to only appear together, under one name.

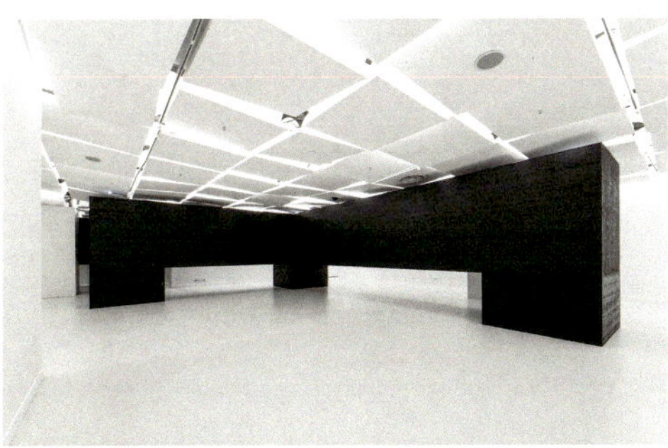

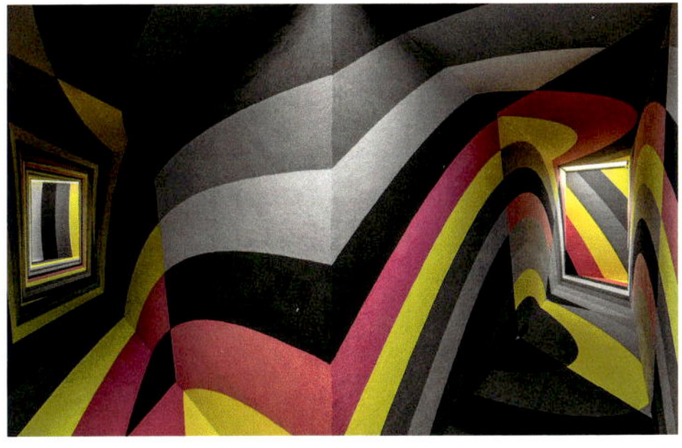

A.▶ BEAUTIFUL TUBE #6, 2019, Galerie des Galeries, Galerie Lafayette, Paris F

SL ▶ At the time we were already inspired by artist pairs like Anna & Bernhard Blume or Fischli/Weiss who appeared as duos or groups.
DB ▶ Recently we thought what we'd have sounded like if we'd used our mothers' surnames – Läderach/Siegenthaler!

DG ◀ Along with the scale, a hallmark of your creativity is your humour. Many of the works aren't just meant to be viewed but can also be used; others feign a usability or slyly sabotage it. How does this balancing act work?

DB ▶ The decisive aspect is the double or multiple ambiguities. We use humour as a means to relativise the reverence for the authority of the work. In the process, what's important to us is to dose it sparingly, not cynically, and not so as to make it obvious.
The humour often results from an initial irritation, particularly in the case of something ostensibly functional that's in fact completely unusable but just looks as if it were: the short moment of pausing before recognising the absurdity of it.

SL ▶ Humour is also important when we share working. A lot of things have to be negotiated and discussed when you work together. We contradict each other in our arguments, and sometimes it's tedious, which is where the levity of humour helps us find a way out. At the end of the day we actually do like working together, otherwise we would have fallen out long ago. But we likewise use humour in our work in order to question hierarchies or dominance, for instance in those pieces that express a scepticism about architecture with a faint smile.

DB ▶ We're interested in matches and disruptions: construed moments, such as for the sic! art space in Lucerne – incidentally our smallest model, made using 3D printing. In this case an immaculate white structure blends with the run-down shed; its proportions and its form make it look as if it fits precisely into the setting, while at the same time throwing it completely into contrast and giving itself an alien look.

LG ◀ How do you find the forms for these moments?

DB ▶ First of all we visit the venue and try to get a visual feel for it and analyse it, but similarly its use, its history, its surrounding, etc. That way we find out how we can

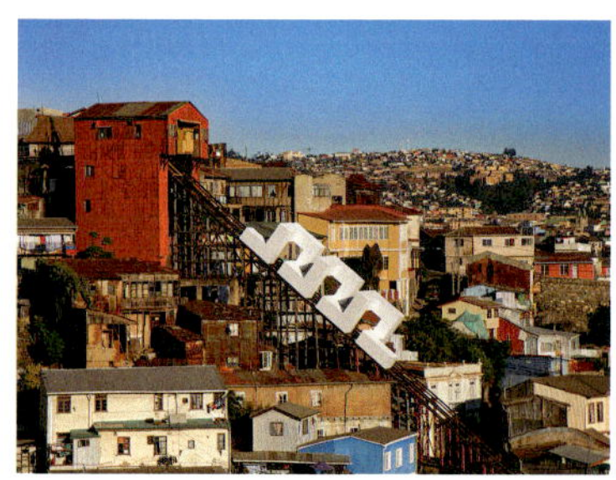

B.▛ SPIRAL #3, 2013, Monjas, Valparaiso CL

reply to it and which material or which form fits best. The material then encompasses the specifications and the dimensions with which we work. We don't trim a panel just because we think 10 centimetres shorter would be better. This means that our thinking incorporates a degree of pragmatism from the outset.

SL ▶ We always keep a good equilibrium with the existing architecture – it's important to us to respect the context. On top of that, certain paths are predefined – not as a signature but as rules of the game. I think this aspect is extremely fascinating. Artists are completely free and in fact could do everything anew and differently every day, but nonetheless this self-imposed constraint is widespread and interesting. And it's a lot of fun to arrange the tools and then to iterate the scope within the "rules".

Success for us is when the thing injects a certain logic and when people assimilate it – say in Le Havre where the gigantic UP #3 structure gets used as a pavilion, with people sitting under it, picnicking, smoking shisha. When that happens, it's perfect [G.▀].

DG ◀ Your works are mostly situated in public spaces. Were museums too small for you?

DB ▶ The proverbial hermetic white cube blocks out the surroundings, making it far harder to incorporate other factors than in public spaces. That's the reason that we decided to turn outwards.

SL ▶ The thing that intrigues us is less the narrow frame and far more the fluctuating context: public spaces, art spaces, alternative spaces, museums, or also indoor or outdoor spaces, whereby obviously each of them entails completely different determining factors, users or viewers, disruptive elements, etc.

DG ◀ Some of your works get purchased and remain longer than planned – what role does time play for you as a factor?

DB ▶ Yes, sometimes we plan the works for the duration of an exhibition but it then stays in situ for longer. Sometimes this is because it gets bought, or sometimes the money is simply lacking to dismantle it, as for example with SPIRAL #3 in Valparaiso in Chile [B.▀].

SL ▶ Intrinsically we think in terms of the logic of impermanence. Everything inflatable is ephemeral – and we take pleasure in that. If you plan for the long term right from the start, you're more constrained.

DB ▶ Brief durations provide a lot more freedoms. White-varnished structures live from the allure that they're white.

LG ◀ Do you also find these freedoms in various other disciplines?

SL ▶ It's often said that we oscillate between design, art and architecture, but that's not quite right. Right from the start we've always worked within an art reference system; our milieu is made up of artists; almost all of our works are created for art exhibitions. What we simply do is to take the liberty of applying strategies from other related fields in our art.

DB ▶ This isn't something we feel awkward about doing. If you want to make a bar for the Kunsthalle Bern then you have to use tools from architecture and design. Having said that, we don't see ourselves in any way as virtuoso designers or architects.

LG ◀ Does this also explain your affinity for art-in-architecture projects?

DB ▶ We started out with photography and screen prints, which we also did on order – LP covers or posters for musicians, and such like. The thing that motivated us was always about making or making it ourselves, which is still possible here in our factory studio. That way we were always able to also keep our commissioned work closely aligned to our own work. This, and precisely the fact that we work together, meant that we never differentiated between commissioned works and "free" works.

SL ▶ A lot of artists strictly divorce their studio work from percent-for-art commissions and avoid including it in their portfolios. We don't change the way we work and we don't differentiate. Our belief is that we're equally free to develop an idea almost whatever the context is we find ourselves in.

DB ▶ What we're interested in is the process – from the very outset to final completion. We love all the stages, and similarly always want to keep as much control over it as we can.

DG ◀ What part do prototypes play for you as a stage between the model and the finished work?

SL ▶ We've got our practical experience to draw on and a range of colours we work with, which means that prototypes aren't usually necessary. We only make a prototype when something's completely new or needs to be checked on a 1:1 scale.

DB ▶ Prototypes are above all vital in clarifying technical issues. But we do our best to have everything already properly nailed down at the theoretical level.

LG ◀ The models now suddenly provide an overview in a small space. What's surprised you most?

DB ▶ Up till now we'd never thought about showing all the models in an exhibition. For us they represented a kind of alternative archive, which as opposed to the photographic documentations was never conceived to be published or put on show. We were totally amazed at the sheer quantity that emerged from out of the compactus and how suddenly you can recognise a huge spectrum.

SL ▶ It's much much easier to trace developments within a single group of works or between variations and to compare them.

DG ◀ Would L/B exist without cigarettes?

SL ▶ That's indeed one really anachronistic element!

DB ▶ Difficult to imagine!

A MODEL IS A MODEL IS A MODEL

JACQUELINE BURCKHARDT

At the end of March 2023, I went to see Sabina Lang and Daniel Baumann (L/B) in their studio in Burgdorf. They had pushed two long rows of tables together and lined up their entire collection of models, one after the other on them: a rudimentary layout of the exhibition in the Teufen Zeughaus. They had not yet made their selection from 96 items.

They showed me their digital isometric drawing of the gallery divided into three aisles, where the models would be placed on shelves suspended in between the columns. A new COMFORT work would cover the walls and windows all around with openings front and back to access the exhibition. COMFORT is what L/B call a spectacular series of ephemeral, site-specific installations of bloated, inflated polyester tubes that stick to the facades like gigantic parasites, sometimes towering above them, padding the corners of buildings and forcing themselves on and through windows. As sculptures for cultural events, they reflect a celebratory tradition that has prevailed for centuries.

In Teufen, their golden, semi-matt COMFORT #21 completely transforms the ambience of the functional, nineteenth-century building with its plastered masonry and timber skeleton. A comfortable shelter with a touch of glamour welcomes the models, enhanced by the animating, yet soothing sound carpet of air whispering through the tubes. Should the sound die out, the tubes would collapse. This festive, slightly tongue-in-cheek display underscores the significance of these models for L/B. As stand-ins for their most important works, they are on public display for the first time. L/B always scrutinize the context that provides a nest for their works and, since the models are now among themselves, their environs

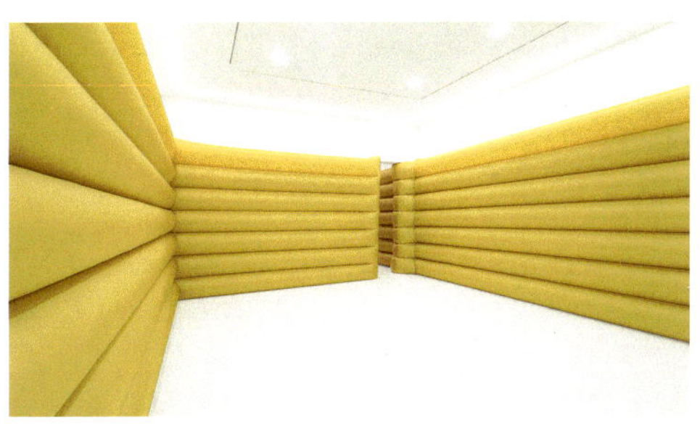

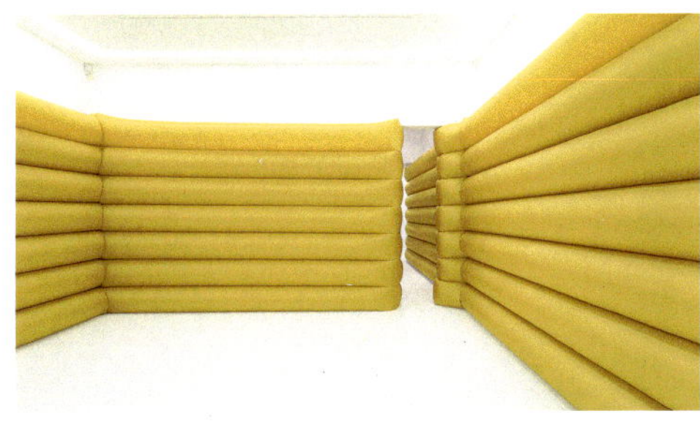

C. COMFORT #8, 2010, Galeria Foksal, Warsaw PL

must be especially well appointed. They have given space the flair of a cabinet of curiosities. Back in 2010, LB's COMFORT #8 took the same approach to cladding the walls of the Foksal Gallery in Warsaw in honour of a venue that has fostered progressive Polish art since the 1960s [C.▛].

Standing in their studio, arrayed as a life-size model of the show in Teufen, made me feel like one of those miniature figures placed in architectural models to illustrate scale. I had to think of how my brother Muck and I set up his model train when we were children. We used to lay out the tracks and switches on a soft landscape that we created by putting pillows and other objects under the carpet. We made railroad stations and tunnels out of cardboard, and models of people and animals out of clay. Scale didn't mean a thing to us. Immersed in our imaginary world, we had no doubt that it was perfectly real and factual. Experiences and impressions of that kind are formative. Muck became an architect and I started out as a restorer. We thank G. F. Schiller for the liberating statement: "Humans are never entirely human unless they play." And working with models is particularly playful.

What better insight into three decades of collaboration than an overview of the models L/B have made? And what better proof that they clearly belong to the species of "artista universale"? The two all-rounders deal in architecture, sculpture, painting, design and hybrids thereof. They have created children's rooms, a cinema, a one-room hotel, lounges, bars, bridges, stairs leading nowhere, diving boards in the middle of a meadow, large-scale abstract paintings on walls and floors with gigantic bands of strong colours, and they have even transformed a racing car into a painted artefact.

Their art is largely site-specific; it is scattered immobile all over the globe or consists of ephemeral installations. As such, it is impossible to present originals. But in contrast to the originals, the models offer intimate insight into the wealth of ideas and thoughts that emerge in the process of developing a project. They bear tangible witness to thinking aloud in anticipation of a phase that changes, develops or is abandoned – step by step. And they also record a past that would otherwise be irrevocable. Models of a project's early stages are mostly cobbled together out of cheap materials (paper, cardboard, Styrofoam) to experiment with shapes, proportions or colour concepts. The models become more elaborate when it comes to solving technical issues of materials and engineering, and to refining colour combinations.

A case in point: viewers can clearly trace the development of L/B's one-room-one-night, four-star HOTEL EVERLAND from initial working model to accurately detailed display model, including all interior fittings. Even the lights can be switched on. When you pick it up, look inside and turn it, you notice that all of the parts are multiples of one basic measurement. I wondered whether L/B had used Vitruvius's anthropometric measurements. Not really, they responded. They work out the dimensions individually from case to case. The basic measurement for HOTEL EVERLAND is 45 centimetres, and for the Zentrum Paul Klee, MODULE #4, it is 40 centimetres [H.▀]. The latter is inspired by the interior of the Klee/ Kandinsky house in Dessau, built by Gropius but with a colour scheme devised by the two Bauhaus professors.

While visiting their studio, I also asked L/B if some of the models were works of art. No, they replied, they are simply pragmatic tools as an aid to keeping track of the process between design and execution. They like being able to refer to them for their own orientation. Jacques Herzog and Pierre de Meuron also mention these advantages and the communicative potential of models in connection with the architectural and material models housed in their purpose-built Kabinett at Dreispitz in Basel.

Even when they use a 3D printer, L/B's models are deeply rooted in the history of art and architecture. The term “modello” goes back to the early Italian Renaissance and is derived from “modulo”, the word for “scale”. But it obviously goes back much further. In the rite of the Roman triumph, victorious commanders presented models of the cities they had conquered. There are mediaeval accounts of Antonio di Vincenzo's immense walk-in model of the Basilica of San Petronio. In 1420, Filippo Brunelleschi built a legendary model of wood, brick and stone to test the structural engineering of the gigantic cupola that he planned for the cathedral in Florence. He always applied meticulously detailed ornamentation to his models as well, using clay and wax – not only to persuade clients of the feasibility and beauty of his project but also to show craftsmen precisely what lay in store for them. The devil was in the detail for this Florentine, who was born in the city of exquisite craftsmanship and who started out as an inventive goldsmith, before going on to become a brilliant engineer.

Around 1450, Leon Battista Alberti wrote “De re aedificatoria”, the first major treatise on construction after Vitruvius's pre-Christian work of the same name. There he writes that an architectural idea must first be precisely envisioned mentally, in the process of thinking, before rendering the idea in drawings, plans and finally in a model. The model is essential to examining the quality of the idea, which is then improved by calling on astute experts, and it also serves to make an estimate of the cost.

All of this applies to L/B's models as well, but with one difference: they visualise poetic alternatives to our world, unlike the models made by architects, engineers or the master builders of the Grubenmann family, whose eighteenth-century wooden models are on display on the floor above L/B's exhibition. LB's art projects are less beholden to the conventions of reason or judicious norms. However, they do adhere to Vitruvius's basic principles of architecture, which are still in place today: “firmitas”, “futilitas” and “fvenustas” (strength, utility and beauty). For L/B, the latter clearly and explicitly takes precedence over all else. “Beautiful” is an adjective in many work titles, as in BEAUTIFUL STEPS, BEAUTIFUL BRIDGE and BEAUTIFUL WALL.

L/B's exacting aesthetic sensibility not only means thorough research into the context and situation in which their work will appear but also drawing up all of their construction plans themselves to ensure the desired outcome. When executing their works, they exhaust the entire array of conventional building techniques or construction methods at their disposal. Their perfectionism leaves no stone unturned, even literally, in the case of HOTEL EVERLAND where the small Bisazza glass mosaic tiles for the bath had to fit perfectly down to the millimetre along the edges and in the corners without breaking a single tile. And for BEAUTIFUL BRIDGE #3, they determined precisely where to add a twist to each baluster of the railing.

However, the two artists also design useful works that invite interaction and even performative involvement, for example the bar on the plaza in front of the Kunsthalle Bern, where it is precariously cantilevered over the embankment down to the river Aare. L/B had been commissioned to build it as a temporary folly in celebration of the institution's centenary in 2018. It is still there today, and will hopefully remain for a long time to come. The design is primarily a tribute in full-scale format to the original black-and-white tiles that were torn out of the lobby of the Kunsthalle in the 1980s. The sides of the bar are bracketed so that the pattern runs from floor to wall and from the top of the wall to the canopy. The brackets are bent at the same angle as the eight corners of the main Kunsthalle gallery, making another subtle reference to the building [I.▛].

L/B's models are a far cry from the utopian visions and weighty subject matter of those on display in Harald Szeemann's spectacular exhibition “Der Hang zum Gesamtkunstwerk” (Tendency toward a Total Work of Art) at Kunsthaus Zürich in 1983: Gaudí's Sagrada Familia, Steiner's Goetheanum, Schwitter's “Merzbau I”, Gabriele d'Annunzio's Vittoriale or Facteur Cheval's Palais Idéal. Szeemann met with sharp criticism at the time from Max Bill and the head of the NZZ's culture section, who accused him of exploiting the models and projecting his own obsessions onto them.

Thomas Demand's models also follow an entirely different trajectory. He selects press photographs of political and social import, which have become inscribed in collective memory, such as the underpass where Lady Di had her fatal accident, a Stasi office that had been trashed after the Wall fell or the President's Air Force One aircraft with gangway. Demand builds exact replicas of these scenes out of paper and cardboard, making them as close to full size as possible. He then photographs his models – always devoid of people – so that the elaborate process of making a built structure does not result in a sculptural work of art but a disconcerting photograph, which proves to be a remake of reality only at second glance. Once the picture has been taken, the model has served its purpose and is destroyed. Made to be photographed, it is like a stage set seen from a specific perspective defined by the sourced image, and, as proof of the illusion, it is better for it to disappear anyway. According to Demand, a formative artistic influence has been photographs of Hitler with Albert Speer in front of the model of the monumental, ice-cold pavilion of the Third Reich at the 1937 World Fair in Paris. Charlie Chaplin showed disturbing prescience of Hitler's diabolical delusions in his satirical film "The Great Dictator" (1940), when he played the Führer tripling about with a miniature model of the Earth, a balloon globe, until it bursts.

L/B's art is unabashed but humane, almost always humorous and at times breathtakingly beautiful. I attended the inauguration in March 2023 of BEAUTIFUL BRIDGE #3 built next to the Bernex tramline in Geneva [D.▀]. I had seen a model of the project years earlier and was immediately enthralled by the sculptural elegance of the bridge, which is indeed a folly, for it bridges nothing although one can sit on the steps, use it as a shelter in the rain and perhaps stage events there. When I saw the work itself for the first time, the rays of the setting sun had bathed the delicate metal railing in golden light, and I realised once again how much the original surpasses its model despite all the ideas it might evoke.

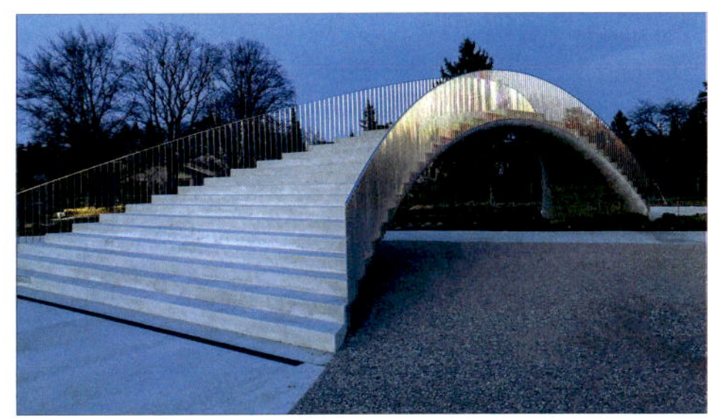

D.▀ BEAUTIFUL BRIDGE #3, 2023, Genève CH

EPISTEMIC TIME CAPSULES

MERET ERNST

L/B agreed on a joint language early on. In an unbroken dialogue, they have always had to constantly convince each other. Their working process allows them to answer the questions they choose to handle jointly. In conversation, they admit that it would be almost impossible for them to paint a picture together. The things that connect them they also communicate as if they were passing balls back and forth to each other.

In tandem, the contexts that they analyse in depth for their works constitute the third pole in generating their ideas. Potential solutions are quickly tested using CAD. But the impact of an idea, even when examined and consolidated in model form, has to be tested in situ and established in xchange with third parties. A constant small team of free-lancers, a network of experts, assist them in realising the works. As a means of communication, the models thus simplify the discussions with participants who require, at a small scale, proof that something will work. Made of paper, card-board or other readily available materials, these items some-times vary in scale from the types of models, mock-ups or prototypes commonly used in architecture or design.[1]

As epistemic objects, the models impart how something should be thought out and constructed so that the intended artistic and social effect is generated.[2] Sometimes the models migrate to where things happen, for instance in the case of COMFORT #4 from 2010, where two rows of windows of a Paris primary school were randomly sewn up with white air tubes. Even if one of the ventilators were to fail, a redundant system guaranteed that the image of a gigantic, textile-like chain of knots remained intact. Each of the tubes was fed four times into one window and then re-emerged. The assembly team used the model on site to determine which connections were the right ones, with the model still bearing the correspond-ing markings.

Lastly, models are time capsules. They anticipate what leaps in dimension achieve in the real-world setting. They

1 For instance, a curtain rail was used for the model of the Ulmberg Tunnel pedestrian underpass – in reality 171 x 3.5 metres – giving a dizzying scale of 1:145.

2 See Sascha Dickel, Prototyping Society: Zur vorauseilenden Technologisierung der Zukunft (Bielefeld: transcript Verlag, 2019), online under DOI: 10.14361/9783839447369.

preserve, as condensed experience, things that have long since been dismantled. The models are stored in a comapctus rolling shelving unit in the cellar of the live-in studio in Burgdorf (in a former electric-motor factory converted in the mid-1980s). If guests come, the models serve as substitute visual material.

While the models slumber in the cellar, the roof of the studio pulsates with an original – the HOTEL EVERLAND [K.▀]. After appearing in Yverdon, Leipzig and Paris, it now funnels the view over the industrial estate in Burgdorf. The idea first found its form in hastily made paper models. The miniature-format, mobile hotel, designed for the Expo.02, is a work of art that can be interpreted as a "mock-up". In the last resort it acts as the one-to-one test bed for the idea of a distinctive hotel, right down to the LP collection, the fully filled mini bar, the reception service or the instructions to guests that they can take the towels with them. Even the guests, who could each only book to stay one night, were part of the experimental set-up, originally offered as an autonomous time capsule. After the mass of visitors had left, the guests remained behind on the exhibition site and could linger over the day's impressions. Erected on poles on the shore of Lake Neuchâtel, the frontally glazed pod provided a view over the lake and the Blur Building ("Cloud") by Diller Scofidio, the defining landmark of evanescence at the Expo.02. Ironically, HOTEL EVERLAND was thought to be a real mock-up, and L/B had to rebuff a number of inquiries about when the mini hotel would be manufactured serially. It is these kinds of productive misunderstandings between model, mock-up and work that occasion the positioning of their works, with the terms "occupation" and "beauty" providing guiding handrails.

The world has always been built and designed; there are no blank spaces anywhere. The sociologist and design theorist Lucius Burckhardt noted that working artistically or designing in public spaces inevitably occurs under conditions of "occupancy":

"Can it be avoided, bypassed; should one accept it, visualise it, poeticise it? And if, then how? […] In our opinion, design does not require space. Far rather it should – under the prevailing circumstances – build on what is already present in the space."[3]

The already-built forms the framework for L/B's interventions. Not only architecture with a capital "A" (although that too because it constitutes a built fact and has a discursive dominance), but also in the commonplace built things we encounter every day. Squares and facades, entrances and

3 Lucius Burckhardt, "Alles ist schon besetzt", in Museum für Gestaltung Zürich and Schweizerischer Werkbund (eds.), Überall ist jemand: Räume im besetzten Land (Zurich: Museum für Gestaltung, 1992), pp. 76–80, here p. 77.

foyers, corridors or inner courtyards – all of these excite L/B's interventions.

The COMFORT work series makes this aspect both poetically and ironically obvious. Huge air-filled tubes writhe through facades and buildings – as if they were searching for a burrow in which they need to comfortably unfurl. This has something erratic, even random, about it. The tubes represent the opposite of the built structure: they are soft, ephemeral, temporary; and they highlight the voids that are inscribed into all architecture. But they are far from harmless. The tubes liquefy what has been built, what pre-exists.

L/B also successfully achieves this in conjunction with a project that at the time was conceived as a criticism of the static, autonomous modern notion of architecture, and actually can only be understood in motion: Bernard Tschumi's Parc de La Villette [E.▛]. For the 2022 "Festival Paris l'été", L/B embellished one of the "follies" in this urban public park in the north of Paris. A light-grey tube winds through Folly N8, and with L/B's "occupation" the built structure becomes the negative of itself.

In his 1983 competition entry for the remodelling of the huge site – one of the 14 Paris "grands projets" during the government of François Mitterrand – Tschumi paid homage to deconstructivism, with Jacques Derrida lending a firm helping hand in pulverising the principles of function, representation and unity. Spread over a 120 × 120-metre grid, Tschumi scattered 26 concrete-skeleton structures clad in bright-red metal sheeting across the site – some of them abstract figurations, others functional pavilions. With this he staked his claim to "realise the largest discontinuous building in the world".[4] Evolved from a cube with an edge length of 11 metres, the follies are punctured by openings and incisions, amplified by geometrical add-ons and protrusions. Like in a lenticular image, the perception of the follies switches between their primary form and their distortions.[5]

L/B's visit there and the discussions with those in charge triggered innumerable variations, such as how a tube could be fed through a folly or how the mountings and the blowers could be incorporated. Before that, however, the job was to select one of the 26 follies. In terms of the ongoing group of works BEAUTIFUL STEPS, the choice seemed almost predetermined. Devoid of any functional use, Folly N8 stands in front

4 Bernard Tschumi, "Parc de la Villette", in Andreas Papadakis (ed.), Dekonstruktivismus: Eine Anthologie, trans. Christiane Court (Stuttgart: Klett-Cotta, 1989), pp. 174–83, here p. 175.

5 The concept was realised between 1982 and 1998. With this deconstructivist gesture, Tschumi "subtly subverted the state-glorifying vision of the French government." Michaela Gugeler, "Der Parc de la Villette – Würfelwurf der Architektur: Das Zusammenwirken von Bernard Tschumi und Jacques Derrida beim Parc de la Villette in Paris", Kritische Berichte, 33, no. 2 (2006), pp. 44–7, here p. 44.

of the park's administrative building, and looking at it, doesn't it include an over-dimensional staircase beginning unreachably at half height and dwarfing the passers-by?

Stairs are architectural features that make a building usable. They mediate between our body size and the building height. They begin and end and begin again at the landings – the interval sign in the act of ascending. As a sculptural element, they make space experiencable. By connecting below and above, they constitute both a function and a symbol of power and social hierarchy.[6] In the work series BEAUTIFUL STEPS, L/B collect stairs and ladders: beside rivers, in street spaces, on facades, indoors. Sometimes the steps lead nowhere or are inaccessible; sometimes they bridge rivers or open up new vistas.

Staged since 2014, BEAUTIFUL STEPS #10 sets an exclamation mark on the north facade of the Casino Forum d'art contemporain Luxembourg. From the inside, seven narrowing steps lead out of the window into the open sky like a diminutive Jacob's Ladder. Anchored permanently to the facade, the gleaming white structure protrudes 3 metres out over the street. Seen from below, it seems abstract and like a functionless alien object that obliges us to look at the facade differently. Except, that is, when someone is standing outside, enjoying the view, and waves back. Aha! A balcony! The steps connect the above and the below, the inside and the outside. And, by adorning the less distinguished north facade, BEAUTIFUL STEPS #10 reverses an architectural hierarchy.

Other stairs and ladders remain unreachable. As part of the "11th Schweizer Plastikausstellung" in Biel in 2009, L/B created BEAUTIFUL STEPS #2 on the Biel Congress Centre, designed by Max Schlup and built from 1960 onwards [J.▀]. L/B analysed how skilfully this building, with its 17 floors, deceives the eye. Schlup patterned the glazed front independently of the ceiling heights of the different floors,

6 See Friedrich-Mielke-Instut für Scalalogie, et al. (eds.), Stair (Venice: Marsilio, 2014), one of 15 brochures accompanying the 14th Architecture Biennale, "Elements of Architecture", curated by Rem Koolhaas.

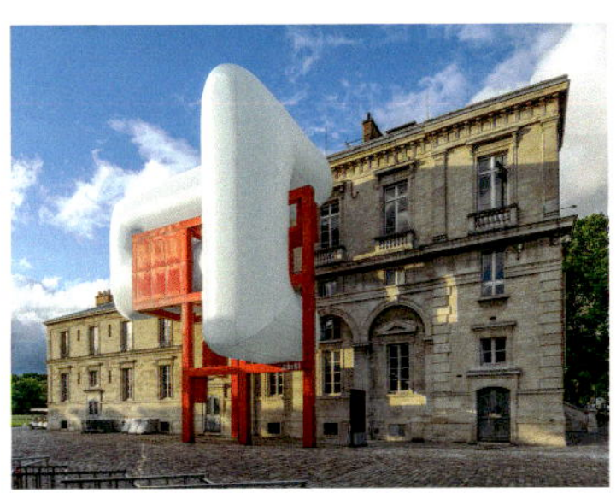

E.▀ COMFORT #20, 2022, Parc de la Villette, Paris F

which is why the tower appears more powerful than it is. The glass frontage is mounted in a two-part exposed-concrete structural frame, its east side formed as a circulation core, while the west side of the frame, detached from the building core, has no function apart from a smoke vent. Onto this blind part of the structural frame, approximately three-quarters of the way up, L/B attached an aluminium set of stairs that appears to lead around the corner from one door to another. In order to match the optical illusion of the building, L/B diminished the stairs and the doors by 20 percent and modified them to fit the real height of the storeys.

The straightforward recognisability leads to a de-deception. It extends an invitation to look more closely at the building at the point where an unintentional beauty implants itself to defy the spartan utility. With his slogan "beauty derived from function or as function", Max Bill strove to harness beauty to serve utility, albeit without being ever quite able to tame it.[7] For L/B beauty in art is meaningless. The labelling of whole groups of work as "beautiful" is a ruse by which to broach precisely this. Because "beauty" is a relational term, it only fulfils itself in the act of seeing, and L/B are correspondingly convinced that their works are consummated by the viewer. And this, moreover, partly explains why they "occupy" public spaces. In the process, the act of viewing has to continuously update the works in order for beauty to become recognisable. We do not stay motionless over time, meaning that the act of re-experiencing results in new interpretations. With the shifting daylight, sometimes the shadow cast by BEAUTIFUL STEPS #2 dissolves into an abstract ornament; and in overcast skies the stairs melt into the grey of the concrete so that they become barely visible.

With their "more is more",[8] L/B run contrary to Ludwig Mies van der Rohe's "less is more". But by no stretch of the imagination do they want their work to be understood as a reference to postmodernism. Their stance, inspired through the punk movement, sets out to defy any type of canonisation. It is not an end in itself; instead it marks their beginnings in the art of the 1990s, characterised by a taste for trash, non-conformity, being out of synch with the times – excess, weirdness, and the rejection of reduction, which itself proved to be a dead end. These are the roots of the particular beauty in L/B's works – a beauty that can be constantly rediscovered. You just have to peer closely enough.

7 Max Bill, "Schönheit aus Funktion und als Funktion", Werk, 36, no. 8 (1949), pp. 272–4.

8 Sabina Lang and Daniel Baumann (eds.), Lang/Baumann: More is More (Berlin: Gestalten Verlag, 2013).

IM KLEINEN DAS GROSSE ENTDECKEN

LILIA GLANZMANN UND DAVID GLANZMANN IM GESPRÄCH MIT SABINA LANG UND DANIEL BAUMANN

Lilia (LG) ◀ All eure Modelle lagern in einem Rollregal. 96 Stück habt ihr aus diesem «Compactus» geholt. Wann habt ihr euer erstes Modell gefertigt?

Sabina (SL) ▶ WHO'S OUT entstand 1992 anlässlich der Bewerbung für die Teilnahme an der Weihnachtsausstellung im Kunstmuseum Thun – eine Installation mit einem 3.20 auf 2.20 Meter grossen schwarz-weissen Selbstportrait, davor ein in den Raum gespanntes Eisengitter von 5 mal 3 Metern. Wir konnten kein fertiges Objekt als Referenz zeigen und mussten beweisen, dass unsere Idee funktioniert. Also haben wir ein Modell gebaut.

Daniel (DB) ▶ Bildbearbeitungsprogramme und 3D-Werkzeuge standen uns damals noch nicht zur Verfügung, der Modellbau war uns nahe und vertraut. Ich hatte Hochbauzeichner gelernt und Sabina war in einem Architektur-Elternhaus aufgewachsen. Modelle zu bauen war etwas, das wir damals gerne taten und bis heute gern tun.

David (DG) ◀ Es ist eine aussergewöhnliche Sammlung von allen in den letzten 32 Jahren gefertigten Modellen. Warum habt ihr sie aufbewahrt?

DB ▶ Wir haben tatsächlich kein einziges weggeworfen. Grundsätzlich archivieren wir alles, sogar unsere allererste E-Mail.

SL ▶ Ja, alles wird aufbewahrt, selbst alle Rechnungen! Wir machen das aber nicht um des Archivierens willen, wir greifen oft auch wieder auf diese Materialien zurück, entnehmen Informationen, die wir zum Arbeiten brauchen.
Im Gegensatz zur Architektur sind unsere Arbeiten flüchtiger, sie verschwinden wieder. Im Modell bleiben sie als Miniatur bestehen und die Dreidimensionalität eines Modells zeigt einen Aspekt, der in der fotografischen Dokumentation so nicht erhalten bleibt.

DB ▶ Lange Zeit haben wir die Modelle in Gestellen irgendwo verteilt im Keller oder im Atelier gelagert. Das sieht man den ältesten Modellen auch an, sie mussten einiges ertragen. An eine Ausstellung mit unseren Modellen hätten wir selbst nie gedacht.

LG ◀ Beim Modellbau ist entscheidend, wofür ein Modell gebaut wird – ob etwas skizziert, überprüft oder präsentiert werden soll. Welche Arten Modelle sind es bei euch?

SL ▶ Es sind Arbeits-, Präsentations- und Ausstellungsmodelle. Von der letzten Kategorie gibt es am wenigsten. Eines da-

von entstand für HOTEL EVERLAND in Paris: ab 18 Uhr war der Zugang aufs Dach nicht mehr möglich, da bereits Gäste im Hotelzimmer waren. Da aber das Palais du Tokyo ungewöhnlich lange Öffnungszeiten hat – bis 1 Uhr morgens! – bauten wir ein Modell für die Eingangshalle des Museums, mit Licht und allen Details, damit die Besucher:innen trotzdem einen realistischen Eindruck des Werkes erhielten.
Die grösste Gruppe sind Präsentationsmodelle: sie sind sehr unterschiedlich ausgearbeitet, es kommt immer darauf an, wem wir sie präsentieren. Für die Diskussion mit Kurator:innen meist eher etwas abstrakter, für Wettbewerbe detaillierter, damit sie auch ohne Erklärungen verstanden werden. Unsere Arbeitsmodelle sind pragmatisch gefertigt, wir nehmen sie zum Ausstellungsaufbau mit und können Informationen daraus ablesen.
DB ▶ Wie zum Beispiel das Modell für die Installation BEAUTIFUL TUBE #6 im Ausstellungsraum der Galeries Lafayette [A.▀]. Hier half uns das Modell zu überprüfen, ob der Teppich am richtigen Ort liegt.

LG ◀ Habt ihr für jedes Projekt ein Modell gefertigt?
SL ▶ Nein, bei weitem nicht. Wenn es nötig ist, eine Idee mit anderen zu besprechen, helfen auch Pläne oder Visualisierungen. Doch zum räumlichen Verständnis ist ein Modell immer sehr hilfreich. Gerade etwa für unsere aufblasbaren Strukturen, die am Computer schwierig darzustellen sind.
DB ▶ Das Modell blieb immer bei uns. Mit der Zeit realisierten wir auch, dass die Modelle oft das einzige sind, das physisch von den ephemeren Arbeiten übrig bleibt. Fertigungstechnisch hat sich nicht viel verändert, ausser natürlich der 3D-Druck, der es viel schneller erlaubt, auch sehr komplexe Modelle anzufertigen.

DG ◀ Manchmal bleiben Modelle kleine Utopien. Gibt es solche Beispiele auch in eurer Sammlung?
DB ▶ Ein gutes Beispiel hierfür ist etwa REVOLVING STUDIO für die Christoph Merian Stiftung im Dreispitz-Areal in Basel. Das Projekt wurde leider nicht realisiert, dennoch bleibt es ein Traum von uns, einmal ein drehbares Haus zu bauen. Es gibt oft auch Ideen, die laufend wieder aufgegriffen und verändert werden, bis sie schliesslich ausgeführt werden können. BEAUTIFUL VIEW #1 in Nanterre bei Paris entstand so [F.▀]. Die Skulptur ist nun 22 Meter hoch. Die erste Idee dafür entwickelten wir ursprünglich für einen Fussballtrainingsplatz bei Zürich, damals aber 40 Meter hoch. Diese Höhe symbolisierte die obersten Ränge des Basler Stadions – das Maximum dessen, was es zu der Zeit im Schweizer Fussball zu erreichen gab.

DG ◀ Im Gegensatz zu den kleinen Modellen sind eure Arbeiten gigantisch – wie ja auch schon das erste Modell zeigt. Warum fasziniert euch diese Grösse?
SL ▶ Als ganz frühe gemeinsame Arbeiten realisierten wir im Dachstock der Reitschule in Bern Projektionen für Konzerte: Mit Hellraum- und Diaprojektoren warfen wir Bilder in den ganzen Raum.

DB ▶ Dort war das Ergreifen, der Rausch ein Thema – dieser wird grösser, je mehr davon. Reduzieren und zurücknehmen hat uns nie interessiert. Und wuchtig daherzukommen war auch Provokation.
SL ▶ Unser Mass war stets: Was können wir gerollt noch im Zug transportieren? Das zeigen auch die Techniken, die wir heute noch anwenden, etwa Tubes oder Wandmalereien, die wir vor Ort aufblasen oder anbringen können.

DG ◀ Wie waren die Neunzigerjahre als Start eurer Zusammenarbeit?
SL ▶ Wir wollten Kunst machen. Anfangs bewegten wir uns in und um die Reithalle, Kollektive waren ein Thema, es gab dort die Möglichkeit, Sachen auszuprobieren, wenn auch die bildende Kunst nie so richtig akzeptiert war. Das «Machen können» war uns wichtig.
DB ▶ Ich habe meine Fotografien in der Reithalle ausgestellt. Da haben wir uns kennengelernt.
SL ▶ Daniel hatte lange Haare und ich keine.
DB ▶ Wir bewegten uns in alternativen Kunsträumen, im Kunstmausoleum in Biel oder im Kunsthaus Oerlikon in Zürich. Wir haben einfach die Nähe solcher Orte gesucht und konnten dort erste Ausstellungserfahrungen sammeln. Ein prägender Ort für uns war dann auch die Kunsthalle Bern, wo wir fast alle Ausstellungen besuchten, an den Vernissagen teilnahmen und dadurch die Kunstszene kennenlernten. Doch in Bern waren die meisten unserer Künstlerfreund:innen fast zehn Jahre älter. Darum haben wir uns früh schon nach Zürich orientiert und in anderen Städten der Schweiz, in Frankreich oder Holland Anschluss an eine jüngere Szene gesucht.

LG ◀ Warum den Doppelnamen?
SL ▶ Ganz zu Beginn hatten wir einzeln ausgestellt, Daniel Fotos und ich Malerei unter dem Titel «Blutige Hände» ebenfalls in der Reithalle, wir probierten vieles aus. Dann gab es eine Ausstellungsmöglichkeit in Leipzig in den ehemaligen Räumen der Galerie Eigen + Art. Wir reisten dorthin und zeigten unsere Arbeiten erstmals zusammen.
DB ▶ Uns nervte, wenn alle fragten: Was ist von dir? Und was hast du gemacht? Sie haben unser Konzept auseinanderdividiert. Ab diesem Moment entschieden wir, nur noch gemeinsam – unter einem Namen – aufzutreten.
SL ▶ Zu der Zeit waren wir schon inspiriert von Künstlerpaaren wie Anna & Bernhard Blume oder Fischli/Weiss. Doppelnamen waren en vogue und es gab einige Künstler:innen in der Schweiz, die als Duos oder Gruppen auftraten.
DB ▶ Letzthin haben wir uns überlegt, wie wir heissen würden, hätten wir die Nachnamen unserer Mütter: Läderach/Siegenthaler.

DG ◀ Neben der Grösse prägt Humor euer Schaffen. Zahlreiche Werke können nicht nur betrachtet, sondern auch benutzt werden; andere täuschen eine Benutzbarkeit nur vor oder sabotieren sie auf listige Weise. Wie gelingt die Gratwanderung?
DB ▶ Doppel- oder Mehrdeutigkeit ist entscheidend. Wir nutzen Humor als Mittel, um den Respekt vor der Autorität des Werkes zu relativieren. Dabei ist es uns wichtig, dass dieser fein

angewendet wird, ohne Zynismus und auch ohne zu offensichtlich zu sein. Der Humor folgt auch oft auf eine anfängliche Irritation, gerade bei etwas vermeintlich Funktionalem, das überhaupt nicht benutzt werden kann, sondern nur so scheint: Im kurzen Moment des Innehaltens bis zum Erkennen der Sinnlosigkeit.

SL ▶ Humor ist auch wichtig in unserer Zusammenarbeit. Vieles muss verhandelt und besprochen werden, wenn man zusammenarbeitet. Wir argumentieren auch gegeneinander, manchmal wird es mühsam und da hilft uns die Leichtigkeit des Humors. Schliesslich arbeiten wir ja gerne zusammen, sonst hätten wir es nicht so lange ausgehalten! In unserer Arbeit wenden wir Humor aber auch als Mittel an, um Hierarchien oder Dominanz in Frage zu stellen. Wie wir zum Beispiel jene der Architektur mit einem feinen Schmunzeln anzweifeln können.

DB ▶ Uns interessieren Passungen und Störungen. Konstruierte Momente, wie etwa für den Kunstraum sic! in Luzern – übrigens unser kleinstes Modell, gefertigt in 3D-Druck. Hier fügt sich eine perfekte weisse Struktur an den heruntergekommenen Schopf. Sie scheint im Grössenverhältnis und der Form genau an diesen Ort zu passen, gleichzeitig kontrastiert sie ihn komplett und wirkt fremd.

LG ◀ Wie findet ihr die Form für diese Momente?

DB ▶ Zuerst einmal besuchen wir den Ort und versuchen ihn visuell, aber auch in seiner Nutzung, seiner Geschichte, seiner Umgebung usw. wahrzunehmen und zu analysieren. So finden wir heraus, wie wir darauf antworten könnten und welches Material oder welche Form dafür passt. Das Material beinhaltet dann Vorgaben und Masse, mit denen wir arbeiten. Wir kürzen eine Platte nicht, nur weil wir denken, zehn Zentimeter kürzer wäre besser. Ein gewisser Pragmatismus wird also von Anfang an mitgedacht.

SL ▶ Wir bleiben immer in guter Balance zum Bestand, es ist uns wichtig, den Kontext zu respektieren. Und dann haben wir – nicht als Signatur, sondern als Spielregeln – gewisse Wege definiert. Das finde ich extrem spannend: Künstler:innen sind komplett frei und könnten eigentlich alles jeden Tag neu und anders machen. Dennoch ist diese selbstauferlegte Einschränkung verbreitet und interessant. Und es macht Spass, sich die Werkzeuge zurechtlegen und dann die Möglichkeiten innerhalb dieser Regeln durchzudeklinieren.

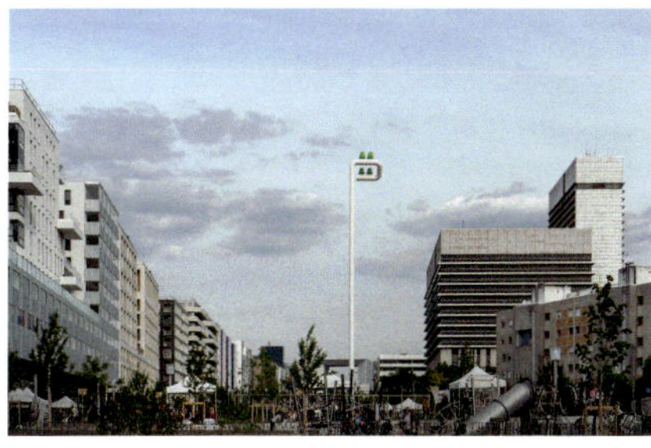

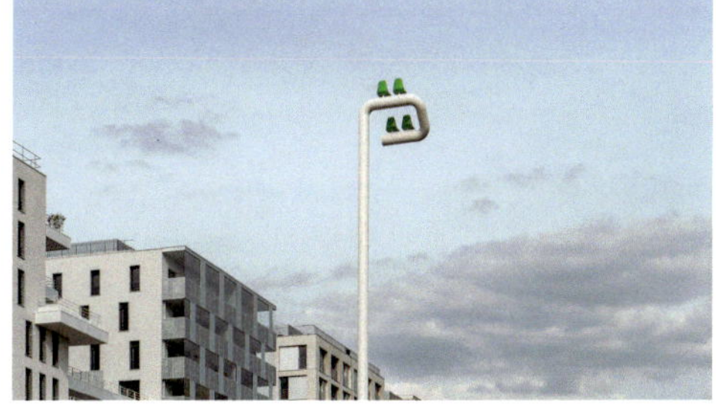

F.▀ BEAUTIFUL VIEW #1, 2019, Nanterre F

Für uns ist etwas gelungen, wenn es sich in eine bestimmte Logik einfügt und wenn es von den Menschen angenommen wird. In Le Havre etwa nutzen sie die gigantische Struktur UP #3 als Pavillon, sie sitzen darunter, picknicken und rauchen Shisha. Perfekt, wenn das passiert [G.▀].

DG ◀ Eure Arbeiten sind meist im öffentlichen Raum zu finden – waren Museen zu klein für euch?

DB ▶ Mit dem hermetischen White Cube wird die Umgebung ausgeblendet und es ist viel schwieriger als im öffentlichen Raum, weitere Faktoren miteinzubeziehen. Aus diesem Grund sind wir auch nach aussen getreten.

SL ▶ Uns interessiert weniger der enge Rahmen als vielmehr der Wechsel des Kontextes: der öffentliche Raum, der Kunstraum, der alternative Raum, das Museum oder auch der Aussen- und Innenraum. Natürlich sind damit jeweils auch ganz unterschiedliche Rahmenbedingungen, Benutzer- oder Betrachter:innen, Störfaktoren usw. verknüpft.

DG ◀ Einige eurer Arbeiten werden angekauft und bleiben länger als geplant. Welche Rolle spielt für euch der Faktor Zeit?

DB ▶ Es kommt manchmal vor, dass wir eine Arbeit für die Dauer einer Ausstellung planen, die dann vor Ort verbleibt. Manchmal ist dies ein Ankauf oder manchmal fehlt auch einfach das Budget für den Abbau wie zum Beispiel bei SPIRAL #3 in Valparaiso, Chile [B.▀].

SL ▶ Wir denken eigentlich eher in der Logik des Vergänglichen. Alles Aufblasbare ist ephemer, das gefällt uns auch. Wenn man von Anfang an für lange plant, ist man eingeschränkter.

DB ▶ Kurze Dauer gibt viel mehr Freiheiten. Weiss lackierte Strukturen leben vom Reiz, dass sie weiss sind.

LG ◀ Findet ihr diese Freiheit auch in den verschiedenen Disziplinen?

SL ▶ Oft heisst es, dass wir uns zwischen Design, Kunst und Architektur bewegen. Aber das stimmt so nicht: Seit Beginn arbeiten wir im Referenzsystem der Kunst, unser Umfeld sind Künstler:innen, die allermeisten Werke entstehen für Kunstausstellungen. Wir nehmen uns einfach die Freiheit, Strategien aus angrenzenden Gebieten in unserer Kunst anzuwenden.

DB ▶ Wir haben keine Scheu davor, dies zu tun. Wer eine Bar

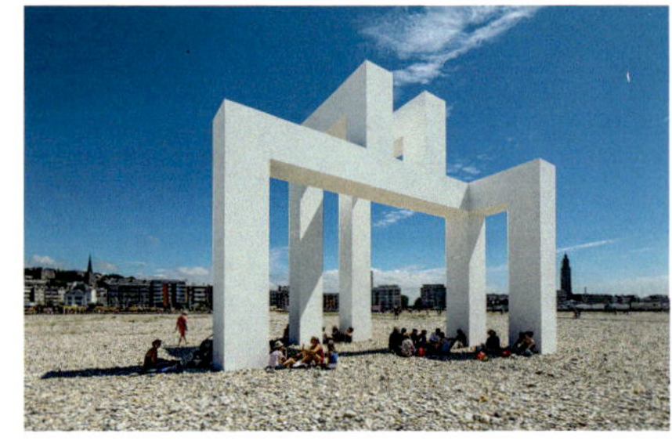

G.▀ UP #3, 2017, Plage Porte Océane, Le Havre F

machen will für die Kunsthalle Bern, muss sich der Werkzeuge aus Architektur und Design bedienen. Wir glauben allerdings nicht, dass wir kompetente Designer:innen oder Architekt:innen sind.

LG ◀ Liegen euch darum auch Kunst-und-Bau-Projekte?

DB ▶ Angefangen haben wir mit Fotografien und Siebdrucken, die wir auch für andere im Auftrag machten, Plattencover oder Plakate für Musiker etwa. Unser Motiv war immer das Machen und vor allem auch das Selbermachen – was hier in der Fabrik immer noch möglich ist. So konnten wir auch Auftragsarbeiten nahe an unserer eigenen Arbeit halten. Dies und der Fakt, dass wir eben zusammenarbeiten, führte dazu, dass wir keinen Unterschied machen zwischen einer Auftragsarbeit oder einer «freien» Arbeit.

SL ▶ Viele Künstler:innen trennen ihre Arbeit im Atelier strikt von Kunst-und-Bau-Aufträgen und vermeiden es, diese in ihr Portfolio zu integrieren. Wir behalten unsere Arbeitsform und machen hier keine Unterscheidung. Wir glauben, dass wir in fast jedem Kontext, in dem wir uns bewegen, genau gleich frei sind, eine Idee zu entwickeln.

DB ▶ Uns interessiert der Prozess von Beginn bis zur Ausführung. Wir lieben alle Stufen und wollen auch immer viel Kontrolle behalten.

DG ◀ Welche Rolle spielt für euch der Prototyp als Schritt zwischen Modell und dem fertigen Werk?

SL ▶ Wir haben Erfahrungswerte und eine Farbpalette, mit der wir arbeiten, daher sind Prototypen oft nicht notwendig. Nur wenn etwas komplett neu ist oder zusätzlich etwas im 1:1-Masstab überprüft werden soll, machen wir einen Prototyp.

DB ▶ Prototypen sind vor allem auch zur Klärung technischer Fragen wichtig. Doch nach Möglichkeit versuchen wir bereits, alles in der Theorie auf den Punkt zu bringen.

LG ◀ Die Modelle bieten nun plötzlich eine Übersicht auf kleinstem Raum. Was hat euch überrascht?

DB ▶ Wir dachten bisher nie daran, alle Modelle in einer Ausstellung zu zeigen. Für uns waren sie eine Art alternatives Archiv, das im Gegensatz zur fotografischen Dokumentation nicht zum Publizieren oder Ausstellen gedacht ist. Wir waren komplett überrascht über die schiere Menge, die da aus dem Compactus kam, und wie plötzlich ein grösserer Bogen zu erkennen ist.

SL ▶ Entwicklungen innerhalb einer Werkgruppe oder Varianten lassen sich so viel deutlicher ablesen und vergleichen.

DG ◀ Gäbe es L/B ohne Zigaretten?

SL ▶ Ein stark anachronistisches Element.

DB ▶ Schwer vorstellbar.

A MODEL IS A MODEL IS A MODEL

JACQUELINE BURCKHARDT

Ende März 2023 besuchte ich Sabina Lang und Daniel Baumann (L/B) in ihrem Atelier in Burgdorf. Auf zwei langen Reihen zusammengerückter Tische war in dichter Folge die vollständige Sammlung ihrer Modelle ausgelegt und rudimentär die Ausstellung im Teufener Zeughaus inszeniert. Noch war die Auswahl von 96 Exponaten nicht getroffen.

Am Computer zeigten sie mir die isometrische Skizze des dreischiffigen Ausstellungsraums: Die Modelle werden auf hängenden Tablaren in den Zwischenräumen der Stützen präsentiert. Eine neue COMFORT-Arbeit verkleidet rundum die Wände und Fenster, um nur zwei Durchgänge offen zu lassen. COMFORT ist jeweils der Titel der spektakulären Serie ephemerer, ortsspezifischer Installationen mit dicken, aufgeblasenen Schläuchen aus Polyestergewebe, die sich wie gigantische Parasiten an Fassaden heften, manchmal diese überragen, Gebäudeecken polstern, sich in Fenster zwängen und anderswo wieder hervordringen. Als Skulpturen für Kulturereignisse gehören sie in die jahrtausendealte Tradition der Festinszenierungen.
Im schlichten Zweckbau aus dem 19. Jahrhundert mit seinem verputzten Mauerwerk und dem Holzskelett verwandelt das goldfarbene, seidenmatte COMFORT #21 das Ambiente gänzlich. Ein behaglicher Schutzraum mit einem Touch Glamour steht für die Modelle bereit, und das feine Säuseln der Luft durch das Gewebe der Schläuche bildet einen animierenden und beruhigenden Soundteppich. Ihr Verstummen würde bedeuten, dass die Schläuche in sich zusammenschrumpfen. Nicht ohne Augenzwinkern drückt die festliche Stimmung aus, wie viel L/B an ihren Modellen liegt. Schliesslich sind sie die Stellvertreter ihrer wichtigsten Werke und werden erstmals öffentlich vorgestellt. L/B bedenken immer mit scharfer Wahrnehmung den Kontext, in dem sich ihre Werke einnisten. Hier sind die Modelle unter sich, daher muss der Raum sorgsam bestellt sein. Es haftet ihm gar das Flair einer Wunderkammer an. Bereits 2010 verkleideten L/B in gleicher Art mit COMFORT #8 die Wände der Galerie Foksal in Warschau als eine Hommage an diesen Ort, der seit den 1960er Jahren ein Zentrum für die progressive polnische Kunst ist [C.▀].

In ihrem Atelier, das selbst als das 1:1-Entwurfsmodell für die Teufener Schau eingerichtet war, kam ich mir wie eine jener Miniaturfiguren vor, die man zur Veranschaulichung der Proportionen in Architekturmodelle platziert. Das weckte Kindheitserinnerungen: wie mein Bruder Muck und ich zuhause seine WESA-Modelleisenbahn aufbauten, den Teppich mit Kissen und anderem unterlegten, um eine bewegte Landschaft zu formen, darauf Schienen und Weichen arrangierten, Bahnhöfe und Tunnel aus Pappe bastelten und Tiere und Menschen aus Modelliermasse kneteten. Massstäblichkeit war uns vollkommen egal. Eingetaucht in die Phantasiewelt waren wir der festen Überzeugung, an etwas Wahrem und Wirklichem zu werken. Solche Erlebnisse und Eindrücke prägen einen. Muck wurde Architekt und ich zunächst Restauratorin. Wir danken G. F. Schiller für den befreienden Satz «Der Mensch ist nur da ganz Mensch, wo er spielt». Mit Modellen umzugehen hat immer etwas besonders Spielerisches an sich.

Die Übersicht auf L/Bs Modelle gewährt den bestmöglichen Einblick in ihre mehr als drei Dekaden Zusammenarbeit. Sie zeigt, dass L/B dem Typus «Artista universale» angehören, Allrounder sind in Architektur, Skulptur, Malerei, Design und deren Mischformen. Zu ihren Entwürfen gehören Kinderzimmer, ein Kinosaal, ein Einzimmerhotel, Lounges, Bars, Brücken, Treppen, die nirgendwo hinführen, Sprungbretter im Feld statt im Wasser, grossflächige, abstrakte Boden- und Wandmalereien mit riesigen Bändern in starken Farben und nicht zuletzt die Bemalung eines Boliden.
Da ihre Kunst vornehmlich ortspezifisch und immobil rund um den Globus verstreut ist oder aus flüchtigen Installationen besteht, ist es unmöglich, die Originale zusammenzutragen. Doch im Unterschied zu den Originalen ermöglichen die Modelle den intimen Einblick in die Fülle an Ideen und Gedankengängen, die in den Entwicklungsphasen eines Projekts aufkommen. Sie sind die greifbaren Zeugen eines lauten Denkens, das einen Zustand antizipiert, der sich dann Schritt für Schritt verändert, entwickelt oder verworfen wird. Unter anderem können sie unwiederbringlich Vergangenes dokumentieren.
Modelle der frühen Arbeitsetappen sind meist skizzenartig aus billigem Material (Papier, Karton, Sagex) gebastelt, auf der Suche nach Formen, Proportionen oder Farbkonzepten. Ausgereiftere Modelle entstehen, um Lösungen für statische oder materialtechnische Probleme zu finden oder um Farbkombinationen auszutüfteln.
Anhand der Arbeitsmodelle ist beispielsweise die Entwicklung von HOTEL EVERLAND, L/Bs mobilem Ein-Raum-eine-Nacht-Vierstern-Hotel, nachzuvollziehen, bis zum detailliert ausgefeilten Schaumodell mit seiner gesamten Inneneinrichtung. Darin können sogar die Lichter angeschaltet werden. Hält man es in

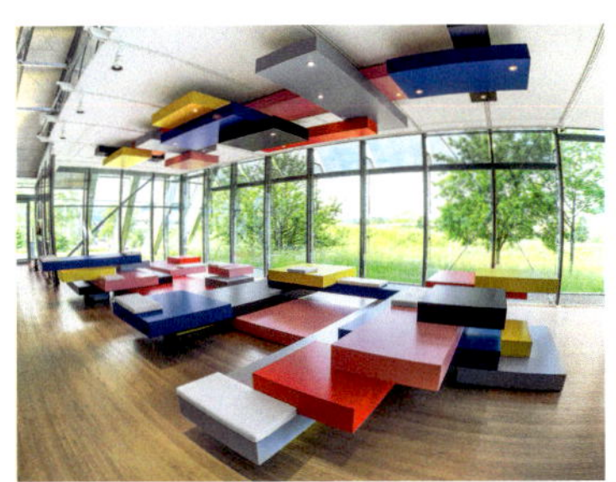

der Hand, guckt hinein und dreht es, merkt man, dass sämtliche Teile einem Grundmass folgen. Ich wollte wissen, ob sich L/B an Vitruvs anthropometrische Grundmasse halten. Nicht wirklich, meinten sie. Von Fall zu Fall arbeiten sie mit einer selbstbestimmten Masspalette. Im HOTEL EVERLAND ist das Grundmass 45 cm, in der Lounge im Zentrum Paul Klee (MODULE #4) 40 cm [H.▀]. Hier beziehen sie sich zudem auf die Farbgestaltung der Innenräume im Dessauer Wohnhaus von Klee und Kandinsky. Der Bau ist von Gropius, aber die Farben bestimmten gemeinsam die beiden Bauhaus-Professoren.
Im Atelier fragte ich L/B auch, ob einige Modelle Kunstwerke seien. Nein, antworteten sie, sie seien lediglich pragmatische Werkzeuge, Arbeits-und Kontrollinstrumente, die in den Etappen zwischen Entwurf und Realisierung eines Werks entstehen. Gut an ihnen sei, dass sie jederzeit als Referenzobjekte zur eigenen Orientierung dienen können. Von diesen Vorzügen und den kommunikativen Qualitäten der Modelle sprechen auch Jacques Herzog und Pierre de Meuron, wenn sie die Sammlung ihrer Architektur- und Materialmodelle im eigens dafür hergerichteten Kabinett beim Dreispitz im Basel vorstellen.
Selbst wenn sie mit dem 3D-Drucker entstehen, haben L/Bs Modelle ihre tiefen Wurzeln in der Kunst- und Architekturgeschichte. «Modello» als Begriff taucht in der italienischen Frührenaissance auf und stammt vom Wort «modulo», Massstab. Aber natürlich gab es sie längst zuvor. Die Römer präsentierten in ihren Triumphzügen die Modelle der eroberten Städte. Im Mittelalter wird von Antonio di Vincenzos riesigem, begehbarem Modell der Kirche San Petronio in Bologna berichtet. Filippo Brunelleschi baute 1420 zur Prüfung der Statik der geplanten gigantischen Kuppel für den Florentiner Dom ein legendäres Modell aus Holz, Backstein und Stein. Er versah seine Modelle stets akribisch mit Verzierungen in Ton und Wachs, nicht nur, um die Auftraggeber von der Machbarkeit und Schönheit des Projekts zu überzeugen, sondern auch, um die Handwerker in alle Details einführen zu können. Für diesen Florentiner, geboren in der Stadt des exquisiten Handwerks, der zuerst ein erfinderischer Goldschmied war, bevor er sich als ein genialer Ingenieur entpuppte, steckten Gott und der Teufel im Detail.
Leon Battista Alberti schreibt um 1450 in «De re aedificatoria», dem ersten und wichtigsten Traktat über das Bauwesen nach Vitruvs gleichnamiger vorchristlicher Schrift, es solle eine architektonische Idee zuerst präzise «innerlich in Gedanken überdacht» sein, um danach in Zeichnungen und Plänen, aber letztlich im Modell entwickelt zu werden. Nur anhand des Modells könne die Qualität der Idee geprüft und unter Beizug von gewieften Fachleuten verbessert werden, und schliesslich diene das Modell auch der Kostenschätzung.
Das trifft alles auch auf L/Bs Modelle zu. Allerdings visualisieren sie poetische Gegenwelten im Unterschied zu den Modellen von Architekt:innen, Ingenieur:innen oder von den Baumeistern aus der Familie Grubenmann im 18. Jahrhundert, deren Holzmodelle im Stockwerk über L/Bs Schau zu sehen sind. L/Bs Kunstprojekte sind weniger gebunden an das gängige Regelwerk der Vernunft oder an zweckdienliche Normen. An Vitruvs heute noch geltenden Grundprinzipien der Architektur,

Firmitas, Utilitas, Venustas (Solidität, Zweckmässigkeit, Schönheit) halten sie jedoch fest. Wobei Venustas bei weitem und explizit den Vorrang nimmt und alles in ihren Dienst g estellt ist. «Beautiful» ist das Adjektiv vieler Titel ihrer Werke: BEAUTIFUL STEPS, BEAUTIFUL BRIDGE, BEAUTIFUL WALL etc. Zu L/Bs ästhetischem Anspruch gehört, dass sie den Kontext, in den sie ihre Kunst stellen, bis ins Detail erforschen und sämtliche Konstruktionspläne für ihre Werke selbst zeichnen, damit sie alles von Beginn an im Griff behalten. Kommt es dann zur Ausführung, kosten sie bis zum Limit die Möglichkeiten der konventionellen Bau- oder Konstruktionsmethoden und -techniken aus. Perfektionistisch widmen sie sich jedem noch so kleinen Element, damit sich etwa die Bisazza-Glasmosaiksteinchen im Bad des HOTEL EVERLAND auf den Millimeter genau bis an die Ränder und Ecken des Bodens einfügen lassen, ohne gebrochen zu werden. Oder sie bestimmen haargenau, wie jede einzelne Stakete des Geländers von BEAUTIFUL BRIDGE #3 leicht verdreht sein soll.
Zudem entwerfen sie durchaus Werke mit Nutzwert, welche zur Interaktion und gar zum performativen Umgang mit ihnen auffordern. Unter anderem die Bar, die abenteuerlich vom Vorplatz der Kunsthalle Bern über den Aarehang hinausragt. Als eine temporäre Folly wurde sie 2018 zum 100-jährigen Jubiläum der Institution bei L/B in Auftrag gegeben. Doch gibt es sie bis heute und hoffentlich noch auf lange Zeit. In erster Linie ist sie eine Reminiszenz im 1:1-Format an den originalen schwarz-weiss gemusterten Fliesenboden, der in den 1980er Jahren aus der Eingangshalle des Gebäudes herausgerissen wurde. An den Seiten schräg zweifach gefaltet, wird der Boden in der Bar zur Wand und oben zum Vordach. Diese Faltungen haben das Winkelmass der acht Ecken im Hauptsaal der Kunsthalle, worin sich eine weitere subtile Referenz an das Haus entdecken lässt [I.▀].

Wie anders aufgeladen waren hingegen die Modelle in Harald Szeemanns spektakulärer Ausstellung «Der Hang zum Gesamtkunstwerk» 1983 im Kunsthaus Zürich: Gaudís «Sagrada Familia», Steiners «Goetheanum», Schwitters «Merzbau I» Gabriele d'Annunzios «Vittoriale» oder der «Palais Idéal» des Facteur Cheval. Sie waren die Repräsentanten utopischer Visionen und schwerer Inhalte. Szeemann heimste sich damals scharfe Kritik von Max Bill oder dem NZZ-Feuilletonchef ein, die ihm vorwar-

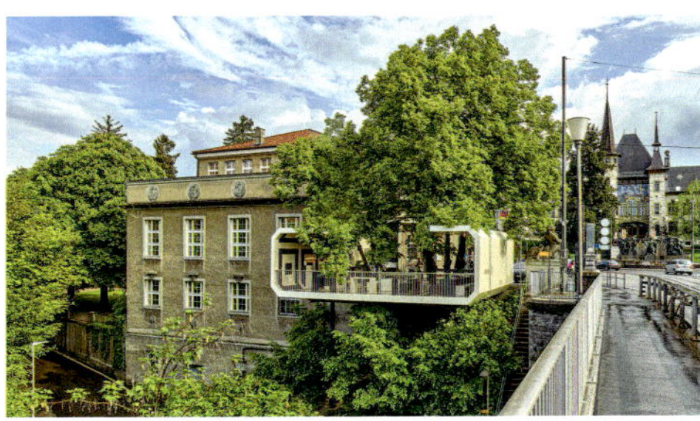

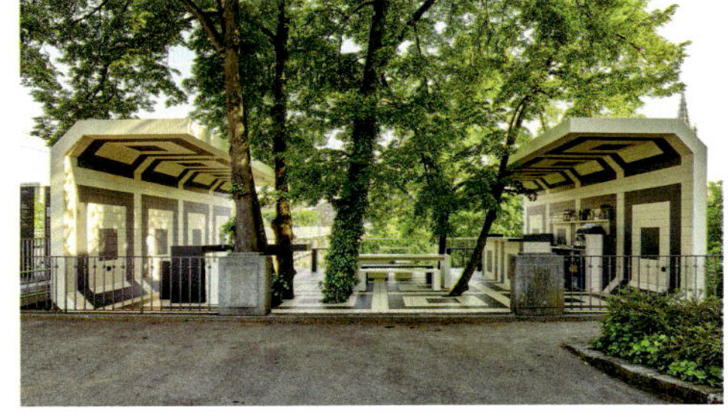

I.▀ MODULE #5, 2018, Kunsthalle, Bern CH

fen, er missbrauche die Modelle, um seine eigenen Obsessionen in sie hineinzuprojizieren.
Einem ganz anderen Zweck als jenem von L/B dienen beispielsweise auch Thomas Demands Modelle. Er wählt Pressefotografien mit politischen und gesellschaftlichen Sujets aus, die sich ins kollektive Gedächtnis eingeschrieben haben, wie etwa die Unterführung, in der Lady Di tödlich verunfallte, ein zerwühltes Stasi-Büro nach dem Mauerfall oder das amerikanische Präsidentenflugzeug Air Force One mit Gangway. Danach baut er die Szene detailgetreu und möglichst lebensgross, aber stets unbevölkert in einem Modell aus Papier und Pappe nach, um dieses in einer Fotografie festzuhalten. Am Ende des aufwendigen plastischen Prozesses ist dann nicht das gebaute Gebilde das Kunstwerk, sondern die irritierende Fotografie, in der sich das Remake der Realität erst auf den zweiten Blick feststellen lässt. Das Modell hingegen, einmal fotografiert, hat endgültig ausgedient und wird zerstört. Denn bühnenbildartig ist es für die Fotografie nur auf den einen perspektivischen, von der Vorlage gegeben Blickpunkt hin angefertigt worden, und als Beweisstück der Illusion ist es sowieso besser, wenn es verschwindet. Demand sagt, unter den wichtigsten künstlerischen Inspirationen seien für ihn die Fotografien von Adolf Hitler mit Albert Speer vor dem Modell der monumentalen, eiskalten Ehrenhalle gewesen, dem Pavillon des Dritten Reichs in der Weltausstellung 1937 in Paris. Charlie Chaplin ahnte, wohin Hitlers teuflische Wahnvorstellungen führten, als er in seiner Satire «The Great Dictator» (1940) Hitler spielte, der mit dem Miniatumodell der Erde, dem Ballon-Globus, tänzelt, bis dieser zerplatzt.

Dreist, aber menschenfreundlich, selten ohne Humor und manchmal von geradezu atemberaubender Schönheit ist dagegen L/Bs Kunst. Im März 2023 konnte ich an der Einweihung von BEAUTIFUL BRIDGE #3 bei der Tramlinie Bernex in Genf teilnehmen [D.▘]. Ich kannte das Projekt seit Jahren vom Modell her und war bereits damals eingenommen von der skulpturalen Eleganz der Brücke, die nichts zu überbrücken hat, aber Sitzgelegenheit und Regenschutz bietet und zu Veranstaltungen anregen will. Als ich dann dieses Werk erstmals live sah und die Strahlen der untergehenden Sonne das feine metallene Brückengeländer golden aufleuchten liessen, zeigte sich mir einmal mehr, wie sehr das Original sein Modell mit all den Vorstellungen, die es anzuregen vermag, übertreffen kann.

EPISTEMISCHE ZEITKAPSELN

MERET ERNST

L/B haben sich früh auf eine gemeinsame Sprache geeinigt. Im nie abreissenden Dialog müssen sie sich gegenseitig überzeugen. Ihr Arbeitsprozess lässt es zu, dass sie Fragen, die sie behandeln wollen, auch gemeinsam beantworten können. Würden sie zusammen ein Bild malen, wäre das kaum möglich, stellen sie im Gespräch fest. Was sie verbindet, vermittelt sich auch in der Art und Weise, wie sie sich gegenseitig die Bälle zuspielen.

Der Kontext, den sie für ihre Werke eingehend analysieren, bildet in ihrem Gespann die dritte Instanz, die Ideen liefert. Mögliche Lösungen testen sie rasch im CAD. Doch die Wirkung einer Idee, selbst wenn sie im Modell kontrolliert und gefestigt ist, muss vor Ort überprüft und im Austausch mit Dritten durchgesetzt werden. Ein beständiges kleines Team von Freelancer:innen, ein Netzwerk von Fachleuten hilft bei der Umsetzung. Als Kommunikationsmittel vereinfachen Modelle so das Gespräch mit Akteur:innen, die den Beweis im kleinen Massstab brauchen, dass etwas funktionieren wird. Aus Papier, Karton oder anderen, vorgefundenen Materialien gefertigt, verlassen diese zuweilen den Massstab, wie er bei Modellen, Mockups oder Prototypen in Architektur und Design üblich ist.[1]

Als epistemische Objekte vermitteln die Modelle, wie etwas gedacht und konstruiert werden muss, damit die beabsichtigte – künstlerische, gesellschaftliche – Wirkung entsteht.[2] Zuweilen wandern die Modelle an den Ort des Geschehens. So bei COMFORT #4, das 2010 zwei Fensterreihen einer Pariser Grundschule mit weissen Luftschläuchen nach dem Prinzip des Zufalls vernähte. Ein redundantes System garantierte, dass selbst wenn ein Ventilator aussteigen sollte, das Bild einer riesigen, textil wirkenden Kette von Knoten gewahrt blieb. Jeder Schlauch führte viermal in ein Fenster und kam wieder hervor. Welcher der richtige Anschluss war, vermittelte dem Aufbau-Team vor Ort das Modell. Es trägt heute noch die entsprechenden Markierungen.

1 So diente eine Aluschiene als Modell für die Unterführung Ulmbergtunnel (171 x 3.5 m), was zu einem abenteuerlichen Massstab von 1:145 führte

2 Sascha Dickel, ‹Prototyping Society – Zur vorauseilenden Technologisierung der Zukunft›, Science Studies, transcript, Bielefeld 2019. Online: DOI.org (Crossref), DOI: 10.14361/9783839447369.

Und schliesslich sind Modelle Zeitkapseln. Sie nehmen vorweg, was in einem Massstabssprung an Ort und Stelle realisiert werden wird. Sie bewahren, was längst wieder zurückgebaut ist, als kondensierte Erfahrung. Eine Compactus-Anlage im Keller des Burgdorfer Wohnateliers, einer ehemaligen Elektromotorenfabrik, die Mitte der 1980er Jahre umgewandelt wurde, bewahrt die Modelle auf. Kommen Gäste, dienen diese als Ersatz für die Werke, die anderswo sind.

Liegen im Keller die Modelle, so wartet auf dem Dach ihres Ateliers ein Original, das HOTEL EVERLAND [K.▀]. Nach seinen Einsätzen in Yverdon, Leipzig und Paris kanalisiert es den Blick nun in die Gewerbezone Burgdorfs. In flüchtigen Papiermodellen hatte die Idee erste Form gefunden. Das mobile, für die Expo.02 entworfene Kleinsthotel ist ein Kunstwerk, das als Mockup interpretiert werden kann. Schliesslich testete es die Idee eines besonderen Hotels eins zu eins – bis hin zur Plattensammlung, der ausgestatteten Minibar, der Rezeptionsdienste oder dem Hinweis an die Gäste, dass sie die Badetücher mitnehmen dürften. Die Gäste, die nur je eine Nacht buchen durften, wurden Teil dieser Versuchsanordnung, die ihnen für den ursprünglichen Expo-Einsatz eine autonome Zeitkapsel anbot. Nach dem Ansturm der Massen bleiben die Gäste auf dem Ausstellungsgelände zurück und konnten so nachklingen lassen, was sie tagsüber erfahren hatten. Auf Stelzen am Ufer des Neuenburgersees aufgestellt, erlaubte die vorne verglaste Kapsel den Blick auf den See und die «Wolke» von Diller & Scofidio, dem Wahrzeichen der Vergänglichkeit an der Expo.02. Ironischerweise wurde das HOTEL EVERLAND als reales Mockup für bare Münze genommen, und L/B mussten einige Nachfragen abwehren, wann das Mini-Hotel denn nun in Serie hergestellt würde. Es sind solche produktiven Missverständnisse zwischen Modell, Mockup und Werk, die Anlass zu einer Positionierung ihrer Werke geben. Die Begriffe «Besetzung» und «Schönheit» bieten dazu ein Geländer.

Die Welt ist immer schon gebaut und gestaltet, nirgends gibt es eine Leerstelle. Der Soziologe und Designtheoretiker Lucius Burckhardt beobachtete, dass die künstlerische oder gestalterische Arbeit im öffentlichen Raum unter den Bedingungen der «Besetzung» geschehe:

«Kann man sie vermeiden, umgehen, muss man sie akzeptieren, sichtbarmachen, poetisieren? Und wie? […] Unserer Meinung nach braucht Gestaltung keinen Raum. Vielmehr muss sie sich, unter gegebenen Bedingungen, auf das stützen, was im Raum schon vorhanden ist.»[3]

Das Gebaute setzt Rahmenbedingungen für die Eingriffe von L/B. Nicht nur Architektur mit einem grossen A – weil sie gebaute Tatsache und diskursmächtig ist – sondern auch das

3 Lucius Burckhardt, «Alles ist schon besetzt», in: Lucius Burckhardt und Museum für Gestaltung Zürich (Hrsg.), ‹Überall ist jemand, Räume im besetzten Land›, Museum für Gestaltung, Zürich 1992 (Wegleitung, 383), S. 77.

Vorgefundene, das, was anscheinend «immer schon da war», ohne einem größeren Plan zu folgen. Plätze und Fassaden, Eingänge und Empfangsräume, Korridore oder Innenhöfe regen L/B zu Interventionen an.

Die Werkreihe COMFORT macht das ebenso poetisch wie ironisch deutlich. Riesige, luftgefüllte Schläuche schlängeln sich durch Fassaden und Gebäude. Als ob sie sich eine Lücke suchten, die sie brauchen, um sich bequem auszubreiten. Das hat etwas Unberechenbares, gar Zufälliges. Die Schläuche stehen für das Gegenteil der gebauten Struktur, sie sind weich, ephemer, temporär und sie machen auf die Leerstellen aufmerksam, die jeder Architektur eingeschrieben sind. Doch harmlos sind sie nicht. Die Schläuche verflüssigen das Gebaute, Gegebene.

Das gelingt L/B auch bei COMFORT #20, einem Projekt, das seinerseits die statische, autonome moderne Auffassung von Architektur kritisiert und eigentlich nur in der Bewegung verstanden werden kann: Bernard Tschumis Parc de La Villette [E.▀]. Für das Festival Paris l'été bespielten L/B 2022 eine der Folies in diesem urbanen Volkspark im Norden von Paris. Ein hellgrauer luftgefüllter Schlauch windet sich durch die «FOLIE N8». Mit L/Bs «Besetzung» wird die gebaute Struktur zum Negativ ihrer selbst.

In seinem Wettbewerbsvorschlag von 1983 für die Umgestaltung des riesigen Geländes, einem der 14 Pariser «grands projets» aus der Regierungszeit François Mitterrands, erwies Tschumi dem Dekonstruktivismus seine Referenz. Jacques Derrida half kräftig mit, die Prinzipien Funktion, Repräsentation und Einheit der Form zu pulverisieren. Im Raster von 120 x 120 Metern verteilte Tschumi sechsundzwanzig mit knallrot lackierten Metallplatten bekleidete Betonskelettbauten über das Gelände, teils abstrakte Figuration, teils nutzbare Pavillons. Damit bekräftigte er seinen Anspruch, «das grösste diskontinuierliche Gebäude der Welt zu realisieren»[4].

4 Bernard Tschumi, «Parc de la Villette», in: Andreas Papadakis und Christiane Court (Hrsg.), ‹Dekonstruktivismus: eine Anthologie›, Klett-Cotta, Stuttgart 1989, S. 175.

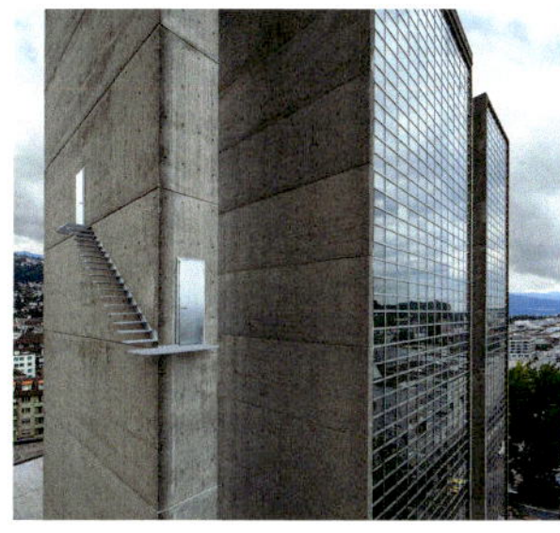

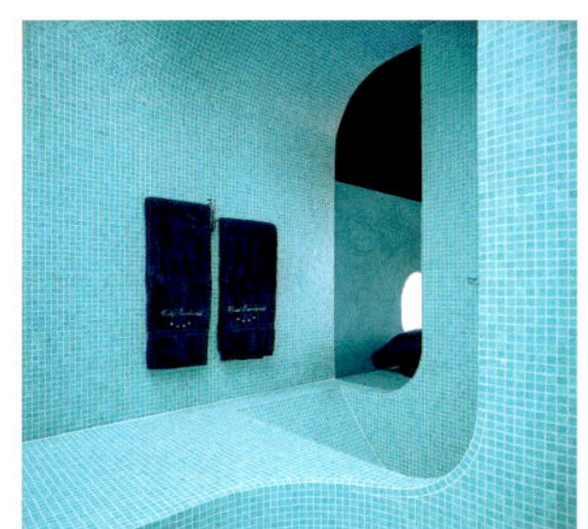

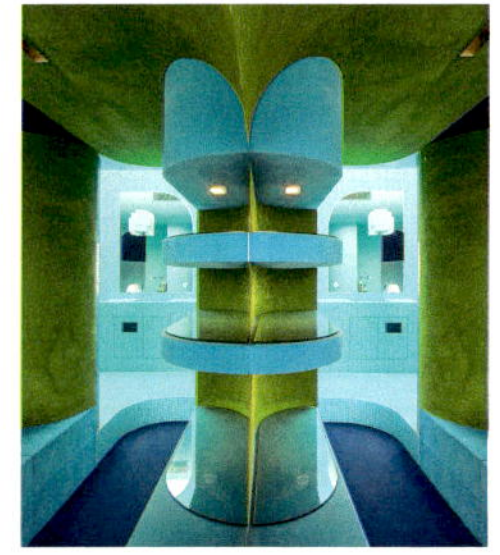

J.▀ BEAUTIFUL STEPS #2, 2009, Biel-Bienne CH

K.▀ HOTEL EVERLAND, 2002, Yverdon CH

Entwickelt aus einem Kubus von knapp 11 Metern Kantenlänge sind die Folies von Öffnungen und Einschnitten durchbrochen; geometrische Zusätze und Ausstülpungen erweitern sie. Wie in einem Kippbild changiert die Wahrnehmung der Folies zwischen der Grundform und deren Störung.[5]

Der Augenschein vor Ort und das Gespräch mit den Verantwortlichen ergab unzählige Varianten, wie ein Schlauch durch eine Folie geführt werden kann, wie die Befestigung und das Gebläse zu integrieren sind. Davor galt es, aus den 26 Folies eines auszuwählen. Mit Blick auf die Werkgruppe BEAUTIFUL STEPS scheint die Wahl zwingend. Ohne Gebrauchsfunktion steht «FOLIE N8» vor dem Verwaltungsgebäude des Parks. Ist da nicht eine übergrosse Treppe, die unerreichbar auf halber Höhe beginnt und die Passant:innen verzwergt?

Treppen sind Kleinarchitekturen, die uns ein Gebäude verfügbar machen. Sie vermitteln zwischen unserer Körpergrösse und der Gebäudehöhe. Sie beginnen und enden und beginnen auf den Treppenabsätzen, den Pausenzeichen in der Aufwärtsbewegung. Als skulpturales Element lassen sie uns Raum erfahren. Indem sie Unten und Oben verbinden, sind sie sowohl Funktion als auch Symbol der Macht und sozialer Hierarchien.[6] In der Werkreihe BEAUTIFUL STEPS versammeln L/B Treppen und Leitern: am Fluss, im Strassenraum, an Fassaden, in Innenräumen. Manchmal führen die Treppen ins Nichts oder sind unzugänglich, manchmal überbrücken sie Flüsse oder eröffnen neue Perspektiven.

BEAUTIFUL STEPS #10 setzt an der Nordfassade des Casino Forum d'art contemporain Luxembourg seit 2014 ein Ausrufezeichen. Von innen führen sieben sich verengende Stufen wie eine kleine Jakobsleiter aus einem Fenster in den Himmel. Dauerhaft in der Fassade verankert, ragt die weiss strahlende Struktur drei Meter über den Strassenraum hinaus. Von dort betrachtet wirkt sie abstrakt und wie ein funktionsloser Fremdkörper, der uns die Fassade neu sehen lässt. Es sei denn, jemand steht draussen, geniesst den Blick in den Himmel und winkt zurück. Ah – ein Balkon! Die Stufen verbinden Unten und Oben, Innen und Aussen. Und BEAUTIFUL STEPS #10 dreht die Hierarchie um, indem es die weniger repräsentative Nordfassade des Gebäudes aufwertet.

Andere Treppen und Leitern bleiben unerreichbar. Im Rahmen der 11. Schweizer Skulpturenausstellung in Biel 2009 entwickelten L/B BEAUTIFUL STEPS #2 am Bieler Kongressgebäude, das Max Schlup ab 1960 konzipiert hatte [J.▀]. L/B analysierten, wie geschickt dieses Gebäude mit seinen 17 Geschossen die

5 Umgesetzt wurde das Konzept zwischen 1982 und 1998. Mit dem dekonstruktivistischen Gestus habe Tschumi «den staatstragenden Anspruch der französischen Regierung in subtiler Weise unterlaufen». Michaela Gugeler, «Der Parc de la Villette – Würfelwurf der Architektur Das Zusammenwirken von Bernard Tschumi und Jacques Derrida beim Parc de la Villette in Paris», in: ‹Kritische Berichte /2› (2006) S. 44.

6 Rem Koolhaas (Hrsg.), ‹Fundamentals: 14th international architecture exhibition›, Marsilio Venedig 2014.

Wahrnehmung täuscht. Das Raster der Glasfront zeichnete Schlup unabhängig von der Deckenhöhe der Stockwerke. Deshalb erscheint das Hochhaus mächtiger als es ist. Die Glasfront ist in einen zweigeteilten Sichtbetonrahmen eingehängt, dessen Ostseite als Erschliessungskern ausgebildet ist; die Westseite des Rahmens, losgelöst vom Gebäudekern, ist mit Ausnahme eines Kamins ohne Gebrauchsfunktion. An diesem Teil des Rahmens brachten L/B auf fast drei Viertel der Höhe eine Aluminiumtreppe an, die über Eck von einer Tür zu einer anderen zu führen scheint. Um der optischen Täuschung des Gebäudes gerecht zu werden, haben L/B Treppe und Türen um 20 Prozent verkleinert und an die Höhe der realen Geschosse angepasst.

Die leichte Wiedererkennbarkeit bereitet die Ent-Täuschung vor. Sie lädt dazu ein, das Gebäude genauer zu betrachten, dort, wo sich das absichtslos Schöne gegen die spartanische Nützlichkeit einnistet. Mit «Schönheit aus Funktion oder als Funktion» hatte Max Bill die Schönheit in den Dienst des Gebrauchs genommen, ohne ihrer ganz habhaft werden zu können.[7] Für L/B ist Schönheit in der Kunst bedeutungslos – die Bezeichnung ganzer Werkgruppen als «Beautiful» ein Kniff, genau darüber zu sprechen. Weil Schönheit ein relationaler Begriff ist, erfüllt sie sich erst in der Betrachtung; entsprechend sind L/B überzeugt, dass ihre Werke durch die Betrachter:innen vervollständigt werden. Hier liegt wohl auch ein Grund, weshalb sie den öffentlichen Raum «besetzen». Dabei muss die Betrachtung die Werke immer wieder aktualisieren, um Schönheit zu erkennen. Weil wir im Lauf der Zeit nicht stehen bleiben, führt das Wieder-Erleben zu neuen Interpretationen. In bestimmten Lichtverhältnissen löst sich der Schattenwurf von BEAUTIFUL STEPS #2 in ein abstraktes Ornament auf. Bei grauverhangenem Himmel verschwinden die Treppen so sehr im Betongrau, dass sie kaum noch sichtbar sind.

L/B stellen sich mit ihrem «More is More»[8] gegen Ludwig Mies van der Rohes «Less is more». Doch keinesfalls wollen sie ihr Werk als Referenz an die Postmoderne verstanden wissen. Ihre Haltung, die durch den Punk gegangen ist, widersetzt sich jedweder Kanonisierung. Sie ist nicht Selbstzweck, sondern markierte ihren Einstieg in die Kunst zu Beginn der 1990er Jahre. Geprägt war er durch die Lust am Trash, dem Nicht-Konformen, dem aus der Zeit Gefallenen – dem Überschüssigen, Schrägen und der Absage an das Dogma der Reduktion, das sich als Sackgasse entpuppte. Darin liegt eine besondere Schönheit, die in L/Bs Werken immer wieder aufs Neue erlebt werden kann. Man muss nur genau hinschauen.

7 Max Bill, «Schönheit aus Funktion und als Funktion», in: ‹Das Werk: Architektur und Kunst = L'oeuvre : architecture et art› 36/8 (1949), S. 272–274.

8 Sabina Lang, Daniel Baumann (Hrsg.), ‹Lang/Baumann: More is More›, Die Gestalten Verlag, Berlin 2013.

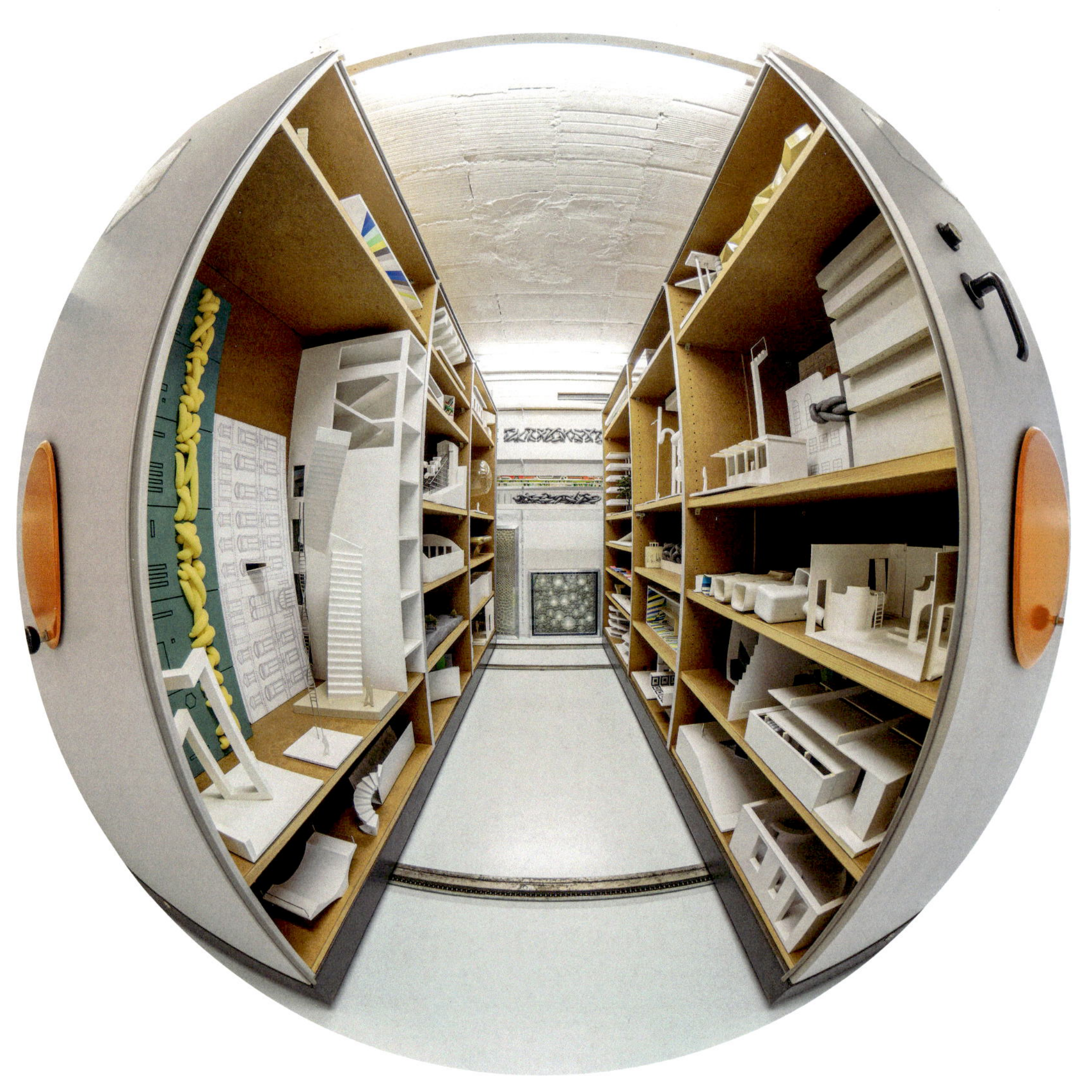

INDEX

01 Working model for GOLDEN TABLE #2
1:5 | cardboard, tape | 19 × 24 × 50 cm
2011 Kultur- und Kongresszentrum, Thun CH
permanent sculpture, brass

02 Presentation model for GOLDEN TABLE #2
1:10 | polyurethane rigid foam, enamel
7.5 × 9.5 × 50 cm
2011 Kultur- und Kongresszentrum, Thun CH
non-realised variant

03 Presentation model for
BEAUTIFUL ENTRANCE #7
1:50 | FDM 3D print, paint
11 × 34.5 × 9 cm
2018 Kantonsschule, Wettingen CH
permanent installation, concrete

04 Presentation model for E9
1:50 | concrete, acrylic glass,
power cable, LED | 51 × 45 × 31 cm
2011 Studentenwohnhaus, Zürich CH
not realised

05 Presentation model for VORNAMEN
1:100 | wood, felt | 18 × 6 × 73.5 cm
1997 Holzfachschule, Biel CH
not realised

06 Presentation model for E15
1:100 | polystyrene, paint, model trees
15 × 37 × 75 cm
1996 Staldenkehr, Burgdorf CH
permanent installation, concrete

07 Presentation model for WAVES
1:12 | steel, enamel, foamcore
60 × 34 × 14 cm
2016 Mobiliar Monbijou, Bern CH
not realised

08 Presentation model for BEAUTIFUL TUBE
1:40 | FDM 3D print, paint
8.5 × 59.5 × 16.5 cm
2023 Aldea, Bergen NO
installation, wood

09 Working model for UP #5
1:33 | FDM 3D print, paint
16 × 27 x.13 cm
2022 Open House, Parc Lullin, Genthod CH
sculpture, wood

10 Presentation model for UP #3
1:50 | FDM 3D print, paint
20.5 × 35 × 31 cm
2017 Un été au Havre, Plage
Porte Océane, Le Havre FR
permanent sculpture, concrete

11 Working model for UP #1
1:200 | SLA 3D print | 6 × 6 × 4 cm
2014 sic! Raum für Kunst
Elephanthouse, Luzern CH
installation, wood

12 Presentation model for SPIRALS #3
1:100 | wood, FDM 3D print,
paint, metal grid | 35 × 14 × 47 cm
2013 Of Bridges & Borders,
Ascensor Monjas, Valparaiso CL
installation, wood

13 Presentation model for UP
1:30 | FDM 3D print, paint
31 × 20 × 25 cm
2020 Bäder Baden, Baden CH
not realised

14 Working model for UP #4
1:35 | FDM 3D print, paint
26 × 15 × 15 cm
2020 Rolex Learning Center EPFL,
Lausanne CH
sculpture, steel

15 Presentation model for UP #7
1:40 | FDM 3D print, paint
45 × 15 × 15 cm
2023 Roche, Basel CH
permanent sculpture, steel

16 Presentation model for BEAUTIFUL VIEW #1
1:50 | brass, enamel | 46 × 18.5 × 14 cm
2019 Quartier Nanterre Coeur Université,
Nanterre FR
permanent sculpture, steel

17 Presentation model for DIVING PLATFORM
1:150 | provided plaster model,
SLA 3D print, paint | 5 × 66 × 35 cm
2014 Labyrinthe, Luxembourg LUX
not realised

18 Presentation model for BEAUTIFUL STEPS
1:150 | provided plaster model,
SLA 3D print, paint | 5 × 66 × 35 cm
2014 Labyrinthe, Luxembourg LUX
not realised

19 Presentation model for BEAUTIFUL STEPS
1:50 | SLA 3D print, copper
6.5 × 10 × 9 cm
2014 Labyrinthe, Luxembourg LUX
not realised

20 Presentation model for PLACES DÉPLACÉES
1:20 | foamcore, print on cardboard,
SLA 3D print | 51.5 × 36 × 27 cm
2019 Stade, Lausanne CH
not realised

21 Presentation model for S42
1:33 | stainless steel | 54 × 14 x 14 cm
2013 Aargauische Gebäudeversicherung,
Aarau CH
not realised

22 Presentation model for BEAUTIFUL STEPS #16
1:25 | wood, paint, stainless steel
58.5 × 31 × 34 cm
2018 Biozentrum, Universität Basel,
Basel CH
permanent installation

23 Presentation model for BEAUTIFUL STEPS #15
1:25 | brass, enamel, wood, paint
72 × 14 × 14 cm
2013 Siedlung Paradies, Zürich CH
not realised

24 Presentation model for BEAUTIFUL BRIDGE #3
1:40 | wood, stainless steel, FDM 3D print
70 × 40 × 11 cm
2023 Art & Tram, Genève CH
permanent sculpture, concrete

25 Presentation model for E3
1:30 | FDM 3D print, paint,
stainless steel wire | 6.7 × 25 × 12 cm
2016 Weide, Kortrijk BE
not realised

26 Presentation model for T15
1:25 | wood, FDM 3D print, paint
13 × 37 × 16 cm
2019 Glattpark, Opfikon CH
not realised

27 Presentation model for BEAUTIFUL STEPS #11
1:25 | FDM 3D print, paint
26 × 25 × 51 cm
2016 Landeskrankenhaus, Feldkirch AT
permanent sculpture, concrete

28 Presentation model for T12
1:25 | FDM 3D print, paint, model plants
27 × 27 × 23 cm
2016 Roche, Kaiseraugst CH
not realised

29 Presentation model for BEAUTIFUL STEPS #13
1:20 | FDM 3D print, paint
18 × 13 × 21 cm
2015 Direktionsgebäude Mobiliar, Bern CH
sculpture, aluminium

30 Presentation model for BEAUTIFUL STEPS
1:30 | FDM 3D print, paint
51 × 41 × 15 cm
2022 Lumière, Paris FR
not realised

31 Presentation model for BEAUTIFUL STEPS #7
1:33 | wood, cardboard, 3D print, paint
20 × 25 × 45 cm
2013 Rives de Saône, Rochetaillée, Lyon FR
permanent sculpture, concrete

32 Presentation model for BEAUTIFUL STEPS
1:20 | wood, polyurethane rigid foam,
enamel | 69 × 25 × 35 cm
2010 Mobimo Tower, Zürich CH
not realised

33 Presentation model for S20
1:33 | SLA 3D print, wood, cardboard,
acrylic glass | 14.5 × 22 × 16 cm
2018 Bibliothèque nationale, Luxembourg LUX
not realised

34 Presentation model for WAVE
1:20 | model tree, FDM 3D print, paint
42 × 40 × 30 cm
2022 Verwaltungszentrum, Chur CH
not realised

35 Presentation model for SPIRALE
1:25 | model tree, FDM 3D print, paint
30 × 38 × 22 cm
2020 Les Vergers, Meyrin CH
not realised

36 Presentation model for S2
1:40 | SLA 3D print, enamel
12 × 20.5 × 18.5 cm
2017 Plateforme 10, Lausanne CH
not realised

37 Working model for SPIRALS #1
1:3 | tinplate, glue | 28 × 7.5 × 40 cm
2010 edition of 5 copper objects

38 Working model for Spirals #1
1:3 | tinplate, wood, glue
30 × 7.5 × 39 cm
2010
copper object, non-realised variant

39 Presentation model for T3
1:100 | polyurethane rigid foam, enamel
42 × 45.5 × 45.5 cm
2012 Chevrolet, La Chaux-de-Fonds CH
not realised

40 Presentation model for GOLDEN TABLE
1:60 | polyurethane rigid foam, wood,
fabric, enamel | 14 × 27 × 46 cm
2004 private collection, Sarnen CH
pool table

41 Working model for COMFORT #6
1:100 | wood, cardboard, PE joint
filler profile | 22.4 × 27 × 40.5 cm
2009 Museumsnacht, Westside, Bern CH
non-realised variant

42 Working model for COMFORT #6
1:100 | wood, cardboard, PE joint filler
profile | 26 × 33 × 41.5 cm
2009 Museumsnacht, Westside, Bern CH
inflatable

43 Working model for COMFORT #3
1:8.6 | polyurethane foil, wood, paint
43 × 28 × 60 cm
2005 KBB, Barcelona ES
inflatable

44 Working model for COMFORT #8
1:23 | foamcore, cardboard, PE joint filler
profile | 29 × 47 × 16 cm
2010 Foksal, Warszawa PL
inflatable

45 Presentation model for COMFORT #19
1:72 | FDM 3D print, PE joint filler
profile | 20 × 20 × 16 cm
2022 Welt in der Schwebe, Kunstmuseum,
Bonn DE
inflatable

46 Working model for COMFORT #6
1:100 | wood, paper, PE joint filler
profile | 54 × 39 × 3 cm
2008 La noche en blanco, Fundacion
Telefónica, Madrid ES
inflatable

47 Working model for BREATHING PILLOWS
1:50 | wood, paint, welded foam pillows
16.5 × 36 × 57 cm
1995 De Fabriek, Eindhoven NL
inflatable

48 Working model for COMFORT #4
1:50 | wood, paint, stainless steel,
PE joint filler profile
13 × 8.5 × 119.5 cm
2015
inflatable, non-realised variant

49 Working model for COMFORT #4
1:50 | wood, paint, stainless steel,
PE joint filler profile | 13 × 8.5 × 60 cm
2015 Contemporary Istanbul, ICEC Congress
Center, Istanbul TR
inflatable

50 Working model for COMFORT #4
1:50 | print on cardboard, MDF,
PE joint filler profile
42.5 × 133 × ca. 2 cm
2010 Nuit Blanche, Ecole Elementaire de
Belleville, Paris FR
inflatable

51 Working model for COMFORT #4
1:50 | wood, print on cardboard,
PE joint filler profile | 33.5 × 20 × 31 cm
2011 Hoehenrausch 2, OK Offenes Kulturhaus,
Linz AT
inflatable, non-realised variant

52 Working model for COMFORT #4
1:50 | wood, paint, PE joint filler profile
36 × 106 x ca. 4 cm
2012 Glow 2012, de Bijenkorf, Eindhoven NL
inflatable

53 Presentation model for COMFORT #20
1:50 | FDM 3D print, paint
29 × 32 × 18 cm
2022 L'Air des Géants, Parc de la Villette,
Paris FR
inflatable

54 Presentation model for BEAUTIFUL STEPS #10
1:50 | wood, print on cardboard,
SLA 3D print | 41 × 77 × 7 cm
2014 Casino, Luxembourg LUX
permanent installation

55 Working model for COMFORT #12
1:100 | foamcore, print on cardboard,
PE joint filler profile | 14.4 × 43 × 39 cm
2013 Struktur und Zufall, Wilhelm-Hack-
Museum, Ludwigshafen DE
inflatable, wall paintings

56 Presentation model for BEAUTIFUL WALL #23
1:20 | wood, paint | 108.5 × 17.5 × 41 cm
2012 Schweizerische Nationalbank, Zürich CH
permanent wall painting

57 Presentation model for BEAUTIFUL BRIDGE #2
1:75 | wood, FDM 3D print, paint,
print on cardboard | 20 × 63 × 30 cm
2016 Tokyo Art Flow,
Futakotamagawa Station area, Tokyo JP
wall painting

58 Working model for BEAUTIFUL WALLS #14
1:95 | print on paper | 4.4 × 7.5 × 24.5 cm
2005 Malereiräume, Helmhaus, Zürich CH
wall painting

59 Working model for BEAUTIFUL WALLS #14
1:40 | foamcore, cardboard, print on paper
11 × 20 × 59 cm
2005 Malereiräume, Helmhaus, Zürich CH
wall painting

60 Presentation model for BEAUTIFUL ENTRANCE
1:50 | print on paper, acrylic glass
12 × 11 × 40 cm
2010 Gassmann Areal, Biel CH
not realised

61 Presentation model for
BEAUTIFUL APARTMENT #1
1:100 | print on paper | 4.5 × 9.5 × 17
4.5 × 9 × 5.5 cm
2011 Kashiwano-ha, Kashiwa JP
not realised

62 Working model for BEAUTIFUL WALLS #22
1:20 | print on cardboard
42 × 23.5 × 29 cm
2012 The Old, the New, the Different,
Kunsthalle, Bern CH
wall painting

63 Working model for BEAUTIFUL TUBE #6
1:46 | print on paper, steel, enamel
4 pcs. 5.5 × 40 × 40 cm
2019 Galerie des Galeries,
Galerie Lafayette, Paris FR
installation, wood, carpet

64 Presentation model for TUNNEL MALEREI
1:100 | wood, cardboard, paint
7 × 21 × 119 cm
2002 Worb CH
not realised

65 Presentation model for STREET PAINTING #3
1:117 | aluminum profile, print on
cardboard | 2 × 185 × 4 cm
2012 Ulmbergtunnel, Zürich CH
permanent floor painting

66 Presentation model for BEAUTIFUL CEILING
1:33 | foamcore, wood, paint, print on
paper | 11.5 × 33 × 58 cm
2013 Nationale Suisse, Basel CH
not realised

67 Working model for BEAUTIFUL WALL #25
1:145 | aluminum profile, print on
cardboard | 3 × 3 × 180 cm
2013 KVA Energiezentrale Forsthaus, Bern CH
non-realised variant

68 Working model for BEAUTIFUL WALL #25
1:145 | aluminum profile, print on
cardboard | 3 × 3 × 159 cm
2013 KVA Energiezentrale Forsthaus, Bern CH
permanent painting

69 Working model for BEAUTIFUL WALL #25
1:50 | wood, paint, print on cardboard
9 × 8.5 × 81 cm
2013 KVA Energiezentrale Forsthaus, Bern CH
non-realised variant

70 Presentation model for BEAUTIFUL WALL #25
1:33 | wood, print on cardboard,
power cable, LED | 14 × 163 × 13 cm
2013 KVA Energiezentrale Forsthaus, Bern CH
permanent painting

71 Working model for 47. MIGROS ARTIST'S CARRIER BAG
1:40 | printed paper | 12.4 × 4.5 × 8 cm
1999 Zürich CH
paper bag

72 Presentation model for SPIRALS #5
1:50 | tinplate, enamel | 15 × 62 × 2 cm
2018 Rehaklinik, Bellikon CH
permanent installation

73 Presentation model for BEAUTIFUL ENTRANCE
1:50 | wood, cardboard, print on acrylic glass | 46.5 × 46 × 20.5 cm
2011 Roche, Basel CH
not realised

74 Working model for BEAUTIFUL CAR #2
1:15 | FDM 3D print, paint
10.5 × 17 × 34 cm
2015 private collection, Wien AT

75 Working model for BEAUTIFUL CAR #1
1:15 | FDM 3D print, paint
10.5 × 17 × 34 cm
2014 private collection, Wien AT

76 Presentation model for REVOLVING STUDIO
1:60 | PBF 3D print, motor
21 × 23 × 15 cm
2012 Christoph Merian Stiftung, Dreispitz Areal, Basel CH
not realised

77 Working model (outer shape) for HOTEL EVERLAND
1:50 | cardboard | ca. 8 × 9 × 22 cm
2002 Expo.02, Arteplage, Yverdon CH
mobile one-room hotel

78 Working model (outer shape) for for HOTEL EVERLAND
1:50 | cardboard | ca. 8 × 9 × 22 cm
2002 Expo.02, Arteplage, Yverdon CH
mobile one-room hotel
non-realised variant

79 Working model (carpet) for HOTEL EVERLAND
1:50 | print on paper | 5 × 6.5 × 19 cm
2002 Expo.02, Arteplage, Yverdon CH
mobile one-room hotel
non-realised variant

80 Working model (carpet) for HOTEL EVERLAND
1:50 | print on paper | 5 × 6.5 × 19 cm
2002 Expo.02, Arteplage, Yverdon CH
mobile one-room hotel

81 Working model (interior design) for HOTEL EVERLAND
1:10 | polystyrene, paper, paint
33 × 35 × 109 cm
2002 Expo.02, Arteplage, Yverdon CH
mobile one-room hotel

82 Exhibition model for HOTEL EVERLAND
1:20 | PBF 3D print, power cable, LED | 23 × 23 × 60 cm
2007 Palais de Tokyo, Paris FR
mobile one-room hotel

83 Working model for WHO'S OUT?
1:20 | wood, paint, photograph on baryta paper, wire | 25 × 26 × 49 cm
1992 Weihnachtsausstellung, Kunstmuseum, Thun CH
installation

84 Presentation model for LOBBY
1:50 | paper, cardboard | 10 × 18 × 45 cm
2004 Kunsthalle, St. Gallen CH
long-term installation

85 Presentation model for CHILDISH BEHAVIOR #4
1:20 | cardboard | 17 × 25 × 32 cm
2004 private collection, Wien AT
children's room

86 Working model for LOUNGE #1
1:25 | foamcore, cardboard
15 × 37 × 38 cm
2003 Joburg Bar, Cape Town ZA
permanent installation

87 Working model for OPEN
1:33 | foamcore, print on cardboard
21 × 40.5 × 21 cm
2012 Grand Palais, Bern CH
installation, wood

88 Working model for BEAUTIFUL CURTAIN #2
1:10 | thermoformed PS, print on cardboard
32 × 73 × 6 cm
2015 Direktionsgebäude Mobiliar, Bern CH
permanent installation, non-realised variant

89 Presentation model for MODULE #4
1:25 | wood, FDM 3D print, paint, acrylic glass | 40 × 50 × 96 cm
2016 Zentrum Paul Klee, Bern CH
permanent installation

90 Presentation model for BEAUTIFUL TUBE #1
1:20 | FDM 3D print, cardboard, wood, paint
16.5 × 62 × 30 cm
2011 Wroclaw Contemporary Museum, Wroclaw PL
permanent installation

91 Presentation model for MODULE #5 (Kunsthalle Bar)
1:50 | FDM 3D print, steel plate, paint
20 × 17.5 × 22.5 cm
2018 100-Jahr-Jubiläum, Kunsthalle, Bern CH
long-term installation

L/B

SABINA LANG and DANIEL BAUMANN have been collaborating since the beginning of the 1990s. They live and work in Burgdorf, Switzerland. www.langbaumann.com

AUTHORS

LILIA and DAVID GLANZMANN co-lead the Zeughaus Teufen.

DR. JACQUELINE BURCKHARDT 1984–2017 co-founder and editor of the art magazine Parkett. 2009–2017 director of Sommerakademie at Zentrum Paul Klee in Bern.

DR. MERET ERNST 2003–2021 head of the editorial department for culture and design at the magazine Hochparterre. Since 2021 lecturer in design history and theory at the Basel Academy of Art and Design.

NORM (DIMITRI BRUNI, MANUEL KREBS and LUDOVIC VARONE) was founded 1999 in Zurich.

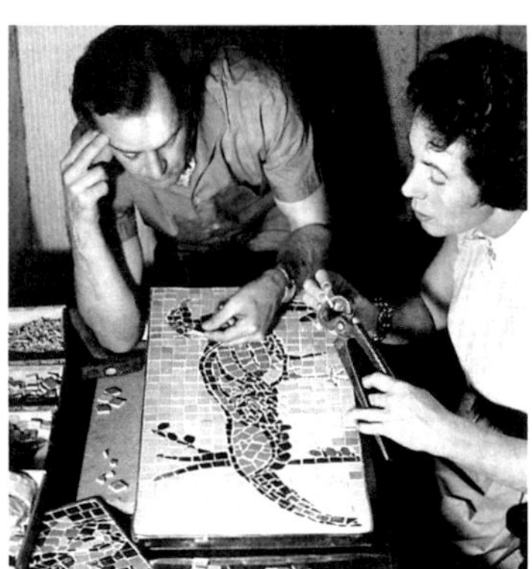

Ein gemeinsames Hobby ist ein gutes Rezept für den Bestand einer Ehe

L/B MODELS

This book has been pubished on the occasion of the exhibition
LANG/BAUMANN. 96 MODELLE, Zeughaus Teufen, from 1st July to 1st October 2023.

Edited by Lilia and David Glanzmann

Proofreading Thomas Skelton-Robinson (English), Karin Prätorius (Deutsch)
Translations Catherine Schelbert, Thomas Skelton-Robinson

Design NORM, Zürich
Photography L/B, except for:
Antonio Corcuera (B.▰ SPIRAL #3, 2013, Monjas, Valparaiso CL)
Jacqueline Buckhardt (D.▰ BEAUTIFUL BRIDGE #3, 2023, Genève CH)
Caspar Martig (I.▰ MODULE #5, 2018, Kunsthalle, Bern CH)

Typeface LL Riforma Mono
Paper Munken Polar / Novatech gloss
Printed by DZA Druckerei zu Altenburg GmbH, Germany
Made in Germany

Team Lang/Baumann
Jörg Bosshard, Simon Fuchser, Stella Lang ♥, Gregor Stritt

Team Zeughaus Teufen
Birgit Widmer, David Glanzmann, Fiammina Catti, Laura Wohlgensinger,
Lilia Glanzmann, Nadja Tarnutzer

ZEUGHAUS TEUFEN is a cultural initiative of the GEMEINDE TEUFEN,
supported by the KULTURFÖRDERUNG KANTON APPENZELL AUSSERRHODEN.

zeughaus GEMEINDE TEUFEN

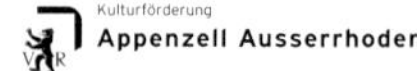

Published by Verlag Scheidegger & Spiess
Niederdorfstrasse 54
8001 Zurich / Switzerland
www.scheidegger-spiess.ch

ISBN 978-3-03942-166-4

Scheidegger & Spiess has been the recipient of a structural subsidy
for 2021-2024 from the Federal Office of Culture.

This publication is kindly supported by

BINDING SÉLECTION D'ARTISTES - SOPHIE UND KARL BINDING STIFTUNG,
ERNST GÖHNER STIFTUNG,
JUBILÄUMSSTIFTUNG DER MOBILIAR GENOSSENSCHAFT,
LANDIS & GYR STIFTUNG,
STANLEY THOMAS JOHNSON STIFTUNG,
DR. GEORG UND JOSI GUGGENHEIM-STIFTUNG,
ERNST UND OLGA GUBLER-HABLÜTZEL STIFTUNG,
STIFTUNG ERNA UND CURT BURGAUER,
SWISSLOS / KULTUR KANTON BERN,
KULTUR STADT BERN.

N° 104 im Programm der Binding Sélection d'Artistes
ERNST GÖHNER STIFTUNG
die Mobiliar
LANDIS&GYR STIFTUNG

STANLEY THOMAS JOHNSON STIFTUNG
DR. GEORG UND JOSI GUGGENHEIM STIFTUNG
Ernst und Olga Gubler-Hablützel Stiftung
Ema und Curt Burgauer Stiftung

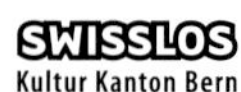

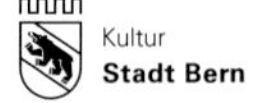